A SMALL BOY AND OTHERS

Edited by Michèle Aina Barale, Jonathan Goldberg,

Michael Moon, and Eve Kosofsky Sedgwick

A SMALL BOY AND OTHERS

Imitation and Initiation in American Culture

from Henry James to Andy Warhol

BY MICHAEL MOON

Duke University Press ✦ Durham and London 1998

© 1998 Duke University Press
All rights reserved
Printed in the United States of America on acid-free paper ⊗
Typeset in Quadraat by Tseng Information Systems, Inc.
Library of Congress Cataloging-in-Publication Data
appear on the last printed page of this book.

To Marcie Frank and Eve Kosofsky Sedgwick

CONTENTS

ACKNOWLEDGMENTS

Completing a project that has turned out to be centered in the 1960s and, frequently, on the topic of childhood has made me mindful of how many of the pleasures of the culture of that decade I first shared with my siblings, Bob, Eleanor, Bill, Tony, Charlie—all dedicated connoisseurs of music, movies, and personalities even then. My sister-in-law, Jean F. Moon, was my first friend who shared my fascination with the art and writing of the period. Well before the '60s began, my mother, Mary Catherine Townsell Moon, had already set me on my way as the multimedia aesthete I have remained by making me my first hand puppet, showering me with picture books and phonograph records, and always staunchly supporting my efforts to understand and practice culture making. I thank her for passing on to me her deep enjoyment of and respect for those processes.

I contemplate with sadness the irony for me that my father Sylvester F. Moon, who was born the year Henry James published *A Small Boy and Others*, 1913, has died this year, 1997, as I complete a work of the same title. This book, undertaken as a work of mourning, must remain one for me to a degree I could not have anticipated when I began it.

The way this book has remained steadily focused on New York has also given me many welcome opportunities to reflect on my youth there, which I rejoice in having squandered in the company of Millie Seubert, Leslie Dwinell, and Mary Lamasney, and on the streets of a city that was passing through one of its most culturally vibrant periods. Thanks to Nick Deutsch for first taking me to the Ridiculous Theatrical Company, to see Charles Ludlam perform his play *The Bourgeois Avant-Garde*. Thanks to Hal Sedgwick, too, for sharing many New York aesthetic adventures with me.

From the time I became at all aware of queerness as a human possibility to the time I came out in the late '70s and for years thereafter, the work of four queer New York artists excited and sustained me, continually expanding my notion of the powers of what we now call queer performativity. Andy Warhol, Charles Ludlam, Jack Smith, and Ethyl Eichelberger all died untimely deaths, all but Warhol's AIDS-related, between 1987 and 1990. I intend this book, however inadequate, to convey my gratitude to them and my profound respect for them for having kept alive for several more decades the splendid and perilous cultural role of *monstre sacré*. While in this book I have tended to emphasize what I see as the strength and power of their work, I want to say that being aware of how fraught an undertaking it was to become any one of these figures, and to maintain the achievement over a productive career of many years, much increases my admiration for each of them.

Portions of this book have appeared in essay form: "A Small Boy and Others" in Hortense J. Spillers, ed., *Comparative American Identities*; "Flaming Closets" in *October* (winter 1989), where it benefited from the editorial attention of Douglas Crimp; "Screen Memories" in Jennifer Doyle, Jonathan Flatley, and José Esteban Muñoz, eds., *Pop Out: Queer Warhol*; "Outlaw Sex and 'The Search for America'" in a special issue of *Quarterly Review of Film and Video* edited by Fabienne Worth; and "Oralia" in a special issue of *Women and Performance* edited by José Muñoz.

A grant from the American Council of Learned Societies for Recent Recipients of the Ph.D. enabled me to undertake research for this book in earnest, and a research fellowship at the Center for Critical Analysis of Contemporary Culture at Rutgers University helped me complete it. In addition to the already considerable boons of the Center, for which I thank George Levine, Bruce Robbins, and Carolyn Williams, I also began to enjoy there the enduring friendship of Julie Graham.

A long procession of gifted and inspiring graduate students has passed through Duke in recent years. For their interest in and responses to various parts of this project I thank Amanda Berry, Lara Bovilsky, Adam Frank, Daniel Itzkovitz, Katie Kent, Aaron Kunin, José Muñoz, Ada Norris, John Vincent, and Gustavus Stadler—especially Dan, for inviting me to write about Yiddish theater and queer theater, and Gus, for stimulating conversations about the whole project around the time I was finishing it.

Stanley Fish and Marianna Torgovnick, in their respective tenures as chairs of Duke's English department, have encouraged me and helped make time and other resources available to me at the beginning and end of my work on this book. Catherine Beaver and Roz Wolbarsht stepped in and saved the day—several days, in fact—at a crucial point in the production of the manuscript.

I am grateful to Michael Warner and Lauren Berlant for their friendship and for their respective writings on queer cultural transmission and public cultures of intimacy. Thanks, too, to Stephen Orgel for his hospitality to me and my work from its inception, to Barbara Herrnstein Smith for her warm and enthusiastic responses and for her unflagging intellectual energy, and to Sharon Cameron for continuing interest and support. Judith Butler has also fostered my work with unfailing generosity and kindness, and often on unconscionably short notice. Thanks to Esther Frank for opening a window on the Yiddish language for me, as she has done for many others. Coediting *American Literature* with Cathy N. Davidson for the past six years has provided me with an invaluable model of personal kindness and professional magnanimity. I continue to appreciate as I enjoy the collegial friendship of Nahum Chandler, Wahneema Lubiano, Janice Radway, Kathy Rudy, Laurie Shannon, and Irene Silverblatt. Ken Wissoker has been a wonderful editor and remains a valued friend, as does Richard Morrison; thanks to both, and to two anonymous readers for Duke University Press, whose generous and very thoughtful evaluations of the manuscript helped me reenvision it in its final form. Thanks to Paul Kelleher for copyediting the manuscript with such intelligent care.

The interest that Jonathan Goldberg has taken in this work makes it more valuable to me. He and I alone can know the care he has taken with it, and of me, during the years of its composition—and this despite his finding *Flaming Creatures* insufferable, and *Terminator* a far superior model of cinematic and artistic possibility. This book is dedicated to the two other friends closest to what I feel is at the heart of it, Marcie Frank and Eve Kosofsky Sedgwick. Marcie and I happily share many pockets of sensibility (Dryden, Cronenberger, Irma Vep), and, over the years, she has contributed many hours of constructive criticism, comparative fan's notes, and friendly enthusiasm to this project in a way that has constantly renewed it for me.

Those who know me know I might not have written a book like this one, about matters I care about as much as I do these, without the example and encouragement of Eve Sedgwick, who has wholeheartedly helped this project along in innumerable ways, material and spiritual. Eve, let me tell you a story. Circa 1970, I heard Elisabeth Schwarzkopf in one of her absolutely final farewell recitals, this one at Goucher College. That evening, after she gave a studiedly ravishing performance of Schumann's *Der Nussbaum*, the audience sat transfixed as the pianist played the closing measures of the song. Just before he finished, a loud, stage-whispered "BRAVISSIMA!" erupted from the back of the auditorium, shattering the silence. Everyone immediately turned to see who had such bad concert manners. Those of us who recognized her were excited to realize that it was the great dramatic soprano Rosa Ponselle, who had started out singing opposite Caruso and had gone on to have a glorious career. When the audience began to applaud, Schwarzkopf smiled enigmatically and bowed mildly, first to one side and then the other. Then she extended her hand in Ponselle's direction and slowly began to lower her body in a deep curtsy, farther and farther forward and down, until her bowed head almost touched the floor. She held the pose for longer than seemed possible before she gracefully rose back up. It was the most dramatic event of the performance. The story is still told in Baltimore opera-queen circles, where it is known as "the night Betty B. went to the floor for Rosa." Eve, with these words, I go to the floor for you.

INTRODUCTION

I began writing this book out of a desire to explore the extraordinary creativity and originality of gay men's contributions to modern culture at several moments of the past century when gay identities were in particularly volatile states of transformation. From its beginnings the project exerted a shuttling motion that repeatedly led me back and forth between the turn of the century and the 1960s—both periods when gay lives and gay culture-making were under especially intense pressure, equaled only by the impact of HIV/AIDS on us during the past two decades.

To my surprise, literary and theatrical performances of a wide range of kinds from the early years of the century and from the sixties exhibited certain consistencies and continuities as well as differences from each other, illuminating each other in what often seemed to me to be rather strange lights. What I saw as Nijinksy's resistance to the lethally oppressive ways in which his dancing was gendered by his contemporaries helped me understand how I could find the perversely withholding quality of Jack Smith's performances in "underground" film of the 1960s a moving and productive practice rather than merely a negative one. Similarly, analyzing the highly ritualized beating scene in David Lynch's Blue Velvet made it possible for me to see how its fusion of elements of a children's game with a performance of violent homoerotic desire between an older man and a younger one made more salient and more comprehensible similar aspects of E. T. A. Hoffmann's "The Sandman," Freud's essay on the uncanny, which takes "The Sandman" as its principal text, and Henry James's "The Pupil." By the time I came to study the art and writing of Joseph Cornell, his continual movement back and forth between his dual obsessions with the ballet and opera of the Romantic period and the female pop stars of his own day, from Hedy Lamarr to Patty Duke, not only made sense to me but seemed an almost inevitable working-out of more of the connections that have linked many different varieties of queer production and performance of recent times with the artistic practices of the last century.

In repeatedly moving through these circuits, I found that my project soon began to exceed the chronological limits I had initially set for it, which began at the turn of the century, in the years following the Wilde debacle, and extended forward in time as far as the work of Jack Smith, Kenneth Anger, Andy Warhol, and others in the New York "underground" during the stormy decade leading up to Stonewall. As I continued writing through the early '90s I only eventually came to realize how steadily and continuously the violent and transformative effects of the HIV/AIDS pandemic, by then in its second decade, had been exerting a magnetic pressure on the project from its inception—indeed, from before then.

At that point I took as my heuristic the question, what if we took as a provisional starting point for our analysis (rather than Wilde) a figure such as Henry James, who had in many ways a much less readily legible relation to the emergence of homosexual identity in his lifetime? Using James's determinedly and painstakingly antisensational model of a major queer culture-making career might yield us a considerably different set of templates for delineating both our expectations of queer art and for specifying our terms for its frequently—reliably—expectation-defying surprises. It has been my hope that looking at figures like James and David Lynch alongside each other might help us perceive other kinds of continuities in the uncanny processes of culture-building than the ones that are relatively familiar to us already. The brutally imposed necessity of learning to rethink and re-imagine many queer lives in relation to massively widespread illness and untimely death made the search for more kinds of connections and continuities in modern queer culture seem an urgent necessity of emotional and intellectual survival rather than merely an academic topic or a "collecting interest."

One pole for thinking about my concerns in this book had seemed to present itself immediately and unproblematically from its beginning: that was the rich fascination several of the artists I am treating—James and Warhol, for chief examples—had with their own thoroughly queer childhoods, not only as material for recollection and representation but as a primary source of models for innovative artistic practices. "A small boy" has consequently been a leading figure in the *imaginaire* from which this project derives its terms from its beginning in some of the sections on James and Warhol and Smith. The processes that seem to me to have been formative of modern queer childhood—of uncanny perception and imitation, of initiation and self-initiation, of the gradual recognition of one's desires and the production and transmission of images and narratives of these desires—are among the primary elements in my accounts of how "a small boy" enables each of several of the highly influential artistic careers under consideration in these pages.

The task of identifying the "others" of the book's title has been in contrast a gradual process. In James's memoir of his early life, from which I have borrowed the title for this project, the "others" of "A Small Boy and Others" signifies all the persons, beginning with his large extended family and including their friends and associates, his boy contemporaries, his tutors, favorite authors and artists, and other initiators who, taken together, comprise his formative sense of the world and its range of inhabitants and of possible relations between them. For me, haunting each of the figures of the "small boys" considered herein is the highly improbable person he became (what relative, doting or not, could ever have imagined that some small child was likely to become Henry James, Joseph Cornell, Andy Warhol, or Jack Smith?), and the similarly unpredictable artistic career he fashioned. These "small boys" are also haunted for me by their eventual intimate association as artists and as persons with untimely deaths—those of others as well as with the possibility of their own. Precociously "acquainted with grief" as protoqueer children growing up in for the most part violently homophobic milieus can be, as adults they became—to a considerable degree against their wills—exemplary mourners of loss and searching students of the effects of illness and death on survivors.

In exploring James's writing alongside such works as Andy Warhol's cartoon paintings, Kenneth Anger's *Scorpio Rising*, or David Lynch's *Blue Velvet*, I am seeking to defamiliarize both sides of the comparison—to trouble some prevailing assumptions both, on the one hand, about James's status making him in any way off limits to analysis as in some ways one queer culture-maker among others, supposedly by virtue of his canonical position as "great author" or "genius," *and*, on the other hand, about the power and complexity of much popular—including Pop—art since World War II.

The queerness—the daring and risky weirdness, dramatic uncanniness, erotic offcenteredness, and unapologetic perversity—of James's writing continues to demand to be addressed. "I am that queer monster the artist, an obstinate finality, an inexhaustible sensibility," James famously wrote in a late manifesto-letter to Henry Adams (March 21, 1914), and if we give that word "queer" any less force and range than he does, it is our failure of nerve and imagination, not his.

Recovering some increased sense of the "monstrous" and outrageous qualities of James's work can help us rethink the meanings of some of the most "transgressive" art of more recent times—Warhol's soup cans and perversely "pointless" films, Kenneth Anger's preening leather boys, Jack Smith's "flaming" drag queens. A generation ago, in his influential essay, "The Performing Self," Richard Poirier made a strong polemical intervention in the then dominant version of Americanist cultural studies by insisting on what he saw as the similarities in the "self-advertising" authorial performances of Henry James and Norman Mailer. Although for many readers in the intervening quarter-century since the end of the 1960s Mailer will have come to occupy a considerably more modest place than he formerly did, one may still admit the aptness and suggestiveness of Poirier's comparison *for its time*. I hope that the kinds of comparative questions this study raises may similarly contribute to the production of an expanded critical field, and help foster an atmosphere in which juxtaposing the works of a supposed mandarin "master" such as James or someone who has similarly been seen primarily as a renewer of high-culture traditions such as Nijinsky with those of various queer artists of subsequent generations may become a more readily available mode of critical and theoretical procedure.

Focusing on the range of texts I consider in this project has also involved me in negotiating other highly contested terrains in several ongoing debates about culture: relations between "public" art (Henry James's novels, Joseph Cornell's boxes) and more "private" work (James's letters, Cornell's journals), between high and popular cultures, between various subcultures (both elite and popular) and a larger mass culture, and between writing and other kinds of "performance" in the expanded sense of the term, and, finally, the relation between writing and visual images—paintings, photographs, films.

. . . the first thing we love is a scene.
—Roland Barthes, "Ravishment," A LOVER'S DISCOURSE

Henry James may once again serve as exemplary figure for exploring the relations between word and image, linguistic and visual representation, seeing and speaking (or writing), relations that have figured as primary topics of much recent theoretical exploration.[1] James took a passionate interest in looking at and writing about painting, in attending the theater, reviewing what he saw there, and writing plays; his writing engages at many moments the complex interactions between various modes of composing a scene or a series of scenes—in writing, in painting, in theatrical performance. "Scene" is a key term and scene making a recurrent topic of the retrospective introductions to his novels and tales gathered in *The Art of the Novel*. Like a number of the other artists I consider in this book, James restages scenes of childhood initiation into the powers of scene making that occur in uncanny spaces. These spaces confuse the question of whether the child (and by implication the reader) is inside or outside the scene produced; the activities of imagining the scene and imaginarily entering and departing it, reducing it to miniature scale or alternatively opening it out into "life-size," are notable features of this writing. These scenes are also represented as occurring in uncanny temporalities, which confuse the question of whether the scene being rehearsed in writing actually occurred in the artist's childhood or was produced in the reconstructive psychic time or timing of what Freud called *Nachträglichkeit*—the "memory" that at least partially rewrites and restages an earlier event or experience in a way that crystallizes a set of meanings that may not have been available to oneself in childhood.

I imagine these small protoqueer boys—James or Cornell or Warhol, for example—searching the images they encounter, either in written or in visual form, with a particular hunger to see represented some of the elements of their own most compelling feelings, desires, fantasies, and fears—images that can be not only glimpsed but gazed at, stored in memory, retrieved, and thereby subjected to something like the full intensity of desire; images that, following the technologies of the visual that proliferated between the development of photography and the development of the motion picture, can also be mentally cropped, framed, sequenced and resequenced, "zoomed in on," flipped through, run in reverse, run in slow motion, set to music and provided with spoken narration, copied, captioned, and recast. For many such boys, early memories of strong affective and erotic responses are just as likely to be about a person and/or a body or body part seen or read about in a story, a photograph, a film, or on stage or television as they are to be about the body of a "real" person (i.e., someone in his own immediate environment). This book focuses on a series of instances of an adult artist's productive revisitation of a remembered scene of himself as a protoqueer child "looking to be" (as the colloquial phrase has it) ravished by images of his own desire, experiencing such ravishment and gradually learning to exploit various aspects of the fantasied/remembered initiatory scene for his subsequent work.

As Roland Barthes renarrates the scene of what he calls "ravishment," or "love at first sight," it is not the other person in the scene who inspires or impels love and desire in the beholder as much as it is the scene itself, and the air of suddenness and happy (at least to begin with) fatality that can be ascribed to it:

> Stepping out of the carriage, Werther sees Charlotte for the first time (and falls in love with her), framed by the door of her house (cutting bread-and-butter for the children; a famous scene, often discussed): the first thing we love is *a scene*. For love at first sight requires the very sign of its suddenness (what makes me irresponsible, subject to fatality, swept away, ravished): and of all the arrangements of objects, it is the scene which seems to be seen best for the first time: a curtain parts: what had not yet ever been seen is discovered in its entirety, and then devoured by the eyes; what is immediate stands for what is fulfilled: I am initiated. . . .[2]

Henry James's earliest memories of theatergoing, and his own accounts of his ravishment by a series of scenes (from both plays and paintings) from the ages of five or six to twelve, are highly consonant with the way Barthes elevates the impact of the scene itself and its initiatory force over any of the elements that constitute the scene (including the figure of the "beloved-at-first-sight").

In recalling his first play, James remembers attending a performance of *Comedy of Errors*. He nominated this his "prime initiation" into "that world of queer appreciations" that was the very mixed scene of the American theater of circa 1850, in which bravura acting in Shakespeare and virtuosic opera-singing both bulked large, alongside (often on the same bill with) a wide variety of Barnumesque hokum, wild melodrama, and farce. This mixture is figured first of all for the "infant" James by "the way the torment of the curtain was mixed" as he sat waiting for the play to begin, as it seemed to him to exude "half so dark a defiance and half so rich a promise." "One's eyes bored into it in vain," he remembers feeling.[3]

His attendance at a performance of *Uncle Tom's Cabin* at Barnum's Museum sometime not long afterward seems to have marked for him his initiation as a critic (as his attendance at *Comedy of Errors* later marked for him his initiation as a playgoer, or his first visit to the Louvre at the age of twelve retrospectively represented for him what he called his initiation into "style"). Harriet Beecher Stowe's sensational (and sensationally successful) antislavery novel represented for James a kind of limit case of how far a book could exceed the supposed boundaries of print to become primarily and even overwhelmingly a visual phenomenon: the book had, James writes, "above all the extraordinary fortune of finding itself, for an immense number of people, much less a book than a state of vision" (159). Experiencing his own much mediated version of this "state of vision" in childhood, James recalls that "we attended this spectacle just in order *not* to be beguiled, just in order to enjoy with ironic detachment and, at the very most, to be amused ourselves at our sensibility should it prove to have been trapped and caught. To have become thus aware of our collective attitude constituted for one small spectator at least a great initiation" (162–63). What James recalls "wondering" about is his boy companions' response to the drama, "where the absurd, the absurd for *them*, ended and the fun, the real fun, which was the gravity, the tragedy, the drollery, the beauty, the thing itself, briefly, might be . . . held to begin." "Uncanny though the remark perhaps," he goes on, "I am not sure I wasn't thus more interested in the pulse of our party, under my tiny recording thumb, than in the beat of the drama and the shock of its opposed forces" (163).

Two kinds of figures stand out in this recollection of James regarding his "great initiation" as a critic. One is the thoroughly mixed charge of the theatrical experience for himself and his companions — compounded of absurdity, fun, gravity, tragedy, drollery, and beauty. The other is the vocabulary of capture, both in the "sensibility" intermittently "trapped and caught" by the drama and the collective pulse taken by the "tiny recording thumb." The desire to "trap" and re-trap ostensibly incongruous combinations of affective and aesthetic tones and registers constitutes a driving force in the work not only of James but of all these artists. The fantasy of successful pupillary capture, the subjection of beloved images and scenes (often highly "mixed" ones) to radical processes of framing and reframing and of storage and retrieval in the eye of memory, is an impelling one across several media in many of the narratives of artistic production retold in this book.

Given this range of fascinations, it is unsurprising that the early-twentieth-century showman and "escape artist" Harry Houdini was a figure emblematic of a set of strong desires for a number of these artists, early and late in their lives. Charles Ludlam is said to have been at work on a play about Houdini, in which he planned to star, shortly before the time of his death from AIDS-related causes in 1987. Houdini was also the boyhood hero of Joseph Cornell, who had seen him perform at the Hippodrome, and wrote a talk about him while a student at Andover. In the talk he voiced his pleasure at the spectacle of "Houdini before seventy thousand people, hanging in midair, escap[ing] from very special constructed shackles and handcuffs." "I am going to give a speech on Houdini if I get called on in English class," he wrote to his mother, only to write again a little later, with his own brand of spectacular diffidence, "I was all ready to give a speech on Houdini, but was not called on. I will save it for another time."[4] As his biographer Deborah Solomon points out, Cornell was likely drawn to Houdini's genius for "disappearing acts." But a recent biography of Houdini suggests another component of Houdini's art that no doubt contributed to the widespread fascination with his performances that has gone largely unremarked: his penchant for performing his stunts (and posing for publicity photographs) as nearly nude as circumstances permitted. In doing so, Houdini carried the magician's ritual assurance, "Nothing up my sleeve," to a logical extreme.[5]

Throughout the modern era, the male body has been turned into spectacle in many different modes and by means of a wide variety of representational techniques, ranging from the Winckelmannian cult of the heroic male nude in the postrevolutionary French painting that James first encountered on his initial and initiatory visit to the Louvre to the displays of beefcake models in postwar physique magazines, Leni Riefenstahl's or

Minor White's high-modernist photographs of male nudes, and the physical self-displays of the hustler-actors of Warhol's films. We have in recent years acquired some tools to aid our understanding of how any given instance of the representation of the male body inevitably not only reveals some desires but also masks or screens while it may also exclude some other desires.[6] The performative effects of the range of representations of male bodies I consider in this book vary widely; while the ubiquity of male bodies and their parts may seem to the unsympathetic or phobic viewer to constitute a single monotonous scene, one of endless repetition, this book argues to the contrary that over the past century written and visual images of male physical desirability have been conscripted to tell an indeterminably wide array of stories.

Hypermimesis

Popular representations of gay men have for a long time now suggested that there is something hypermimetic about our behavior: to the degree that we are visible or legible to the "general population," that apparency has often depended on our being recognizable as imitation women—either actually in drag or effeminate in manner. More recently, the impersonation of hypervirile men has been added to our repertoire in the popular imagination. A profusion of theoretical work, from Esther Newton's and Severo Sarduy's to Judith Butler's, has dislodged some of the binarisms that have bound a broad range of historically queer roles and identities—butch, femme, drag queen, leatherman—to an ontology of inauthenticity and failed imitation.[7]

Rather than disavowing queer hypermimeticism, this book embraces its practices and effects. Yet from its beginnings, the present project has sought to examine queer imitations not so much on their own terms as in the ways in which they have frequently manifested themselves throughout the past century in relation to queer practices of initiation and self-initiation. What does it mean to initiate someone into something? "To induct into membership by or as if by special rites" is one routine dictionary definition; "to instruct in the rudiments or principles of something" is another. "To instruct someone in some secret knowledge" is a common subvariant of the latter definition. Few of us are actually inducted or sexually initiated into being queer and part of some queer community in quite the way the homophobic fantasy of organized, militant, recruiting homosexuals would have it. But the scene of sexual instruction and initiation remains a charged fantasy-space, probably for many of us (it is, after all, one of the most commonly reported and frequently represented fantasies across a range of sexualities). And for many queers, the erotic overtones of such scenes color many other fantasies and memories of ours about the long stretches of time many of us have spent turning ourselves into makers and transmitters of various components of queer culture.

In his commitment to thinking erotic and artistic imitation and initiation together, Gérard de Nerval—one of Joseph Cornell's primary models as an artist—is an exemplary figure. From one limited perspective it may be possible to understand Nerval's prolonged amorous obsession with the actress Jenny Colon as a heterosexual attachment, but from several others it seems appropriate to call it "queer," in its excessiveness, in its own theatricality, in its morbidity, and not least in its fusion of "practical" futility with imaginative and artistic fertility. Of the series of severe mental and emotional crises he underwent during the years after her death, as he continued to cultivate his vision of her and of what he saw as her avatars, Nerval wrote, in the closing words of his novel *Aurelia* (1854), "I compare the series of ordeals through which I passed to that which, for the ancients, represented the idea of a descent into the underworld"—that is, the classical idea of ritual sacred initiation.[8] Similarly, in the closing words of his novel *Angélique* (1850), Nerval evokes the most canonical of such initiatory passages, the words of the Sybil of Cumae to Aeneas as he seeks entry into the underworld in book 6 of the *Aeneid: facilis descensus Averno*, "the way down to Avernus is easy" (it is the route back up to the surface of the earth from the underworld that is difficult). However, in the brief colloquy that precedes this particular recursion to the classical model of initiatory rites, Nerval has linked imitation specifically to literary practice: "You have imitated Diderot," his interlocutor tells him; "who imitated Sterne," he replies; "who imitated Swift," his interlocutor rejoins—and they continue in this fashion, extending the copying farther and farther back: "who imitated Rabelais," "who imitated Petronius," "who imitated Lucian," "who imitated the author of the Odyssey." Interestingly, unlike the other objects of writerly imitation included in this genealogy, "the author of the Odyssey" is not named except in this periphrastic fashion. Did Nerval perhaps think, as Samuel Butler did, that "the author of the Odyssey" was a woman?

Whether he did or not, his declining to name the ur-poet of ancient Western epic at the structural climax and point of origin of his own account of his literary tradition neatly destabilizes the otherwise uninterrupted and untroubled regression to the sources of his own practice staged at the end of *Angélique*. In the ideal world according to Nerval, one can become initiated, but, ultimately, no one initiates. All imitate.

Such acts of momentarily or thoroughly queered imitation abound in the pages that follow; consider, for example, the sense in which the young Joseph Cornell may be said to be imitating his idol Houdini when he prepares an admiring speech about his spectacular exploits, only to find himself "not called on" to deliver it, and writing home that he "will save it for another time." When gay S-M writer John Preston addresses the matter of queer-male initiation and performance directly in his article, "The Theatre of Sexual Initiation," he devotes the bulk of his attention to describing activities at the Mineshaft, a well-known gay sex-club of the 1970s.[9] Preston argues that the performances of various sexual acts by some gay men for informal audiences of other gay men who wandered from room to room of the club provided rites of initiation to gay men who were barred from such common rites of passage for many young men in modern industrial societies as athletic competition and service in the military. What Preston's otherwise valuable account does not address is the question of why a scene like the Mineshaft was populated mostly by "regulars," and, if its primary function was, as he argues, initiatory, why many men went there not once ("for initiation") but many times, over a period of months or years. What this gap in his account suggests is that the queer theater of initiation is not about "one-time" experiences, but about the restaging of fantasies and/or memories of or desires for "first-time" experiences, endlessly. Iterability is, of course, a crucial feature of imitation, but it is not ordinarily thought of as a primary feature of initiation. Seeing repetition as a feature of "the theater of initiation" may help one begin to see how imitation and initiation are more closely related than they are ordinarily considered to be. Many narratives of queer desire suggest that this may be the case.

Chapter 1 of this book concerns Henry James's representations of the disorienting effects of imitation on desire, in James's tale "The Pupil," of a boy's and his young tutor's love for each other. The chapter rereads the tale, first in relation to Freud's essay on "The Uncanny" and E. T. A. Hoffmann's tale "The Sandman," from which Freud derives his theory of the workings of the uncanny, and then in relation to a series of scenes of eroticized beating and mock-lovemaking between the two principal male characters in David Lynch's Blue Velvet. The chapter explores a series of continuities among these texts (along with Kenneth Anger's Scorpio Rising) as well as the differences between their respective representations of the initiation of a younger male by an older one through ritualized or literal beating and erotic contact.

Chapter 2 considers closely Henry James's representations of what he calls his own "initiation into style" as a twelve-year-old boy visiting the Louvre for the first time in A Small Boy and Others. The chapter examines at length the significance of James's claim that his boyhood initiation as an artist took place not in relation to a set of literary texts (as one might expect), but amidst the display of a celebrated collection of "queer" (his recurrent term) images: the intensely male-homoerotic mythological and history paintings associated with the French Revolution and the First Empire (e.g., Jacques-Louis David's paintings of Roman and Spartan heroes, Girodet's Sleep of Endymion, Géricault's Raft of the Medusa).

Vaslav Nijinsky seems to have recognized and resisted the ways in which contemporary audiences saw his performances as a dancer as inherently excessive in an incoherent combination of ways (e.g., as too athletically masculine and, at the same time, as too effeminately graceful). Chapter 3 considers the alternately withholding and explosive dynamics of Nijinsky's performance as a paradigm for much controversial and "difficult" stage and film performance later in the century. This chapter focuses on the relatively little known but highly influential example of filmmaker and performance artist Jack Smith, director of Flaming Creatures (1963), and his modes of both imitating and resisting the fascinated and withholding attitudes of his audience.

Chapter 4 examines a highly transformative moment in the career of Andy Warhol, circa 1960, when he abandoned his attempts to gain recognition as an artist by producing mimetically realistic representations of male-homoerotic images (drawings of idealized male bodies and body parts) and, in their place, recoded the cartoon images that he remembered having eroticized as a child (Superman, Dick Tracy, Popeye) as revised images of not only his desire for other men but also his desire for artistic "popularity" and success on a mass scale.

Chapter 5 takes up the topic of mimesis and male prostitution. Representations of hustler-and-john relations served as a major trope for a crisis in "American manhood" in the fiction and film of the 1960s, in the work of James Baldwin, John Rechy, and in the American reception of the novels of Jean Genet. The chapter compares Warhol's ironization of relations of imitation and initiation between males in his film *My Hustler* with John Schlesinger's domesticizing mainstreaming of the same emblematic relations in his Oscar-winning film *Midnight Cowboy*.

Celebrated for the "boxes" he constructed and exhibited from the late 1930s to the 1970s, Joseph Cornell has only begun to be recognized as someone who produced a massive and important writing project during his lifetime. A large volume of his journals and working notes appeared in 1993, providing a tantalizing sample of what is said to be thirty times as much material still awaiting editing and publication. Chapter 6 concerns Cornell's lifelong imitation in his boxes and writing of a wide range of performance by women of the nineteenth and twentieth centuries. Cornell's muse-subjects extend from the first generation of female stars of Romantic ballet and opera, to Marianne Moore and Susan Sontag, as well as to Patty Duke, Lauren Bacall, and Hedy Lamarr. As he imitates women's performance, Cornell also engages in a simultaneous mimetic revision of the writing of such male muses and exemplars of his as Nerval, Whitman, and Proust. In doing so, he reveals himself to be one of the most notably successful cultivators and practitioners of the arts of "disorienting" desire. As is the case with the previous subjects of this study, recognizing the effects of some of the crosscurrents of imitation and initiation in his art and writing helps us recognize hitherto largely unrecognized kinds of affinities between his work and that of some of the other most influential artists and writers of the past century.

Chapter 7 returns to Henry James in order to locate him in a milieu which he visited but with which he has not often been associated: that of the turn-of-the-century Yiddish theater in New York City. Questions of literary and theatrical performance, as these are inflected by notions of linguistic and artistic purity and hybridity, provide a basis of common concern between James and some of the leading playwrights of the Yiddish theater. Charles Ludlam and Ethyl Eichelberger, leading figures in queer theater of the 1970s and 1980s, considered the thoroughly "mixed" Yiddish theater to have constituted an indispensable forerunner to their own brand of mongrel and outraged tragicomedy. Despite his avowed dedication to what he already saw as the lost cause of maintaining the purity of the English language, James's openness to recycling the devices of popular art of many kinds in his writing throughout his career suggests that as an artist he may have had more in common with some of the *shund-* (trash-) loving playwrights of the Yiddish theater or the leaders of the queer "theater-of-the-ridiculous" movement than we are used to recognizing.

ONE ✦ A Small Boy and Others: Sexual Disorientation

in Henry James, Kenneth Anger, and David Lynch

In this chapter I am concerned with a group of texts that have been produced over the past century: chiefly, Henry James's "The Pupil" (1891), Kenneth Anger's film *Scorpio Rising* (1963), and David Lynch's *Blue Velvet* (1986). Each of these texts draws much of its considerable uncanny energies from representing heavily ritualized performances of some substantial part of the whole round of "perverse" desires and fantasies, autoerotic, homoerotic, voyeuristic, exhibitionistic, incestuous, fetishistic, and sadomasochistic. Particularly striking are the ways in which all these texts foreground the mimed and ventriloquized qualities of the performances of ritual induction and initiation into "perverse circles," which they represent, rather than attempting to de-emphasize the mimetic secondariness of these representations, as realist texts and ordinary pornography both commonly do. Since René Girard launched his influential critique of the object-theory of desire twenty-five years ago, his argument that it is not the putative object of desire but mimesis that is primary in the formation of desire has been usefully elaborated by a number of theorists.[1] Of these, Mikkel Borch-Jacobsen's recent rereading of Girard's hypothesis "against" some similarly fundamental hypotheses of Freud's has been highly suggestive for my own current project. "[D]esire is mimetic before it is anything else," Borch-Jacobsen writes.[2] Rather than focusing on simple triangulations of desire among persons, as he criticizes Girard for doing, he attempts to theorize the thoroughly disorienting effects mimesis has on desire ("[D]esire is not oriented by pleasure, it is (dis)oriented by mimesis . . ." [34]).

In the texts I am looking at, I want to consider some of the ways in which sexuality is not so much oriented by its object, by the perceived gender or age, race, social class, body type, style of dress, and so on, of its object, as it is *disoriented* by mimesis. There are many more people who respond strongly (whether or not they recognize or acknowledge any positive component to their response) to images of male-male sadomasochism, for example, than there are people who identify themselves as gay-male sadomasochists—this at least became clear in the aftermath of the controversy surrounding the Corcoran Gallery's cancellation of its projected exhibition of Robert Mapplethorpe's photographs. The reason for this strong response is not simply because these images induce the viewer at least momentarily to violate (painfully and/or pleasurably, depending on one's point of view) the general interdiction of sadomasochistic object-choice among males in our society, for just such object-choices flourish in many institutional settings; relations of inflicting and receiving psychological and physical pain, with the sexual element of this interchange suppressed or not, are considered not shocking aberrations but ordinary and even necessary practice in the military, prisons, many corporate organizations, athletic teams, and schools of all levels. It is the domestication of many of these procedures into "discipline," the daily practice of institutional "law and order," with only those interchanges that are most flagrantly sexually enacted isolated and stigmatized as "sexual perversion," that conduces most of us to disavow our insiders' knowledge of sadomasochistic pleasures most of the time.

As with other kinds of largely disavowed knowledges, the knowledge of ostensibly minority pleasures like sadomasochism plays constantly around the margins of perception of the "normal" majority—that most audacious of theoretical fictions. If in an important sense *no* desire is our own—that is, originates with us; if desire is indeed primarily induced by imitation, mimed and ventriloquized, then it is impossible to maintain our ordinary "orienting" notions of which desires we are at home with and which ones we are not. Powerful images of ostensibly perverse desires and fantasies disorient our currently prevailing assumptions—symmetrical and pluralistic—about our own and other people's sexual orientations by bringing home to us the shapes of desires and fantasies that we ordinarily disavow as our own. In forcing us to recognize at least liminally our own familiarity or "at-homeness" with these desires these images produce *unheimlich*—uncanny—effects. In the texts I am discussing, the process of inducing uncanny effects is inseparable from the related process of inducing effects of what I am calling sexual disorientation, to denote the position of reader- or viewer-subjects at least temporarily dislocated from what they consider their "home" sexual orientation and "disorientingly" circulated through a number of different positions on the wheel of "perversions," positions that render moot or irrelevant our current basic "orienting" distinction, homo/heterosexual. I am interested in doing this not in order to try to efface this distinction, which on the gay side has been so murderously enforced over the past century, never more so than it is today, but to the contrary to extend our thinking about the dependence of both so-called high and popular culture during the same period on the sexually "perverse" for their energies and often for their representational programs.

Roy Orbison's 1963 song "In Dreams" figures importantly in Blue Velvet. It begins, "A candy-colored clown they call the sandman tiptoes to my room every night, / Just to sprinkle stardust and to whisper, 'Go to sleep, everything is all right.'" Orbison's "candy-colored clown they call the sandman" has commonly been taken to mean—as so much figurative writing in pop music of the 1960s and after has been—simply "drugs," in this case "downs" or "sleepers." Without discounting this entirely, I want to press on the intertextual relation of the "sandman" of Orbison's and Lynch's texts with that of E. T. A. Hoffmann's 1816 story "The Sandman" and Freud's 1919 essay "The Uncanny," which takes Hoffman's story as its model literary text.

In Hoffmann's story, a young student named Nathanael believes that an old instrument-peddler who calls himself "Coppola" is the same man who, as the lawyer Coppelius, used to pay mysterious nocturnal visits to Nathanael's father, until the night the boy's father was killed by an explosion and fire in his study, from the scene of which Coppelius supposedly fled. During this time the child Nathanael had developed the fixed notion that old Coppelius was the nursery-fable figure "the Sandman" in the flesh—rather repellent flesh, little Nathanael thinks.

Freud interprets the story's uncanny effects as proceeding from castration anxieties, which it registers around the figure of Nathanael, who displaces his fear of castration by his father onto his father's evil and uncanny double, Coppelius.[3] As is the case with so many of Freud's key formulations, we get only the "heterosexual plot" of the "sandman" narrative in his reading of it. Neither Freud nor any of the other readers who have published interpretations of the story has to my knowledge made anything of the narrative's continuous engagement with a thematics of male-male

17

sadomasochism and pedophilia, as when Nathanael says that Coppelius had "mishandled" or "manhandled" him once when he caught the boy spying on him and his father, violently twisting his hands and feet and moving as if to pluck out his eyes.[4] Later in the story Nathanael claims Coppelius "had entered him and possessed him" at the time he caught him spying (292). Nathanael's "madness" takes the form of a series of hysterical outbursts in which he keeps crying, "Whirl round, circle of fire! Merrily, merrily! Aha lovely wooden doll, whirl round!" (304, 308). It is possible to see how the hallucinatory contents of his delirium may derive from a premature and precocious induction into the "perverse" "circle of fire" he enters when as a child he spies on the mysterious nocturnal activities of his father with Coppelius. He keeps hysterically mistaking his relation to the "lovely wooden doll"; in the second half of the story he falls in love with the girl-automaton Olympia, a figure that is on one level of his confused thoughts an image of his physically invaded child self and on another an image of his infantile perception of the phallus of the father and/or Coppelius as a terrifying and powerful machine ("wooden doll, whirl round!"). Lacan speaks of one of the primary significations of the phallus as being its character as the visible sign of the sexual link or what he calls the "copula," [5] and Nathanael's belief that Coppelius renamed himself "Coppola" after his attack on him and his alleged murder of his father underscores Coppelius's position as phallic terrorist in Nathanael's story.

Part of the uncanny power of Hoffmann's "The Sandman" no doubt derives from the undecidable relation of this "perverse" narrative to the familiar oedipal one about Nathanael's relation to his father and his female sweethearts that psychoanalytic theory has privileged. Hoffmann's text reveals with stunning force how thoroughly any given reader, including Freud and subsequent critics of "The Sandman," may be both "at home" and "not at home," simultaneously and in undecidable combination, with these powerful and "perverse" undercurrents. The film Blue Velvet, too, oscillates between a conventional, linear, oedipal plot and a circular, "perverse," and ritualistic one. The trajectory of the oedipal plot of Blue Velvet is also racist, sexist, ageist, and homophobic in the ways to which the oedipal so readily lends itself: a young man must negotiate what is represented as being the treacherous path between an older, ostensibly exotic, sexually "perverse" woman and a younger, racially "whiter," sexually "normal" one, and he must at the same time and as part of the same process negotiate an even more perilous series of interactions with the older woman's violent and murderous criminal lover and the younger woman's protective police-detective father. This heterosexual plot resolves itself in classic oedipal fashion: the young man Jeffrey destroys the demonic criminal "father" and rival Frank, rescues the older woman, Dorothy, from Frank's sadistic clutches, and then relinquishes her to her fate and marries the perky young daughter of the good cop.[6]

But that is not the whole story of the film: there is an anarchic second plot that emerges intermittently but unmistakably in which subject positions and transferals of identities and desires are highly volatile. Young Jeffrey arrives at film's end at the object of his oedipal destination, the high-school student Sandy (notice how the name of even this character, the only principal one in the film supposedly located well outside the "perverse" circuits it traverses, links her with Orbison's and Hoffmann's uncanny "sandmen"), but he is frequently swept off course from this oedipal trajectory, not only by his attraction to and involvement with Dorothy, "the Blue Velvet Lady," but by his only marginally less intense "involvement" with her lover Frank and the other men who surround him. There are two moments in the film that I shall discuss at some length in which the supercharged valences of male-male desire are represented with particular graphic power. In these scenes, characters enact a whole series of uncanny relationships between males of different ages, social classes, and supposed sexual orientations — orientations that get thoroughly disoriented when they get swept near the flame of "perverse" desire that flows around the figures of the chief sadomasochistic pair, Frank and Dorothy.

Anyone who watches *Blue Velvet* with "The Sandman" in mind may well be struck by how densely intertextual the film is with the story, not only in its repeated evocations of the figure of "the sandman," but also in its "perverse" plot: as in Hoffmann's "The Sandman," a young male gets unexpectedly initiated into a circle of sadomasochistic and fetishistic desires. Lynch's characters, like Hoffmann's, indulge in a round of spying and retributive and eroticized beating on each other, and of mimed and ventriloquized desire. Early in the film the young man Jeffrey hides in Dorothy's closet and spies on her. When she catches him, she forces him to strip at knifepoint and subsequently introduces him to sadomasochistic sex, as both direct participant and voyeur. When on one occasion later in the film Frank catches Jeffrey leaving Dorothy's apartment, he forces both of them to come with him for what he calls a "joyride," the first stop of which is at Ben's, where Jeffrey is preliminarily punched a time or two (by Frank and Ben) and Ben, looking heavily made-up, lip-synchs Roy Orbison's song about "the candy-colored clown they call the sandman," until he is interrupted by a grimacing Frank, who manically orders everyone present to get on with the "joyride."

The initiation ritual to which Frank is subjecting Jeffrey at this point in the film is extremely ambiguous: the younger man is being intimidated and frightened away from Frank and his circle of perversions at the same time as he is being forced and welcomed into it. The contradictions do not stop at the figure of Jeffrey; they extend to everyone present at the scene of initiation: in Frank's obvious pleasure *and* pain during Ben's lip-synching; in Ben's "suave" behavior toward Frank, as Frank calls it, and Ben's sadistic behavior toward Jeffrey (he hits him in the stomach), as well as in Ben's being both male and "made-up" (i.e., wearing cosmetics); in Dorothy's being brought to Ben's both to be terrorized and punished and to be allowed to see her small child, who is being held there; in the mixed atmosphere of Ben's place, which appears to be a whorehouse with a staff of mostly grandmotherly looking whores, several of whom are sitting around a coffee table, suburban-homestyle, chatting with Ben when Frank and his party arrive. Ben's lip-synching of "In Dreams" functions as both a kind of "tribute" to Frank and also as a kind of threat to Jeffrey that some uncanny figure called "the candy-colored clown" or "sandman" is going to "get him"—but, as one sees in the pain Frank registers in his face during the latter part of the lip-synch, this figure "gets" Frank, too; he seems almost on the verge of breaking down before he yanks the tape from the player and orders everyone to "hit the fuckin' road."

When Frank, Dorothy, Jeffrey, and the others make their next stop it is at a deserted spot far out in the country. Here Frank starts hyperventilating and playing sadistically with Dorothy's breasts. Unable to remain in the voyeuristic position in which he has been placed for the moment, Jeffrey first orders Frank to "leave [Dorothy] alone" and then leaps forward from the backseat of the car and punches Frank in the face. Frank orders Raymond and his other henchmen to pull the boy out of the car and to put the song "Candy-Colored Clown" ("In Dreams") on the car's tape player. The action between Frank and Jeffrey becomes most densely ritualistic at this point. Frank smears lipstick on his mouth and kisses it onto Jeffrey's lips, pleading with him to leave Dorothy alone (the same thing Jeffrey had ordered him to do a minute before), and threatening to send him "a love letter" if he does not, explaining to him that by "a love letter" he means "a bullet from a fuckin' gun." "If you get a love letter from me, you're fucked *forever*," Frank tells Jeffrey. He then starts speaking to Jeffrey the words of the song playing on the tape player: "In dreams I walk with you, / In dreams I talk to you; / In dreams you're mine, all of the time, / We're together in dreams." Frank then wipes the lipstick from the boy's lips with a swatch of blue velvet, instructs the other men to "hold him tight for me," and, to the crescendo of the song's chorus ("It's too bad that these things / Can only happen in my dreams"), begins to beat Jeffrey mercilessly. As Jeffrey presumably loses consciousness, the music and the scene fade out.

When Lynch has Frank mouth the words of the song a second time, this time directly to a Jeffrey whom he has ritually prepared for a beating by "kissing" lipstick onto his mouth and wiping it off with a piece of blue velvet, it is as though Lynch is both daring the viewer to recognize the two men's desire for each other that the newly discovered sadomasochistic bond that unites them induces them to feel *and* at the same time to recognize the perhaps more fearful knowledge that what most of us consider our deepest and strongest desires are not our own, that our dreams and fantasies are only copies, audio- and videotapes, of the desires of others and our utterances of them lip-synchings of these circulating, endlessly reproduced and reproducible desires. Lip-synching is the ideal form of enunciation for the ritualized and serious game of "playing with fire"—that is, with the game of inducing male homosexual panic and of making recognizable, at least in flashes, the strong S-M component of male-male violence—that Frank, Ben, and Jeffrey play: lip-synching a pop song allows Ben to "come on" to Frank, and Frank in turn to "come on" to Jeffrey, singing about how "In Dreams" they possess the man to whom they're singing—without doing so in any way that "counts" for more than the fantasmatic and mimicked moments the two pairs of men share.

The lip-synch/lipstick initiation to which Frank subjects Jeffrey ritualistically enacts the rupture between the sayable and the unsayable about the intense sadomasochistic bond between them, both as they transact this bond through their shared involvement with Dorothy, and as it threatens, just at this point in the film, to bypass mediation through her—that is, to become simply a male-male S-M relationship. It also marks the point of lack on the part of both men of an "original" voice or "original" utterance and the consequently ventriloquistic character of their—and our—desires. The fascination with other men's lips, with men kissing each other, especially in the context of a sadomasochistic relationship, and with the look of smeared lipstick on men's lips—all these bespeak the generally enforced misrecognition of many men most of the time of the relation between their own ostensibly "normal" male heterosexuality and their relation to the penetrable orifices of their own and other males' bodies; it is a sign of the "scandal" of the liminal gendering—one might say the minimal gendering—of the mouth and anus, the repression of which "scandal" so much energy and anxiety in straight-male relations are invested in concealing and revealing, as is evident in the most basic buzzwords of male-male abuse, "cocksucker" and "asshole" and "faggot," a set of terms and relationships of male-male power into which almost every small boy in our culture is interpellated as a crucial part of his elementary education. The "candy-colored clown they call the sandman" whom Ben and Frank mimic (the "made-up" and intensely flashlit look of both their faces as they lip-synch is a sign that they are "clowning") is a figure for the circulation through the men in these scenes of a mostly disavowed familiarity with, and in varying degrees, adeptness at, sadomasochistic desire and practices between males.

It would be a significant oversight to ignore the roles of the women in these scenes—Dorothy especially and the other woman who joins the "joyride" at Ben's—in the initiation ritual carried out on Jeffrey. Dorothy moves over to the driver's seat when Frank and the other men drag Jeffrey out of the car to beat him, but her real position remains abject: she shouts, "Frank, stop! Frank, stop!"—to no avail—then lays her arms and her head on the steering wheel and weeps, as Frank carries on with the ritual violence in which she is relegated to the position of a Stabat Mater who can't bear to look. The other woman who has joined the group is unfazed, is perfectly "at home," with the scene of male-male sadomasochism she has been transported to witness: she climbs out of the car onto its roof, where she dances to the strains of "In Dreams," combined with the rhythmic sound (the "beat") of Frank's fists falling on Jeffrey's body, with the mechanical imperturbability of Olympia, Nathanael's automaton-sweetheart in Hoffmann's "The Sandman."

It is surely relevant to the way women in this scene are relegated to positions of either abjection or affectlessness to mention that, as Lynch had it

in the original script for Blue Velvet, Frank was at this point in the film supposed to rape Jeffrey, to enact literally his telling Dorothy, in response to
her fearful question when they leave Ben's, "Where are we going?" "We're
takin' your neighbor [Jeffrey] out to the country to fuck."[7] Lynch's decision
to film the scene "otherwise," to transmute Frank's violation of Jeffrey and
his body from a literal rape to a symbolic ritual, raises questions about the
way males and male bodies are privileged in this film and the way women—
again, Dorothy especially—are abjected in it. It is important in this connection, for example, that the representational economy of nakedness in
the film is initially presented as a gender-symmetrical one: Jeffrey spies on
Dorothy undressing as he hides in her closet, and when Dorothy discovers
him she forces him to undress while she watches. But there is no scene performed by a male that corresponds to the climactic one late in the film performed by Rossellini, when, as Dorothy, she comes staggering, naked and
incoherent, out into the street where Sandy's drunken ex-boyfriend and his
buddies are picking a fight with Jeffrey. Dorothy's punctual arrival, nude,
at a second scene of male-male violence has the effect of rescuing Jeffrey
from a second beating; catching sight of her, the drunken ex-boyfriend first
asks Jeffrey mockingly, "Is that your mother?" (thereby voicing for Jeffrey
and the viewer the oedipal anxieties the film frequently both engages and
mocks), but even the drunken teenage boy seems to lose interest in baiting
Jeffrey when he sees how badly off Dorothy really is. There is a dynamic relation between Jeffrey's being let off the hook—not only from the violence
being immediately threatened at this point in the narrative but from any
real threat of violence for the rest of the film—and Dorothy's being reduced
at this climactic moment to a literal vision of staggering naked abjection.
The excessive and appalling degree to which Dorothy and her body are exposed to the general gaze at this point serves the other characters and their
director-author to underwrite the "happy ending" that subsumes Jeffrey
and Sandy and, supposedly, Dorothy and her little son (her lover Frank and
her husband both die in the violence at the end of the film). We should also
recognize how it serves retroactively to underwrite Lynch's sublimation of
male-male rape in the scene between Frank and Jeffrey into a beating that
leaves sexual violation enacted only on a symbolic plane.

One of the most pervasive fantasies informing the "perverse" initiation
rituals I'm discussing and the uncanny, sexually disorienting effects they
produce is that of a person's being able to ravish and hold captive another

person by the unaided agency of a powerful gaze, and the attendant danger of this gaze's making its director more rather than less highly susceptible to other people's gazes (in Blue Velvet, for example, Frank tries repeatedly to control Dorothy's and Jeffrey's gazing behavior toward him). The fantasy of the pupil of the eye as the focal point of visual and erotic capture is at the core of Henry James's tale "The Pupil," which treats a series of visual and erotic captures and struggles to escape both into and away from a "perverse" circle constituted by a brilliant little boy, his loving and beloved tutor, and the boy's mother, who is attractive and socially ambitious but perpetually financially embarrassed. The precincts of James's fiction may seem remote from those of a recent and flagrantly "perverse" film like Blue Velvet, but they are not as far apart as they may at first appear. Despite James's own announced distaste for the project of some of his contemporaries of representing "perversion" relatively openly and sensationally—Wilde's Dorian Gray, for example—James's own literary explorations of the circulation of "perverse" desires are elaborate and searching, and remarkably unconstrained by contemporary standards of gentility and prudery. "The Pupil" was summarily rejected by the editor of the Atlantic Monthly, one of the very few times one of James's fictions was declined by the journals to which he regularly contributed. James professed to be unable to understand why, but it may well have been because it produced the same kinds of discomfort in the editor that an anonymous critic writing in the Independent expressed a few years later in response to The Turn of the Screw. "How Mr. James could . . . choose to make such a study of infernal human debauchery . . . is unaccountable," the reviewer writes, going on to say, "The study . . . affects the reader with a disgust that is not to be expressed. The feeling after perusal of the horrible story is that one has been assisting in an outrage upon . . . human innocence, and helping to debauch—at least by standing helplessly by—the pure and trusting nature of children. Human imagination can go no further into infamy, literary art could not be used with more refined subtlety of spiritual defilement."[8] In other words, James's work looked to some of his contemporaries—and may look to us, if we allow it to—the way Blue Velvet looks to us: shocking and disturbing. Or to put it another way, if James were writing today, his work would look more like Blue Velvet than it would like Merchant and Ivory's ponderously reverent period "re-creations" of his novels.

One thing James's work registers continuously that Merchant and Ivory's betrays little feeling for is the investment of "sexiness" in, the fetish-character of, a given epoch's favored fashions in dress and styles of interior decoration. The Paris of the Second Empire was the most formative setting of James's childhood according to his own testimony, and it is a principal setting of "The Pupil." The bourgeois culture of this period may be said to have had its own intense velvet fetish. According to Walter Benjamin in his study of Baudelaire, bourgeois domestic interiors at the latter end of the period had become velvet- and plush-lined carapaces for a social class that seemed to want to insulate itself from the world from which it derived its wealth and power behind a grotesque barrier of such luxury fabrics — in clothing for ordinary and ceremonial occasions, in upholstery and wall coverings, and, perhaps most significantly, in linings for instrument cases, jewelry boxes, and coffins.[9]

"Velvet" is everywhere in James, once one becomes aware of it, and it is there unsurprisingly, given the characteristic settings and concerns of his fiction — freedom and domination, glamour and stigma, during what he calls in the preface to "The Pupil" "the classic years of the great Americano-European legend." When the tutor Pemberton in "The Pupil" wonders resentfully how his penurious employers can manage to keep installing themselves in what the narrator calls the "velvety *entresols*" of the best hotels in Paris, "the most expensive city in Europe," "velvet" still bears the unambiguously positive charge it had carried forty years before in Thackeray's *Vanity Fair*, the repository of so many of James's basic props for signaling fine degrees of upward and downward social mobility, as when Becky Sharp finds herself at one of the peaks of her success being waited on by a "velvetfooted butler."[10] There is a striking detail in the opening lines of "The Pupil," however, that suggests that a luxury fabric could bear a more ambiguous charge as sign late in the nineteenth century. When the characters of Pemberton the tutor and Mrs. Moreen are first introduced, he is called simply "[t]he poor young man" and his new employer Mrs. Moreen is "the large, affable lady who sat there drawing a pair of soiled *gants de Suède* through a fat, jewelled hand. . . ."[11] This description occurs in the second sentence of the story and it is easy enough for one to overlook it as a gratuitous "realistic" detail, but on reflection one can see in what rich detail these images signify "trouble ahead" for Pemberton and even the ambiguous nature of that "trouble." Mrs. Moreen's gesture of drawing her soiled suede gloves through her "fat, jewelled hand" mimes an unspoken desire—not necessarily her own—for her son, who is both the only other person present at this conversation and the most mixed quantity in the story, the figure in it who is neither entirely innocent of the shabbiness or willful moral abjectness of the rest of the Moreen family, nor entirely guilty of it, but rather only tainted or "soiled" with it by unavoidable association. Pemberton squirms with discomfort during this initial (and initiatory) interview because Mrs. Moreen is performing this curious mime of displaying a bit of her dirty laundry to him instead of settling the matter of his salary, which the narrator refers to as "the question of terms." What Pemberton does not see at the beginning of the story is that while his salary is not being discussed, his real compensation for his work—an invitation to desire Morgan—is being repeatedly issued in mime by Mrs. Moreen. His intense but unnamed relationship to her little son—here is the real "question of terms" that is in contest in the story and beyond it—will partake of the mixed character of her "soiled" gloves. Rather than being something that sets them apart from the rest of the Moreen household, the "scandal" of the intimacy between tutor and pupil is perfectly "at home" with the more inclusive "scandal" of the kind of mixed clean-and-dirty surface Mrs. Moreen and the rest of the family show to the world. I shall return to the detail of the soiled gloves a little later on.

When Morgan dies at the story's climax, his body doesn't end up simply in his tutor's arms, as it might if the story were just a pederastic idyll, as I would argue it is not, nor does his body end up in his mother's arms, in the kind of vignette that would anticipate the similar death of little Miles in the arms of his governess at the climax of *The Turn of the Screw*. Rather, the body of the dead boy ends up suspended between his tutor and his mother. When Pemberton sees that Morgan is dead, the narrator says, "[h]e pulled him half out of his mother's hands, and for a moment, while they held him together, they looked, in their dismay, into each other's eyes" (460). The resemblance of this last image in the tale to its first one is striking: the boy Morgan's dead body occupies precisely the place of the dirty suede gloves, but this time instead of merely noticing them unreflectively while Mrs. Moreen pulls them through her hands, Pemberton actively intervenes to draw Morgan's body "half out of [her] hands." Suspended between childhood and manhood (he has grown from age eleven to fifteen in the course of the story) and between mother and tutor, Morgan's body at the moment of death becomes a kind of uncanny puppet, a "soiled" hand puppet like a "soiled" glove. Although Pemberton and Mrs. Moreen have repeatedly quarreled over which of them has made the greater "sacrifice" for Morgan, the boy himself ends up, perhaps not entirely unwillingly, the sacrificial victim of the rituals the three practice, leaving tutor and mother in the utterly abject position of members of a collapsed cult.

I want to consider a little further the possible significance of "soiled" suede as a figure for relations in "The Pupil." Like those of "velvet," the erotic and class associations of "suede" have shifted and mutated considerably over the past century and more. The possible erotic association that makes soiled "suede" rather than velvet the appropriate figure for whatever unnameable bond unites Mrs. Moreen and her little son at the beginning of the story, a bond into which they admit, and with which they secure Pemberton, is primarily a verbal one: English-language guides to proper dress from midcentury forward inform the reader that the newly fashionable fabric "Suède" is "undressed kid." Those who would argue that "undressed kid" could not have meant, even subliminally, "undressed child" to James and his readers because "kid" did not then in that place and time commonly mean "child," need only look in the OED to see that it was precisely in the decade or two before "The Pupil" was written that "kid" as a term for "child" ceased to be "low slang" as it long had been and entered into common use among the English upper class as a term of familiar affection for a child or children of one's own: William Morris writes of the health of his "kid" in a personal letter of the 1860s, and Lord Shaftesbury makes a notation of several happy days spent with his "wife and kids" in his journal of the 1880s. If my translations of the phrase "drawing a pair of soiled *gants de Suède* through a fat, jewelled hand" into "handling dirty undressed-kid gloves" and, possibly, into other permutations of that phrase, including "handling a dirty undressed kid," seem far-fetched, it is only because the erotic wish encrypted, mimed but unspoken, in the text of "The Pupil" is precisely the kind of meaning that requires just such high-intensity translation or decoding—not only because James may have been to some degree unconscious of this meaning but also because of our own resistance to recognizing the access to "perverse" energies that his writing frequently affords us.

Rather than assenting to the notion that texts like "The Pupil" and *Blue Velvet* are historically, politically, and stylistically remote from each other and consequently not susceptible to the same modes of interpretation, I want to argue that the successful obfuscation of these kinds of connections by several successive generations of literary critics has done a deep disservice not only to James's writing but also to the historical and political configuration in which it was produced and to the culture of our own day, which has, for all its differences, by no means resolved the kinds of political and sexual-political conflicts James anatomizes so unsparingly. To indulge an invidious comparison for a moment, I think James's practice in "The Pupil" is if anything more rather than less radical than Lynch's in *Blue Velvet*. The film's marginalization of Ben, the only character in the film explicitly marked as gay, is a sign of this. In effect quarantined from the rest of the film, his appearance is restricted to only one scene, although what he fleetingly represents—ties between men *not* mediated through a captive woman—is not. Lynch's raising the age of his boy-initiate Jeffrey into his early twenties is another significant normalizing gesture on his part; if *Blue Velvet* has been a controversial film, imagine how much more so it would have been if Lynch had followed James's practice in "The Pupil" of making his boy-initiate a *boy*—that is, not over fifteen.[12] Discarding the "heterosexual plot" on which narratives of "perverse initiation" from Hoffmann's "The Sandman" to *Blue Velvet* have traditionally depended, James in "The Pupil" produces his "perverse" plot almost undiluted by normalizing or heterosexualizing measures.

One must look beyond the example of Lynch to someone like Kenneth Anger, I think, to find work that explores the dynamics of "perverse" desire as uncompromisingly as James does. Anger is one of the figures who represents something closest to a "direct route" between figures like James and Lynch. In thirteen segments of complex montage, each set to a different pop tune of the two-or-three-year period before the film was made—the ancestors of today's ubiquitous rock videos—Anger's film shows the members of a motorcycle gang preparing for a race by tinkering with their bikes, dressing up in elaborate fetish gear, snorting cocaine, and performing a series of rituals including a mock orgy-and-torture session. These fetishistic and largely mock-sadomasochistic preparations culminate in a motorcycle rally in which the bikers race their 'cycles around a track to the tune of such pop-songs as "Point of No Return" and "Wipe-Out"—terms that may well remind us of what the group of texts I've been discussing represent as the traumatic and irreversibly shattering qualities of precocious initiation into "perverse circles."

One way of reading *Blue Velvet* is as a text that Lynch unfolded out of the "Blue Velvet" segment of Anger's 1964 film *Scorpio Rising*. In this segment, as Bobby Vinton croons, "She wore blue velvet," the film represents not a woman in blue velvet but a bike boy (three of them, in fact) in blue *denim* donning black leather and chains. While the song invites its auditor to fantasy a specularized and fetishized girl or woman—a figure like Lynch's Dorothy, "the Blue Velvet Lady"—Anger's film presents specularized and fetishized boys. Rather than the kind of undisrupted miming or lip-synching that characterizes male behavior and serves as a vehicle for a limited range of male-male desires in Lynch's film, Anger's film at moments like the one I am considering drives a wedge between the aural effects and the visual ones it is producing. By representing leather boys "dressing up" to the tune of the song "Blue Velvet," Anger produces the disorienting shock effect—quite successfully, judging from the outraged reception and censorship of the film during the early years of its reception—of placing males in the position of the specularized and fetishized "supposed-to-be-female" figure of sexist—and heterosexist—representational regimes.

The kinds of erotic and erotically disorienting substitutions in which *Scorpio Rising* deals, of which the blue-velvet bike-boys episode is a chief example, are certainly an important aspect of the pleasures of Anger's text. Another aspect of this pleasure I would not overlook is the one common to this as well as to all of the other texts I have been discussing of representing the fetish—whether it be velvet or suede, denim or leather—as a primary focus of the various "perverse" desires all these texts mime; in them, the fetish is an exemplarily disoriented marker of desire, not itself either the object of desire or simply the kind of substitute phallus it is in classical Freudian theory but something—at least as much a practice as it is an object—that locates itself undecidably between mimetic desire and the indefinitely wide range of objects on which that desire may fasten. *Scorpio Rising* literalizes more thoroughly than any other text of which I am aware not only the priority of mimetic desire over object-desire but also the priority of the fetish over other "perverse" investments.

One further link from Anger back to James's milieu passes through the figure of Aleister Crowley, someone whose work and career have been perhaps even more important for Anger than those of the two gay film directors whose influence is most obvious in his work, Eisenstein and Cocteau. A generation younger than James and exactly the kind of cultivator of a "perverse" public image that James strenuously avoided associating himself with, Crowley began his career as a member, along with Yeats and others, of the occult society of the Order of the Golden Dawn. Crowley spent most of his career performing and writing about forms of ritual magic based on "perverse" sexual practices, and Anger has been an avowed disciple of his since boyhood. Anger's precocity was the first very notable fact of his own career; the story of its beginning reads like one of the tales of always-premature, "perverse" initiation I have been considering. Left on his own one weekend by his parents when he was seventeen, Anger, no doubt fulfilling many suburban parents' worst nightmare about their offspring, made a film starring himself about a seventeen-year-old boy who is "picked up" by a gang of sailors and raped and disemboweled by them. That the atmosphere of the film is lyrical and witty rather than horrific suggests that Jean Genet might have had little to teach this boy-filmmaker about "perverse" desires and their representation. As the narrator of "The Pupil" says of Pemberton the tutor's efforts to fathom the remarkable resourcefulness and resilience of his little charge, "When he tried to figure to himself the morning twilight of childhood, so as to deal with it safely, he perceived that it was never fixed, never arrested, that ignorance, at the instant one touched it, was already flushing faintly into knowledge, that there was nothing that at a given moment you could say a clever child didn't know. It seemed to him that *he* both knew too much to imagine Morgan's simplicity and too little to disembroil his tangle" (437). Like little Morgan and his tutor and the other "small boys" and young men that figure in these texts, we all often find ourselves possessing what seems to be both more knowledge than we can use and less than we need when we try to think about such difficult issues as our own relations to children and young people, including our students, and our no less complicated relations to our own child selves. Those uncanny figures, as James writes, sometimes seemed to know their most painful lessons almost before they learned them. As I think the examples I have been discussing suggest, we have much to learn from these child-figures when they return to haunt us with their uncommon knowledge of the "perverse" energies that impel desire.

In the Memory Palace of Henry James

The "legend of the Master" continues to pervade many aspects of our understanding of Henry James and his writing. According to the legend, the "Master" was as a writer a fascinated, voyeuristic chronicler of the powerful effects of intimacy—and especially of the betrayal of intimacy—on the lives of others. James's voyeuristic fiction, the story goes, was a displacement of his own lifelong unease with intimate relations. In looking at some of James's writing about his memories of his childhood formation as an artist in relation to a series of crucial transformations in his culture's codes for representing the erotically desirable male body—transformations that for the most part had occurred a generation or more before his birth—I shall be attempting to read out of these writings a different kind of story about James, intimacy, and erotics from the received one.

If James has inevitably been something of a disappointment to some gay readers hoping to find in his work signs of a liberatory sexual program for male-male desire of the kinds available in the writings of some of his contemporaries, such as John Addington Symonds or Oscar Wilde,[1] a distinguishing element of the relation of James's writing to male-male erotics is its intense and strategic anachronism and anatopism. For James, as for a number of his predecessors in aesthetic theory and practice from Winckelmann to Pater, it is ostensibly not male-male eros "in the here and now" that impels the writing; rather, the possibility of fulfilling such desires beckons queerly to the passionate pilgrim or lover of beauty from the shores of other times or other countries. That from the late-eighteenth to the mid-nineteenth century the amateur of art or lover of beauty was perforce a lover of male beauty—but ostensibly the male beauty of other times and places—involves the histories of modern art and regimes of "looking" not only in a kind of foundational anachronism but in a no less foundational male homoeroticism as well.

Some of the places in his writing where James explores his own intimate relations to these "other" times and places most thoroughly are in his late memoirs, A Small Boy and Others and Notes of a Son and Brother. Looking back at his childhood and youth in the 1850s and 1860s from the vantage of 1910–11, when he was nearly seventy, inevitably involves James in extensively anatopic and anachronistic relations in his writing, to "other" countries, cultures, and languages in which he has lived or traveled, to his own past, to the pasts of his predecessors, and to at least the recent pasts of the arts he practices: prose fiction and the critical essay, but also what one might call "the art of the composition and placement of the scene" more broadly understood, both pictorial and dramatic, for which recent painting and theater, respectively, provide some of his most important models.

In chapter 25 of A Small Boy and Others James gives a complex account of what he calls his "initiation" into artistic style at the age of twelve, on the morning of his first visit to the Louvre in July 1855. Tactically suppressing for the time being the question of specifically literary style, James adduces a series of French painters and their works as his most formative models of style, a catalog that extends from some of Elisabeth Vigée-Lebrun's self-portraits and what he calls the "helmetted Romanisms" of Jacques-Louis David—works of the 1780s, the decade culminating in the Revolution—to Théodore Géricault's Raft of the Medusa (1819) and some paintings of Eugène Delacroix and Thomas Couture of the 1840s. In singling out French painting from the time of the Revolution through the first half of the nineteenth century as the rhetorical field in which his own sense of style emerged, James locates his art in a context in which images of the heroic male nude, in both its virile and ephebic versions, had served as the primary medium for representing relations of power and desire.[2]

James's writing, conventionally identified with late-nineteenth-century realist prose fiction, is haunted by this rich, primarily visual and corporeal discourse of male-male eros—a discourse that had fallen into comparative desuetude by the end of the nineteenth century, when it had effectively been replaced by the pathologizing discourses of the etiology, surveillance, prevention, and punishment of what had by then come to be called homosexuality. In locating his initiation as an artist not in the Anglophone literary milieu of the 1850s and 1860s, when he actually began to write, but in the French painterly milieu of the early decades of the nineteenth century, James acknowledges the primacy of the visual representation of the desirable male body for his artistic formation. These visual/visionary modes of apprehending and representing the male body, inaugurated by Winckelmann in the 1750s and 1760s, were disseminated for a couple of generations after his untimely death by a wide range of artists working in various media, including figures as diverse as David, Goethe, and Josiah Wedgwood, and by a number of writers, including some whom James read most assimilatively—Balzac and Byron—as well as one whom he read particularly resistantly: Pater, whose essay "Winckelmann" appeared in 1867 and whose celebrated evocation of Da Vinci's La Gioconda appeared in 1869, in the year of James's first visit to Rome. Both these texts were crucial in the revision of Winckelmann's cult of male beauty and in his much imitated practice of apostrophizing works of art in a "sublime" voice that is a combination of the spectator's and the artistic object's.

James declined as a young man visiting Rome for the first time in 1869 to imitate Winckelmann too directly or too openly (and, by that time, too banally) by in any way repeating his ecstatic praise of the Apollo Belvedere ("I become oblivious to everything else as I look at this masterwork of art, and I myself take on an elevated stance, so as to be worthy of gazing at it. My chest seems to expand with veneration and to rise and to heave . . .").[3] In his letter home to Alice James about his first visit to Rome, when he arrives at the inevitable topic of the celebrated antique sculptures exhibited in the Belvedere in the Vatican—objects considered the epitome of artistic style by several preceding generations of artists—James adopts a coolly knowing tone:

> These clever pieces don't err on the side of realism. My first movement at the Vatican was to run to the Belvedere and get them off my conscience. On the whole they quite deserve their fame: famous things always do. . . . The Apollo is really a magnificent youth with far more of solid dignity than I fancied. The Laocoon on the other hand, strikes me as a decidedly made up affair. . . .[4]

James is representative of the connoisseurs of his generation in distancing himself from the classical sculptures that Winckelmann had installed as supreme artistic masterpieces in the 1760s. By the 1860s, the process of replacing them with a series of "Renaissance" masterpieces—Michelangelo's David, Leonardo's La Gioconda, among others—was almost complete (I can at this point only gesture toward the process whereby this "substitution" was made and mention the names Burckhardt, Taine, and Pater as some of its chief agents).

Although James clearly identifies himself as being an artist on the side of the moderns through both his distancing himself from the canon of classical sculpture and his claiming to have been initiated into artistic style by a series of postrevolutionary French painters, his anachronistic attachment to sculpture and the sculptural manifests itself in various ways in his writing. In the index to his one-volume edition of his biography of James, Leon Edel's first listing under the monitory-sounding category of "Psychosexual problems" is "Fantasies: women as statues." "In most of Henry James's early stories loved women are compared to statues," Edel writes. "Only later does he become aware, if not of their flesh, at least of their heart and mind." [5] Edel provides no complementary account of James's perception of other men, perhaps especially men (real or imaginary ones) whom he found erotically desirable, as statues, yet it would be surprising if, for James and some of his contemporaries who were weaned on the doctrines of neoclassical sculpture and painting, seeing a man as an erotic object were not in some ways related to seeing him fantasmatically as a figure in the discourse of male physical beauty associated with antique sculpture and disseminated by Winckelmann and his many disciples. During the same year James began work on his memoirs of his childhood and youth, Freud published his speculations on homosexual men and what he called their "infatuation with statuary" in *Leonardo da Vinci and a Memory of His Childhood* (1910).[6] For James, his homosexual contemporaries' cult of classical sculpture had been mediated for him by the work of the modern painters whom he adduces as his artistic initiators, from David to Géricault and Delacroix, who were centrally involved in the construction, and later the dismantling, of a pictorial imaginary that took the figure of the beautiful and heroic nude male body as a primary site for representing meaning.

Two related practices formed the core of these artists' academic training: the drawing of the nude either from living models or from classical sculpture. In analyzing French painting of the period in question, art historians routinely identify the models for various figures in a picture as either recognizable friends and students of the painter or as any of a substantial number of classic "antique" postures: the Discobolus, the Barberini Faun, the Dying Gladiator, the Boy with a Thorn in His Foot, and so on.[7]

There is no doubt that James was an intense and mimetic reader of Hawthorne's *The Marble Faun*, which engages in some troubled and disturbing ways both with the erotic meanings of classical sculpture for cultivated nineteenth-century Americans and with the modern cult of the artist. Except in some of his earliest work, such as his own novel about a sculptor, *Roderick Hudson*, the erotic and homoerotic resonances of Greek and Roman sculpture and modern imitations thereof seem defensively muted most of the time. But the effects, erotic and otherwise, of the various cults of the aesthetic, are ubiquitous in James's fiction. Part of the effect of the long-maintained critical insistence on a dyadic understanding of the so-called "international theme" in James's writing—a monolithic "America" versus a similarly monolithic "Europe"—has been to suppress the many differences in the histories of male-male association, friendship, professional rivalry, pedagogy, sodomy, and pederasty, which occur across the range of the geography of James's imagination. I take the major terms (for my present purposes) of this geography to be America, England, France, Italy, and Greece. For James as for many of his Anglophone contemporaries, the eastward and southward course of this reverse trajectory from America and England, when mapped onto a reverse historical trajectory also aimed backward in time, constituted the rudimentary outlines of a master-narrative about not only the history of politics per se (from the experiments of the ancients with republics and democratic polities) but also the general impossibility—or deep immorality—of satisfied sexual desire between males at any time after "the ancient Greeks." By the time James was a young man, the solidly instantiated (and itself solidly anachronistic) myth of the (homo)sexual causes of the "decline and fall of the Roman empire" served as an effective bar against thinking of same-sex desire as anything but individually and socially dangerous and destructive in the modern world.

Whitney Davis has recently written of Winckelmann's strategies for attempting to reinaugurate what he understood as the cycle of ancient homoerotic modes of relation among males in the modern world. Davis is attentive to what Winckelmann's writing envisions as the paradoxical possibility and impossibility of succeeding in carrying out this project. As Davis reads it, Winckelmann's program involves reinstituting something like the reciprocal relations through which he imagines the ancient Greeks transacted male-homoerotic eros: boys who wish to make themselves appear desirable, through their behavior, their appearance, and their imitation of athletic, literary, and philosophical models of male desirability, and men who love such boys and who are involved in the production of the athletic, literary, and philosophical models of the ideal-types, are involved in a complex web of mutual needs and desires.[8] In his late autobiographical writing, I believe, James partially overcomes his earlier self-exclusion from the position of ecstatic admirer of the Apollo Belvedere. If it is not possible for him entirely to enter into a reciprocal relation with such a beautiful and desirable object, neither was it for Winckelmann, and as Davis has shown, this was at least as enabling as it was disabling for him and his program of reinstituting homoeroticism under modern conditions, so to speak. Like Winckelmann but with a redoubled sense of the ultimate impossibility of "success" for such a program, James imagines himself both inside and outside such an imaginary circuit. The violence of such a situation but also the intense pleasures of remaining inside and outside the circuits of male-homoerotic desire leave their marks at many points on James's writing, in which the figures of the dandy, the *flâneur*, the successful artist and author are haunted by the figure of the wounded or dead male body, often that of a boy or young man, a student or a soldier.[9] In James's representations of his initiations, the bodies in question are both his own and those in the pictures. I propose at this point to consider some of James's contemporaries' representations of his body around the time he wrote *A Small Boy and Others*.

An Effeminate Old Donkey

The marble bust of James and the Sargent portrait of him commissioned by his friends as tributes on his seventieth birthday provide ready figures for an image of James that corresponds to the received sense of him as "the Master," notionally delivered from time and circumstance to be presented to posterity in the guise of a powerful senator or a successful financier. Yet not everyone who looked at James, even at the height of his fame and influence during his lifetime, saw the serene and assured "master" of legend. Some of his younger American contemporaries found his appearance and manner outrageous, ridiculous, and contemptible. Harold Frederic, author of *The Damnation of Theron Ware* (1896), referred to James in a letter to a friend as "an effeminate old donkey who lives with a herd of other donkeys around him and insists on being treated as if he were the Pope."[10] Henry Dwight Sedgwick, encountering James unexpectedly on a visit to common friends of theirs in 1901, saw not the worldly and distinguished figure he may have expected but what he calls "a figure of vaudeville": "tight check trousers, waistcoat of a violent pattern, coat with short tails like a cock sparrow—none matching; cravat in a magnificent flowery bow." The James of a somewhat earlier period had been remembered as being over-dressed—C. C. H. Millar recalls "his rather conspicuous spats and extra shiny boots" circa 1890, his air "of having just come from an ultra-smart wedding ceremony"—but ten years later the theatricality of James's dress and behavior seems to have intensified to the point where elements of the grotesque and bizarre have begun to obtrude themselves: Jessie Conrad remembers James's appearance in 1902 having moved her four-year-old son Borys to exclaim, "Oh, Mamma! isn't he an elegant fowl!" [11]

The connotations of the terms in which Frederic ridicules James are all too easy to decode: an "effeminate . . . donkey" is not only stubbornly and stupidly effeminate, but perhaps also a mule, a sexless and sterile creature, a queer, and an "old" one to boot—decrepit, perhaps, and certainly "old enough to know better." Frederic reinforces the implications of what he insinuates about James by insisting that he lives surrounded by "a herd of other donkeys"—that such men move in packs and are particularly absurd and despicable for doing so evidently already being a primary article of homophobic faith. The rest of Frederic's smearing of James derives its charge from old-fashioned American anti-Catholicism ("know-nothingism") of the more hysterical type—priests who claim to be or are celibate must be perverted eunuchs, and the Pope the arch-pervert and arch-eunuch ("Is the Pope Catholic?" and "Does the Pope wear a dress?" being twin classic locutions for suggesting that one's interlocutor is "clueless"). Frederic's assertion that James is not a "lion," as some people regard him, but rather a "donkey," continues the carnivalesque activity of reversing hierarchical orders—in this instance, in a way that complicates the simple exchange of high for low by rendering James's sexuality both suspect and vague (on the scale of potency from stallion to mule, donkey is closer to mule). For Frederic, James is a figure not simply of fun but of the jocular violence of carnival: he is the "Pope" not just of Fools but of beastly although perhaps also "asexual" (eunuch) sodomites. Suggesting that James thinks he's the Pope also efficiently retells the "open secret" that James is not really "American" or even properly "English," but actually an imaginary embodiment of some kind of legendary "Roman," with all the "intimate" anecdotal baggage that such an ascription may carry about

Rome as a "fleshpot," especially a sodomitical and pederastic "fleshpot," for English males on the Grand Tour looking for the famed "libertine license" of the city, and the papal court as a notorious historical site of high-stakes sexual and social intrigue among its male inmates. The association of the Pope and the Vatican with the recently somewhat eclipsed and now "unmanly" cult of the classical male nude completes the catalog of charges enfolded in Frederic's name-calling.

Sedgwick's evocation of James is less violent and phobic than Frederic's, but only in degree. For him, James's offenses are not so specifically that he seems queer *and* imperious but more generally that he insists through his dress and manner—wittingly or not—on other people's noticing his body, both in *toto* and part by part; especially, we gather, the lower parts (short legs, crotch, fat buttocks and belly) emphasized by "tight . . . trousers" and short-tailed coat. The tightness of the clothes and the unmatchedness of the patterns bespeak Sedgwick's own sense of the comic corporeal excessiveness he attributes to James, who in Sedgwick's vision presents his body in all its spectacularity to his (in this case) unwilling viewer not only all decked out but finished at the neck like an outsize gift, complete with "magnificent flowery bow." Sedgwick modulates Borys Conrad's admiring if astonished cry of "elegant fowl" into a more harshly and phobicly phallic register: for him James struts in his outrageous "vaudeville" getup "like a cock sparrow," not simply a clown, but a distinctly modern, sexually exhibitionistic type of clown in tight, snazzy array—a star of the beerier music-hall circuit, or a pimp or hustler.

I have to this point discussed these instances of James's seeming comical, ridiculous, and even offensively absurd in appearance and behavior to some of his contemporaries as departures from "the legend of the Master," but it would perhaps be more useful, as well as more accurate, to think of them as constitutive elements of that "legend"—indeed, Simon Nowell-Smith's 1948 collection of anecdotal material on James entitled *The Legend of the Master* is our primary source for these unflattering images of James in later life as well as for the more familiar reverent and adulatory ones. The anecdotes I have discussed suggest that a combination of an increasingly public effeminacy, an at least slightly grotesque exhibitionism, and a decreasing fear of being perceived as behaving in a ridiculous manner were all conspicuous features of James's habits of self-presentation in the later years of his life. Through cultivating such behavior in the first decade of the new century, James increased his capacity for understanding how he had himself resisted some of the effects of "the great male renunciation" and its increasingly homophobic enforcement throughout the second half of the nineteenth century. In chapter 25 of A Small Boy and Others James is able to make an extensive account of some of "the sources" from which he had "drunk" in his precocious "foretaste . . . of all the fun . . . [he] was going to have, and the kind of life, always of the queer so-called inward sort . . . [he] was going to lead."¹²

James's account of his initiation into style in A Small Boy and Others passes through three phases. There is a kind of pre-initiatory discussion of the kinds of French painting most in vogue when James visited Paris as a boy; Thomas Couture's Romans of the Decadence and The Falconer as well as some of the work of Paul Delaroche and Eugène Delacroix are the principal topics here (341–45). This pre-initiatory moment takes place in the preparatory space of the Luxembourg, where the works of the most celebrated living French artists were displayed — the practice at midcentury still being that even the work of the most highly acclaimed artists was not admitted into the Louvre itself until ten years after their death.

Delacroix found himself an exception to this rule when he was commissioned by Napoleon III to paint a large mural on the ceiling of the newly restored Galérie d'Apollon in the Louvre (completed in 1851). This Galérie is the actual setting of what James calls his initiation into "Style." As James describes it, his boy-self then undergoes a kind of secondary initiation elsewhere in the Louvre. It is in this relation to this phase that James discusses paintings by David, Gérard, Géricault, Girodet, Gros, Guérin, Prud'hon, and Vigée-Lebrun. I want now to look more closely at these three moments and at the images associated with each of them.

James recalls Couture's Romans of the Decadence as having been "recently acclaimed, at that time, as the last word of the grand manner, but of the grand manner modernised, humanised, philosophised, redeemed from academic death . . ." (341). As viewers from Théophile Gautier to Michael Fried have noted, the "orgy" depicted in the painting has long passed its height and is captured by the painter at the moment hangover and exhaustion set in.¹³ Albert Boime, author of the most extensive study of the painting (and of Couture's work as a whole), provides an apparently exhaustive account of possible sources, classical and contemporaneous, for

1. Thomas Couture, *The Romans of the Decadence* (1847). Paris: Musée D'Orsay. Photo © Réunion des Musées Nationaux.

the painting's theme, design, and representations of individual figures, finally concluding that the "*Romans* is a series of unreconciled contradictions."[14] The painting allows viewers to have it both ways, to enjoy the "excessive indulgence" that it allegedly depicts but also to align themselves with the scowling (and fully dressed and, presumably, sober) "philosophers" who look on disapprovingly at the scene from its lower-right-hand corner. While one "philosopher" signals his disapproval by standing with hand on hip and scowling theatrically, the other does so (with equal theatricality) by drawing his voluminous cloak up to his neck with one arm and all the way around his waist with the other, as if to repudiate not only the general disorder of the scene but especially the exposure of the body that is its chief sign — and, for many viewers, probably the picture's chief appeal, then as now. Taken by some of its viewers to be a moral critique of the "decadence" of those classes who prospered most under the July Monarchy, the ostensible politics of the painting proved flexible enough to allow its great popularity to survive the 1848 Revolution and Napoleon III's coup d'état of December 1851, to be one of the most highly acclaimed exhibits in the World's Fair in Paris in 1855, the year James first saw it.

To his twelve-year-old eyes, the painting may have appealed powerfully — if in some ways also painfully — as a supposedly sublime representation of the unhappy end of the "orgy" of the classical revival and especially of the discourses of beautiful and heroic male nudity that had been proliferating since the mid-eighteenth century and that the painting both belatedly exploits and condemns. *Romans of the Decadence* may be the most influential visual representation ever made of the aforementioned myth of the (homo)sexual causes of "the decline and fall of the Roman empire," not least because it evokes the myth only indirectly and implicitly, through its ostensibly moralistic rejection of the "orgy" of the display of male physical beauty in painting and sculpture during the preceding fifty years. Subsequent restagings of the painting as *tableau vivant* in late-nineteenth-century circuses, and its strong and direct influence on the "Roman orgy" set piece in early Italian and American "epic" silent films, thoroughly reinstantiated the scene and the scene of homosexual prohibition toward which it gestures in twentieth-century mass culture.

Yet it is also possible to detect some resistance on James's part to the painting's overwhelming rejection of the erotics of "the antique" male nude and its leading modern disseminators. It was, James writes, "to this master's [i.e., Couture's] school that the young American contemporary flutter taught its wings to fly straightest . . ." (341). On returning from Paris, William James and Henry themselves "flew straight to" the Newport studio of "the Boston painter" William Morris Hunt, who had been one of Couture's American pupils. (As I shall discuss below, it was as an observer of a scene of "life drawing" of a nude male in Hunt's studio that James remembers himself definitively putting aside the practice of the visual arts for literature exclusively.) By imaginarily imbuing the leading young American artists of his boyhood with what Pater had called, after the Greeks, the *pteroû dúnamis*, the "power of the wing," James evokes a number of the most frequently represented and most erotically charged of the male-nude figures in French neoclassical painting, such as Cupid and Zephyr, as well as a series of other mythological figures whose stories conjoin themes of youthful susceptibility with birds and flight—most notably Ganymede and the story of his abduction or rape by Zeus in the form of a great eagle, and of Psyche and her being "uplifted" to be joined with Cupid, to undergo a series of initiatory trials, and ultimately to become a divinity herself, and the mother of Pleasure (*Voluptas*).[15]

The metaphorics of winged flight that emerges in James's comments on the *Romans of the Decadence* expands as he turns to the *Falconer*, Couture's other most famous painting, which James also first saw exhibited in the International Exposition on his childhood visit to Paris. James recalls the impression it made on him in terms that suggest that it had even more significance for him than the celebrated *Romans of the Decadence* did:

> We were in our immediate circle to know Couture himself a little toward the end of his life, and I was somewhat to wonder then where he had picked up the aesthetic hint for the beautiful Page with a Falcon . . . his other bid [besides the *Romans*] for style and capture of it—which we were long to continue to suppose perhaps the rarest of all modern pictures. The feasting Romans were conceivable enough, I mean *as* a conception; no mystery hung about them—in the sense of asking one's self whence they had come and by what romantic or roundabout or nobly-dangerous journey; which is that air of the poetic shaken out as from strong wings when great presences, in any one of the arts, appear to alight. What I remember, on the other hand, of the splendid fair youth in black velvet and satin or whatever and who, while he mounts the marble staircase, shows off the great bird on his forefinger with a grace that shows *him* off, was that it failed to help us divine, during that after-lapse of glory of which I speak, by what rare chance, for the obscured old ex-celebrity we visited, the heavens had once opened. Poetry had swooped down, breathed on him for an hour and fled. (342)

The Falconer represents a spectacularly pretty "page," a richly clad boy out of early-nineteenth-century fantasies of medieval or Renaissance court life, with a half-smiling expression of languorous pleasure on his face as he toys with a large falcon he is holding. Despite its surface differences from the *Romans*, *The Falconer* is in some ways a similar painting; in his elaborate contextualization of the picture, Boime has demonstrated how it, like the *Romans*, may have been understood to be a critique of aristocratic effeteness or "decadence." Boime comments on the strong homoerotic charge this and other paintings of Couture's seem to carry, but he does not relate this aspect of the picture to what one might call the action of the picture as he himself characterizes it: "an exquisite dude toying with the bird for his private amusement."[16] While making much of the art-historical significance of the figure of the falcon, Boime curiously—given his recognition and acknowledgment of its possible homoerotic meanings—fails to con-

2. Thomas Couture, *The Falconer* (c. 1844–45). Reproduced by permission of the Toledo Museum of Art, Toledo, Ohio.

sider what he calls "the motif of gentle lad versus predatory bird" in relation to the myth of the rape of Ganymede, a commonplace in Renaissance art and literature.

For the aging James, the mysterious thing about the *Falconer* is that in it Couture has made a scene of teasing erotic play and display on a boy's part entirely "graceful"—not only acceptable but positively pleasing, appealing, beautiful in the eyes of many viewers. Amidst the textual beating of "strong wings" signaling visitations from "great presences," James in his discussion of the painting rewrites the rape of Ganymede in terms that precisely reverse those of the mythic narrative: rather than being merely passively ravished, the *Falconer* represents for James "[an]other great bid for style and capture of it"—and it is the youth who represents the artist making the "great bid . . . and capture," not the god in the guise of the winged predator. James may have preferred the *Falconer* to the *Romans of the Decadence* because the *Falconer* suggests that there may be a way out—and an erotic way out—of the sexual and political *huit clos* ("No one gets out of here alive") that the *Romans* represents, and that one of the names for it is "style" ("a grace that shows him off"). While the *Romans* depicts a "great bid for style" (the cult of the heroic male nude) exhausted, depleted, "played out," the *Falconer* shows an entirely successful "capture of it [i.e., of style]," which is also a capture by style: "Poetry had swooped down, breathed on him for an hour and fled." The ensuing scene of initiation into "style," which James's remarks about the *Falconer* anticipate, goes a considerable way in specifying what kinds of relations—including what kinds of erotic relations—may be ongoing during "Poetry's" or "style's" ravishing visitations.

After his discussion of Couture, James turns directly to his first experience of initiation in the Louvre. As he wanders through the museum on the morning of his first visit there, he at first finds himself simply "overwhelmed and bewildered" by the grandeur and variety of the designs and ornamentations of the "vast halls":

> To distinguish among these, in the charged and coloured and confounding air, was difficult—it discouraged and defied; which was doubtless why my impression originally best entertained was that of those magnificent parts of the great gallery simply not inviting us to distinguish. They only arched over us in the wonder of their endless golden riot and relief, figured and flourished in perpetual revolution,

breaking into high-hung circles and symmetries of squandered picture, opening into deep outward embrasures that threw off the rest of
monumental Paris somehow as a told story, a sort of wrought effect
or bold ambiguity for a vista, and yet held it there, at every point,
as a vast bright gage, even at moments a felt adventure, of experience. This comes to saying that in those beginnings I felt myself most
happily cross that bridge over to Style constituted by the wondrous
Galérie d'Apollon, drawn out for me as a long but assured initiation
and seeming to form with its supreme coved ceiling and inordinately
shining parquet a prodigious tube or tunnel through which I inhaled
little by little, that is again and again, a general sense of *glory*. (346)

The scene of the Galérie is at first simply one of his boy-self enjoying
a series of transporting pleasures ("I felt myself most happily cross that
bridge over to Style"); a moment later it gets figured as "tunnel" and at the
same time as "tube." To cast the question this double figure raises in the
form of a riddle — "What's large enough for one to walk through and small
enough to take into one's mouth?" — may be one way of beginning to perceive how the primary terms of this scene of pubescent initiation might
emerge from the fantasmatic construction in infancy and early childhood
of scenes of pleasure and danger imaginarily enacted in relation to both
the outer surfaces and the internal depths of the larger bodies and body
parts of adults and older children (the "Others" of the title A *Small Boy and
Others*) that surround one as a small child.

The adult body that is the primary object of this fantasy possesses, for
the infant that imagines it, organs of both the male and female bodies,
in incoherent relation to each other. For example, according to Melanie
Klein and other theorists of infantile fantasy, what subsequently gets identified as "paternal penis" is first located in the infantile imagination in
the "maternal" body, and is to some degree "confused[ ]" (a key Jamesian
term in the passage under examination [347]) with what subsequently gets
identified as "maternal breast." James, in his vivid verbal re-imagining of
this scene recaptures and articulates a sense of this alternately (sometimes
simultaneously) exhilarating and frightening "confus[ion]" of bodies and
body parts, especially of organs of physical pleasure, at the very beginning of the passage, where he speaks of his "impression originally best
entertained" as being that of "those magnificent parts of the great gallery

45

simply not inviting us to distinguish." These "magnificent parts" "only arched over us in . . . endless golden riot and relief, figured and flourished in perpetual revolution, breaking into high-hung circles and symmetries . . . , opening into deep outward embrasures. . . ." Robert Wetherby has pointed out the persistence of an identification in James's writing between "arching" figures and figures of femininity and especially maternity: for example, he wrote of his mother after her death as having been the "keystone" of his family, and named a female character on whom he lavished identificatory energies Isabel Archer. In this passage, the gender of the overarching "magnificent parts" remains less determinate. This set of terms evokes a rapid visual tour through an ensemble of "parts" that disables any stable sense of their having a "proper" location or function except to excite and give pleasure to their observer, and they do so in language that combines terms of formal aesthetic observation ("figured and flourished," "symmetries"—terms we can relate to the phrase "beauty and art and supreme design" later in the passage) with terms of political unrest and revolt ("riot" and "revolution"—terms we can relate to the phrase "history and fame and power" later in the passage).

As the combination of such terms here suggests, "history" in this initiatory scene is by no means incompatible with the fantasmatic production of pleasures of infantile intensity from which the scene draws its energies; it is indeed one of the principal avenues through which what might otherwise degenerate into a torpid scene of pleasure—an infant drowsing at the breast—gets recharged with the energies that keep the scene at a fairly continuously high level of excitement and suspense. In relation to the "riot" of "magnificent parts" playing over and around him, and through which he moves at the same time that he imaginarily takes some of these parts into his own body, James represents his boy self achieving a "most happ[ ]y" "confusion" or "cross[ing]" of ostensibly active and passive pleasures, "happily cross[ing] that bridge" that is "drawn out for [him] . . . long," sucking "again and again" on the "prodigious . . . tube" that presents itself to him.

It is indicative of James's sense that it was the initially "bewildering" effects of the Galérie—especially the effect of circulating body parts and designedly "confus[ing]" parts of bodies with "parts" of other structures and histories—that were the crucial element in precipitating his initiation into "Style" that he omits to describe the actual painted scene that "over-

3. Eugène Delacroix, *Apollo Defeating the Python* (1851). Paris: Musée du Louvre. Photo © Réunion des Musées Nationaux.

arches" the Galérie d'Apollon and gives it its name. This is Delacroix's grand mural of *Apollo Defeating the Python*, which had been painted and installed only a few years before James's early visit, as one of the chief features of the renovations of the Louvre carried out between 1848 and 1851. The mural gives spatial form to precisely the vertiginous movements and the kinds of fantasmatic and eroticized object-relations that animate James's memory of his response to his first sight of the gallery: high overhead in the center of the great ceiling of the gallery, the god Apollo directs a fatal shaft at the enormous coiled serpent awash in the flood below; the bodies of stallions, putti, nymphs, and other figures swirl in profusion around them

47

in a disorienting array of perspectival relations. That Apollo, and specifically Apollo battling the Python, is the subject of Delacroix's mural affirms that the artistic initiation that occurs beneath is that of a modern artist, but one whose erotics and aesthetics retain important ties to the "antique" and specifically to the Winckelmannian cult of male physical beauty, for the Apollo Belvedere, emblematic image and object of this cult, is also supposed to represent the god at the very moment of his triumph over the Python.[17] In resetting the scene amidst a field of "overwhelm[ing]," "bewilder[ing]," and "confus[ing]" space-and-object relations, Delacroix in his mural disrupts what James would later call the "solid dignity" of the Apollo Belvedere and casts the figure aloft (and in a sense adrift) through the defiles of fear and desire in which male-homoerotic possibility can re-emerge under the conditions of modernity. James writes of his initiation under the sign of Delacroix's Apollo as having had "the effect . . . of a love-philtre or fear-philtre which fixes for the senses their supreme symbol of the fair or the strange" (347).

The Galérie d'Apollon was not only the scene of James's childhood initiation as an artist; "many years later," he writes, his memory of the place enabled for him "the instantaneous recovery and capture of the most appalling yet most admirable nightmare of [his] life" (347). Immediately after describing the process of his initiation in the Galérie, he goes on to relate the nightmare that was set there. In his dream, James writes, he woke from sleep to realize with horror that some "awful agent, creature or presence" was approaching his chamber with "straight aggression and dire intent." He springs from his bed and throws himself on the closed door, "defending by the push of [his] shoulder against hard pressure on lock and bar from the other side." "The lucidity, not to say the sublimity, of the crisis," he writes, "had consisted of the great thought that I, in my appalled state, was probably still more appalling" than the marauding creature. James the dreamer, in a "triumph of . . . impulse," forces the door outward and routs his would-be assailant, who in the moment he sees "the tables turned upon him" has become "but a diminished spot in the long perspective, the tremendous, glorious hall . . . over the far-gleaming floor of which . . . he sped for his life, while a great storm of thunder and lightning played through the deep embrasures of high windows at the right" (348–49).

In his account of James's initiation in the Galérie d'Apollon, Leon Edel points out how much the names "Apollon" and "Napoleon" sound like each other in French, and provides a quick sketch of James's lifelong fascination with the glamor of the Empire, evident in his fascination with the Louvre itself, which had first been opened to the public and made a primary site for the display of the loot of imperial conquest by Napoleon himself; Napoleon III's renovations of the Louvre, especially of the Galérie d'Apollon, were a conspicuous part of his bid to associate himself with his imperial predecessor. The legends and homonymic names of Apollo, who had been a primary figure for French imperial power in the visual arts since the time of Louis XIV, and Napoleon, who had embodied the ultimate limits of such power, seem to have continued to signify each other for James from the time of his first visit to the Louvre in 1855 to the making of his written account of it almost sixty years later. The beauty and cruelty of the god and the triumphant and overwhelming—and finally disastrous—career of the emperor interlined each other in a way that made their names a powerful means of invoking the "glory"—composed of both intense love and fear—that James remembers dawning on him in the Louvre.

After discussing James's account of his "most appalling yet most admirable nightmare," Edel "note[s] that to Apollon and Napoleon we must now add another word—*appalling*," and suggests that the "consonance of syllable and association which emerges in this closely-woven chapter of reminiscence" produces a kind of triple invocation, "Apollon–Napoleon–Appalling." According to Edel, in writing chapter 25 of A Small Boy and Others, James resolves the very mixed sets of impulses that impel it—terror and desire, beauty and strangeness, admiration and repulsion—into a set of "balanced alternatives and antitheses" (his Henry James: The Untried Years, in which the discussion appears, was first published in 1953). Yet the terms of this text are not at all "balanced" or smoothly resolved into a kind of zero-sum of positive and negative impulses. If for all the overwhelming glamor they exert over James, he still wants to recognize—to hold onto as a kind of value—how "appalling" Apollo and Napoleon, jointly or singly, are, and how appealing *and* repellent they may at once be, then we may ask what the name, or *a* name, for this "American," or "puritan," kind of guilty fascination might be. I submit that it is a fourth term called up by "*Apollon*," "*Napoleon*," and "appalling": this is the name "Apollyon," "the angel of the bottomless pit" of Revelation 9:11, "whose name in the Hebrew tongue is Abaddon, but in the Greek tongue hath his name Apollyon."

From the same Greek root as "Apollo," "Apollyon" means "the destroyer": "Sin is the Apollyon, the destroyer" (Jeremy Taylor, *Holy Dying* [1651]). The name "Apollyon" would most likely have stuck in James's mind from early contact either with the actual text of or from oral accounts of John Bunyan's *Pilgrim's Progress* (1678), in which Christian's battle with Apollyon is one of the most celebrated episodes. Christian's "adventures" were retold in numerous abridged editions for children throughout the eighteenth and nineteenth centuries, and were staples of pious storytelling; a relative or servant might have read or told James the story of Christian and Apollyon, and omnivorous and retentive reader that he was, he certainly may have read it for himself.[18]

Part of what is so frightening about Bunyan's Apollyon is that he is a "monster" in the sense of the term that he combines in his body the body parts of various beasts: "he was clothed with scales like a fish . . . he had wings like a dragon, feet like a bear, and out of his belly came fire and smoke, and his mouth was as the mouth of a lion." When Christian resists Apollyon's demands that he halt his progress and remain subject to him, the monster falls "into a grievous rage" and the two combat each other "for above half a day." Although Christian is repeatedly wounded in head, hand, and foot by Apollyon's darts, when the two wrestle, Christian finally deals him a terrible blow with his sword. "And with that Apollyon spread forth his dragon's wings, and sped him away. . . ."[19] Like the dreamer in James's nightmare, Bunyan's Christian, at first appalled by an aggressor, stands his ground and succeeds in turning the tables and routing his would-be destroyer. The story of Christian's battle with Apollyon may have given James at a very early moment in his life a narrative resource for imagining the possibility of withstanding the intensities of the onslaughts of "glory" and "style" that were first to visit him as the "magnificent parts of the great gallery" of Apollo "arch[ ]" and "riot" over him, composing their own kind of monstrous body.

The composite bodies of Apollyon, or of Delacroix's mural of Apollo, or of the other "magnificent parts of the great gallery" taken together not only mediate between a "small boy's" body and "the world['s]" body; they suggest how these bodies may interact despite their apparently vast difference in scale. "The world" presents itself to James in this initiatory vision as being, "by an odd extension or intensification," locally and specifically "the Second Empire, which was (for my notified consciousness) new and queer and perhaps even wrong, but on the spot so amply radiant and elegant that it took to itself, took under its protection with a splendour of insolence, the state and ancientry of the whole scene . . ." (347). The "odd extension or intensification" of the scene, its quality of being "new and queer and perhaps even wrong," its "insolence"—all these terms bespeak both the novelty of the scene and the boy's anxiety at entering into it. Phallic and masturbatory signs predominate in James's representation of his boy-self's response to and participation in the scene, as he "felt himself most happily cross that bridge over to Style . . . , drawn out for me . . . long," which we may read as in one sense representing the boy "most happily" feeling his own penis—through the organ itself, but also possibly with his hand—becoming tumescent in response to, and in concert with, the "riot" of body parts above and around him, as the head of the erecting penis ("drawn out for me . . . long") emerges from the foreskin (the "tube"). The aged James, remembering this scene of initiation of his twelve-year-old self, associates its effects with a kind of "flooding" that permeates the designedly overwrought prose style in which he relates it and that carries overtones of such new kinds (for a pubescent youngster) of sexual experiences as ejaculation and orgasm, in relation either to incidental sexual arousal, masturbation, or erotic dreaming—experiences that can initially be both exhilarating and strongly pleasurable and at that same time disturbing and disorienting—powerfully self-fortifying at some levels while disablingly guilt- and anxiety-inducing at others.

The intense pleasures that accompany these sensations ("*glory*") are at once signs of "the world [in one sense, the phallus] . . . raised [i.e., erected] to the richest and noblest expression," but they are also to the boy's mind "new and queer and perhaps even wrong." Significantly, these latter words are his terms for his notion in boyhood of the Second Empire, which even to his "dim historic vision, confusedly though it might be," is both historically illegitimate but also, for the moment, "on the spot," justifying itself to him through a "splendour of insolence," a triumph of style—of the kind a bookish but nonetheless worldly child of the 1850s might associate with Apollo in his myriad artistic manifestations, with Napoleon, or with the "splendid fair youth" of Couture's *Falconer*, himself the ostentatious focus of a complex intersection of autoerotic, homoerotic, and pederastic energies.

I have written above of the possibility that the boy James saw in Couture's *The Falconer* a "way out" of the scene of ruination depicted in the

Romans of the Decadence. I now want to complicate that hypothesis somewhat by momentarily returning to those two paintings in the context of the scene of initiation that follows James's discussion of them in chapter 25. In "cross[ing]" the "bridge over to Style" as a culminating moment in this ritual, the boy James enters and participates in a scene of "endless golden riot and relief"; *The Falconer* can only be a partially adequate picture of the scene of initiation because it reduces the complex scene to a frontal and phallic image of a "splendid . . . youth . . . mount[ing] the marble staircase [to] show[ ] off" himself and his "great bird." The scene of James's initiation as an artist is a dual one, composed of both the fantasmatic scene of the orgy or "riot" of "magnificent parts . . . not inviting us to distinguish" in the Galérie d'Apollon and the more limited or contained scene of a child's or youth's autoerotic, homoerotic, and exhibitionistic pleasure — a scene of pleasure *and* terror and a scene of pleasure in which terror is absent or at least momentarily muted.

There ensues on James's account of his "nightmare" a passage I take to be a repetition of his initiation, or perhaps a kind of secondary initiation. Although he does not mention the location of this experience, it would appear to have taken place one room away from the Galérie d'Apollon, in the Salle des Sept Cheminées, where the work of the most acclaimed French painters of the preceding generation or two (David, Gérard, Géricault, Girodet, Gros, Guérin, Prud'hon, Vigée-Lebrun) were exhibited. James writes:

> The sharp and strange, the quite heart-shaking little prevision had come to me, for myself, I make out, on the occasion of our very first visit of all, my brother's and mine, under conduct of the good Jean Nadali . . . deputed by our parents, in the Rue de la Paix, on the morrow of our first arrival in Paris (July 1855) and while they were otherwise concerned. I hang again, appalled but uplifted, on brave Nadali's arm. . . . I cling to him while I gape at Géricault's Radeau de la Méduse, *the* sensation, for splendour and terror of interest, of that juncture to me, and ever afterwards to be associated, along with two or three other more or less contemporary products, Guérin's Burial of Atala, Prudhon's Cupid and Psyche, David's helmetted Romanisms, Madame Vigée-Lebrun's "ravishing" portrait of herself and her little girl, with how can I say what foretaste . . . of all the fun, confusedly speaking,

4. Théodore Géricault, *The Raft of the Medusa* (1818–19). Paris: Musée du Louvre. Photo © Réunion des Musées Nationaux.

that one was going to have, and the kind of life, always of the queer so-called inward sort, . . . that one was going to lead. (349–50)

Géricault's *Raft of the Medusa* (1819) represents the sufferings from exposure and starvation of a handful of survivors adrift on a raft, after the disastrous wreck of the government frigate the *Medusa* off the west coast of Africa in the summer of 1816. The figures in the painting, about twenty in number, of varying ages and appearances, are arranged mainly in two masses: a pyramidal group on the right-hand side of the composition strenuously tries to signal its plight to a distant ship, while across the lowermost quarter of the picture, in its foreground, on the rear of the raft, lie four nude or seminude corpses of young men; two somber living figures sitting over them appear to be both in mourning and in shock.

James speaks of the *Raft of the Medusa* as having been for him "the sensation, for splendour and terror of interest, of that juncture," and one of the convergences that this "juncture" brings together is the scene of the chaotic group (the "riot" or orgy, as in, for example, Couture's *Romans* or Delacroix's *Apollo*) and the scene of the beautiful, solitary youth. The "splendid insolence" of the Galérie d'Apollon is transmuted here into the dire and tender pathos of the dead youth whose nude body extends off the side of the raft into the lowermost left-hand margin of the picture. The young Delacroix, who is said to have posed for the corpse lying just to the right of this figure (of which we see only the back of the head and the upper back), was one of the first to recognize how the full impact of the image registers only insofar as the viewer becomes imaginarily involved in the scene: one must "believe he has one foot in the water to perceive all of" the painting's merit, he wrote.[20]

If James later remembered his viewing of Couture's *Romans* as a kind of preparatory pre-initiatory rite for his viewing of Géricault's *Raft*, he may have appreciated how thoroughly the *Romans of the Decadence* imitates the *Raft of the Medusa* of a generation before. Albert Boime points out a number of figures and poses that Couture seems to have borrowed directly from the *Raft*. "Above all," he writes, "it is the stroboscopic play of light on the flesh and the various stages of exhaustion, illness and feverish excitement that formally relate these two works."[21] The relation between the specularization of flesh and the stimulation of fear and desire, excitement and exhaustion, point to more than "formal" resemblances between the *Romans* and the *Raft*. Géricault's painting is also an "intense" group scene like James's vision of the "parts . . . rioting" overhead in the Galérie d'Apollon. Unlike the *Romans*, it provides a point of spectatorship not moralistically over-determined like that of the scowling "philosophers" in Couture's painting. "I hang again, appalled but uplifted, on brave Nadali's arm. . . . I cling to him while I gape at" the *Raft of the Medusa*, James writes, reassuming as he does so the anaclitic position of his boyhood self as the child mimes the "hang[ing]" and "cling[ing] of the "appalled" and appalling survivors on the raft, especially the dead youth suspended immediately before his gaze.

Given that the primary subject of *A Small Boy and Others* (or the parts of that subject that "seemed to hang together and . . . to decline mutilation or refuse to be treated otherwise than handsomely" [2]) is the extremely far-flung and variegated character of Henry and William James's education, and the peculiar suitability of such an education for Henry as someone who had been initiated early into the intense cultivation of artistic "style," it should not surprise us that James repeatedly reads the exciting and exhausting, pleasurable and frightening, "group scenes" of his initiation primarily as scenes of instruction. Although the scene of desperate men adrift on Géricault's raft may seem remote from any schoolroom, for a youngster like James who was as fascinated as he appears to have been already at the age of twelve with the formation and training of artists, the scene of the *Raft* may have appeared to be a thoroughly "academic" scene, since it combines the elements of what was called in the art schools the *académie* (the nude drawn from life) and, as I have mentioned was common practice at the time, images of bodies of models taken directly from the inmates of the studio of the painter. The radiant corpse in the lower foreground of the picture is said to have been modeled by one Louis-Alexis Jamar, a pupil of Géricault with whom the painter was sharing sleeping quarters in his studio at the time he was producing the *Raft*. This in itself does not of course constitute "evidence" that master and pupil were lovers, although the situation does bespeak a high level of familiarity and intimacy between the two, and the painter's posing and highlighting of the youth's body and, as Thomas Crow points out, his making the open and extended palm of the dead youth's hand a resonant center of pathos in the painting, does invite the viewer to eroticize the figure in pleasurable as well as disturbing ways.[22]

Art historians sometimes used to fault the *Raft* for manifesting too clearly the traces of the origins of its style in the sculptural poses of neoclassical art. Walter Friedlaender's comments are representative of these: for him, the painting shows signs of being "infected by a somewhat stiff and academic atmosphere," and "its study of the model remains somewhat too evident."[23] For other viewers—including, I am presuming, the boy James—the very qualities that critics such as Friedlaender point out as faults are matters of high merit and strong enjoyment. For them, both the "somewhat stiff and academic atmosphere" of the picture and the evident fascination of the artist with his models and with the process of drawing and painting from the model, especially the nude model, give the picture a particularly marked set of erotic inflections that enlivens what others have seen as its "stiff[ness]" and overdependence on Géricault's preliminary studies of his models (both the living ones and the ones derived from sculpture). When Thomas Eakins, later in the century, photographed and painted himself and his students cavorting in the nude, he limited his representations of these scenes to the idyllic mode. In the *Raft of the Medusa* Géricault seems to have imagined launching himself along with some of his closest associates and pupils on a potentially sublime voyage of exploration into perilous territory—the ungrounding of the beautiful male body as a public sign and guarantor of "virtuous" desire. It is a scene at which James the neophyte artist may well have "gape[d]" with wonder and appreciation.

Having said this, we should note that the beautiful male body, the meanings of which are being ungrounded, is a white one. At the opposite end of the painting from the desolate triangle composed of beautiful dead bodies and their melancholiac guardian, which occupies the foreground, a quite different kind of triangle arises, composed of a group of male bodies turned away from the viewer and signaling excitedly to a far-distant vessel. At the apex of this triangle the viewer sees the bare back and head of an African sailor energetically waving a banner. The emphatic verticality of this figure's torso contrasts markedly with the gleaming paleness of the two nude white corpses extended across the lower border of the composition; indeed, the three figures—black sailor and white corpses—taken together form a larger triangle that subsumes the painting's smaller organizing structures. Perhaps part of the young James's wonder at this image proceeded from the way it may have seemed to him to invert the race hierarchies of his native land and possibly to inaugurate a new political myth of black survival and white vulnerability—circumstances that would have been unthinkable to most whites back in the United States of the 1850s.

Besides Géricault's *Raft of the Medusa*, James mentions several other paintings that figured centrally in giving him his first "foretaste . . . of all the fun . . . [he] was going to have, and the kind of life" he was going to lead: "Guérin's Burial of Atala, Prudhon's Cupid and Psyche, David's helmetted Romanisms, Madame Vigée-Lebrun's 'ravishing' portrait of herself and her little girl . . ." (350). Curiously, James misidentifies the painters of the first two paintings he mentions here. The *Burial of Atala* (1808) was not painted by Pierre-Narcisse Guérin (1774–1833), as James has it, but by another leading artist of the period, Anne-Louis Girodet (1767–1824). Moreover, there appears to have been no painting of Cupid and Psyche by Pierre-Paul Prud'hon (1758–1823) in the Louvre at the time of James's visit or since.[24] The painting of Cupid and Psyche that the young James would have seen in the Louvre on his first visit is the 1798 painting by François Gérard (1770–1837), one of the most famous images of its time. One could pass over these errors of attribution by simply assuming that James misremembered a few of them as he cast his mind back to paintings he had seen over fifty years before—although it is likely that he had revisited them many times in the interim.

However, I want to suggest that there may be substantial issues at stake in his substitution of "Guérin" for "Girodet" and of "Prudhon" for "Gérard." As his biographers have demonstrated, James was fascinated with the opulent grandiosity of the First Empire throughout his life (one recalls that on his deathbed he dictated correspondence in the delirious belief that he was Napoleon) and was widely read in the abundant memoir-literature produced by the public figures of the time. For many twentieth-century readers, the names of these now largely forgotten painters of the Napoleonic era may seem interchangeable, but to connoisseurs of nineteenth-century French painting and of male figure-painting, of which James was certainly one, theirs were names "to conjure with," and their respective biographies were well known.[25]

Given, as we have noticed, that most of the paintings James singles out for mention perform their "bids for style and capture of it" with a considerable degree of eroticization of the male body, I want to speculate that James may have suppressed the name "Girodet" (miscalling him "Guérin") from his memories of his childhood initiation in the Louvre because Girodet, besides being the painter of the Burial of Atala, was also the creator of the no less celebrated and perhaps even more influential painting The Sleep of Endymion (1791), which James could also have seen in the Louvre in 1855, but of which he makes no mention. Girodet's Endymion represents the nude body of a sleeping youth, the upper parts of which are bathed in an erotic glow of radiant moonlight, which betokens the desire and the approach or arrival of the otherwise chaste goddess Diana, who visits Endymion's body as he sleeps. Further figuring desire (Diana's or the youth's or the spectator's?) is a leaping Eros at the youth's feet who dominates the left half of the picture and has the body of a pubescent boy. In contrast with the body of the youth, the middle of whose body lies in shade, the buttocks of the boy Eros shine with moonlight—a particularly notable feature of the painting, as Whitney Davis has pointed out, considering that Eros is facing directly away from the ostensible light source in the picture.[26] Unlike many of the principal figures in the pictures James mentions in the passage under ex-

5. Anne-Louis Girodet, *The Sleep of Endymion* (1791). Paris: Musée du Louvre.
Photo © Réunion des Musées Nationaux.

amination, Eros hangs on no one: he appears to float a little ways above the
ground, poised so as to suggest (to quote Davis) "that the hovering Eros
will momentarily be directly above or astride" the sleeping youth.[27]

For Davis, the representation of Eros and Endymion by Girodet is an example of what he calls

> Winckelmann's contradiction, a rhetorical formation perfectly intelli-
> gible to literate European society after that scholar's murder in 1768:
> The modern artist imitates the forms of classical antiquity, its rep-
> resentations of beautiful boys and perfect youths (or perfect youths
> and physically powerful, dignified men) in sensual association, with-
> out publicly acknowledging their content—"Greek love" as such, the
> sexual activity among boys, youths, and older lovers.[28]

James's rhetoric of "confusion" in his several memorial restagings of his
initiation in the Louvre has some of the same kinds of effects that Winckelmann's rhetoric of "contradiction" does. For James hardly "represses" the
richly male-homoerotic paintings of David and his successors from his ac-

count of his initiation; various of the most famous ones figure importantly in it. One of the most notable features of the *Burial of Atala* itself—the painting James misattributes to Guérin—is the beautiful muscular back of the Europeanized Natchez Indian Chactas in the scene depicted from Chateaubriand's *Atala*. At the moment he swerves away from the name of Girodet and from the sensational and vividly relational depiction of male homoeroticism in Girodet's *Endymion*, James substitutes the name of Guérin, one of whose best-known paintings was his *Aurora and Cephalus* (Louvre, 1810), which, like his *Iris and Morpheus* (Hermitage, 1811), is a blatant attempt to exploit both the "shock" and the appeal of the sleeping nude youth in the *Endymion* while considerably diminishing the homoerotic elements of the picture, especially the kinetic potential of the boy Eros. It is the conjunction of the eroticized youth and boy in the same picture, I believe, that makes James swerve away from it; the "small boy" can be represented in James's "memory palace" as a "solo" figure or as part of a group ("and others"), especially if the group is situated in a rhetorical field marked by affliction, but he cannot become visible as part of a "duo" composed of himself and a "mature" and highly desirable youth. Which is not to say that the figures of Endymion and Eros cannot "slip" into others of the paintings James discusses; for example, one way Girodet's *Endymion* may be understood as "haunting" the text of *A Small Boy and Others* is to imagine that the radiant and extended nude body of the dead youth in Géricault's *Raft of the Medusa* is a kind of revision of the similarly radiant and extended nude body of Girodet's *Endymion*.[29]

It remains for me to speculate about James's substitution of the name of "Prudhon" for Gérard. In "confusedly" mentioning Prud'hon, James may be implicitly readmitting to the text the boy Eros he had just banished from it along with the name "Girodet," for a key painting of Prud'hon (exhibited in the Salon of 1814; it entered the Louvre exactly a century later) portrays *Young Zephyr*, the boy god of the west wind. "Prud'hon's boyish Zephyr," Davis writes, "is, I think, a replication belonging to the same rhetorical field as the figure of Eros in Girodet's *Endymion*."[30] It is important for my present purposes to realize that "Zephyr" is also crucially a figure belonging to the same rhetorical field as Cupid and Psyche themselves. It is Zephyr who comes to the aid of Psyche at the beginning of her initiation, when she has been led to a rock high on a mountain and abandoned to her fate there, and gently wafts her away to the house of Cupid.[31]

A Small Girl as Eros

Among the other paintings James mentions in describing his secondary initiation, I would not want to omit from this series another important figure in James's refiguration of initiatory scenes of intimacy and erotic desire. This is the little girl in Elisabeth Vigée-Lebrun's " 'ravishing' portrait of herself and her little girl." Why does James place quotations marks around "ravishing"? The marks may indicate that "ravishing" is the commonplace term of praise for the picture, one which James wishes to distance himself from by special punctuation marks. They may also serve to emphasize the ambiguity of the meanings of the terms "ravish" and "ravishing," which may in English range from "extremely pretty and pleasing" to "raping." To "be ravished" may mean either "to be seized and taken away by violence" (as in the rape of the Sabine women, or of Ganymede) or "to be overwhelmed with pleasurable emotions" (as in the experience of being ravished by a beautiful appearance, landscape, image, etc.). Vigée-Lebrun's portrait of herself and her daughter is the only image of a "twosome" among all the paintings James mentions; as we have seen, what he calls "Prudhon's Cupid and Psyche" is, rather, a series of paintings by Prud'hon of "solo" Zephyrs or Psyches or Venuses attended by Zephyrs and other boy gods (Cupid, Hymen).

In considering the possible meanings of Vigée-Lebrun's self-portrait in James's "memory palace" it is important to recognize how it is this image that bears the burden of signifying the relationship of the "pair" or "couple," otherwise excluded from visibility. What may be "ravishing" about this image for James is the "contradiction" or "confusion" of a young woman's and a young mother's publicly declaring through her self-portrait her commitment to the social fantasy of antiquity as a period more hospitable than the modern one to intense female desire, including, possibly, desire for other women or girls, as well as male desire for other men or boys.[35] In the 1789 self-portrait-with-child, the artist uses costume to allude to a recent "scandal" in which she was the principal figure; this was her famous "Greek supper," at which she served some "ancient" dishes (e.g., Spartan "black broth") and improvised some "classical" costumes to entertain a group of friends one evening in 1788. The event became a major scandal as the story of the evening was repeated and embellished all over Europe. Vigée-Lebrun claims that a dinner party for a dozen or so guests

7. Elisabeth Vigée-Lebrun, *Self-Portrait à la grecque* (1789). Paris: Musée du Louvre. Photo © Réunion des Musées Nationaux.

that actually cost a modest fifteen francs was rumored abroad to have cost sixty or eighty thousand, until it became a byword for some people for the corruption and extravagance of the French court just before the revolution.[36]

In presenting herself in a painting in the following year embracing her little daughter while herself wearing "Greek" costume, Vigée-Lebrun might be taken by some as intending to refute the charges that she was a "scandalous" woman. It might be truer to the complexity of the situation to resituate the picture in the context of Winckelmannian "contradiction" or Jamesian "confusion," to imagine the artist representing herself as capable of both "maternal tenderness" and affiliation of herself with the cult of the "antique" that some may see as "scandalous." As an internationally visible member of the court and a primary producer of glamorous images of Marie Antoinette, her children, and her female intimates, Vigée-Lebrun could not entirely escape the widespread imputations that sexual activity between women and between mother and child had been among the most reprehensible features of the Queen's and some of her female associates' behavior.[37]

Vigée-Lebrun's relations with her daughter seem to have had their own "scandalous" or "extravagant" dynamics. That she produced at least fifteen paintings and drawings of her daughter during the first seventeen years of the girl's life is some indication of the intensity of her absorption in her relationship with her growing child. The dates of these various compositions suggest that Vigée-Lebrun was most actively engaged in representing her daughter in various roles and activities when the child was seven or eight, again when she was twelve or thirteen, and yet again when she was around twenty.[38] One way of thinking about what appear to be "peak periods" of absorption in representing her daughter in painting on Vigée-Lebrun's part other than in psychobiographical terms would be to notice how these three phases correspond with her male contemporaries' extensive experiments in representing boys as either "cupids" (small boys), "eroses" (pubescent boys), or "heroic youths" (physically mature young men in their late teens or early twenties). Without disregarding the kinds of gendered asymmetries one might well expect to see in an eighteenth-century woman artist's reworkings of a masculinist system of eroticizing males of different ages and male bodies at different stages of physical development, it is possible to see Vigée-Lebrun's portraits of other females at various ages, and especially of her daughter and other little girls, as a complex kind of critical response to the age-gender erotics of her male artist-contemporaries. Seeing Vigée-Lebrun's portraits of her daughter and other girls and young women as moments in a prolonged and complicated debate about the erotics of states of infancy, childhood, adolescence, youth, and maturity in varying relations to each other can be considered part of an effort to restore the missing terms of a representational regime that has often been discussed as if its domination by males, both as painters and figures in painting, were monolithic. Looking at Vigée-Lebrun's work in the context of the effects of a systemic female homosociality in the circles in which she moved suggests that her portraits of other little girls undertaken around the same time that she painted the two so-called *maternités* are informed by a highly contradictory and tense awareness of difference, including erotic difference, among women of different ages.

Vigée-Lebrun became estranged from Julie Lebrun as the young woman entered adulthood, and the mother outlived the daughter by many years, publishing her memoirs in 1835 at the age of eighty and dying seven years later. Since her memoirs, including her account of her prolonged alienation from her daughter, were widely read and discussed in the mid-nineteenth century and after, it is not unreasonable to assume that James may have become aware of at least some of the story in the years between his first look at Vigée-Lebrun's portrait of herself and her daughter and his writing about the memory in 1911–12. If he did, he may have had more than a simply intuitive sense that the picture was one of the ones in the Louvre that had had most to suggest to him as a boy about "the kind of life, always of the queer so-called inward sort . . . [he] was going to lead" (350).

Lost in the woods around Cummington, Massachusetts, one summer afternoon in 1981, my friend Mark and I walked in endless circles and talked
desultorily, exchanging fragments of our life stories. He told me the following anecdote by way of partially explaining why he had become sexually
active only late in youth. When he was twelve, he said, his mother went out
shopping one Saturday afternoon and left him and his two older brothers,
who were thirteen and fourteen, at home by themselves. The oldest boy
proposed they have what he called a Scheherazade party in their mother's
absence, and the other two readily fell in with the plan. He had recently
been talking about what sounded to each of them like a funny and possibly exciting game of "playing harem," and the boys decided to seize the
opportunity to try it out. Giggling, they put on a phonograph record of
Rimsky-Korsakov's *Scheherazade* and launched into simultaneous and up-
roarious stripteases to the music. Once they were undressed, one of the
boys ran into their parents' room and returned with three of their mother's
scarves, which they tied around their by now erect penises as they resumed
their hilarious "harem girl" dances. At this point their mother, having realized she had forgotten her wallet, unexpectedly returned home. The three
"dancing girls" found themselves surprised by a parental whirling dervish
who shouted and cursed at them, threw the phonograph record off the
turntable, and then, her fury still unvented, hurled a chair through one
of the living-room windows. Mark said years later that he was so embarrassed and frightened by the episode that he didn't again indulge in any
form of sexual experimentation—even solo masturbation—for nine years
afterward.

  To the question of why Mark's mother was so upset and angry there is
of course no shortage of answers or explanations: a parent's violent responses to her pubescent sons' enactment of their sexuality; a woman's—a

mother's—rage at a scene of the male sexuality by which she had long felt (if only unconsciously or inarticulately) oppressed; the blind homophobic fury of an at least nominally heterosexual woman at the (to her) astonishingly casual homosexual play of her three sons. It would have been little comfort to Mark and his brothers, and perhaps even less to their mother, to have been told that their behavior in this situation paralleled in some striking ways the plot of the most celebrated Scheherazade party of them all, the 1910 Diaghilev–Ballets Russes production, but I think it is of considerable interest to the student of the dynamics of homoeroticism and homophobia as constitutive elements of modern culture to notice how aspects of the scenario of Diaghilev's influential pseudo-oriental extravaganza in some ways correspond to Mark's story. In the Ballets Russes *Scheherazade*, the shah is told by his brother that he (the shah) is being duped by his wives, that all of them are unfaithful to him. The shah, in a pet, pretends to go off hunting, and leaves his chief wife, the sultana Zobeida, and the rest of the harem to themselves. As soon as he is gone, his wives receive their various "slave" lovers, Zobeida's being the so-called Golden Slave (one of Nijinsky's most celebrated roles). The shah returns unexpectedly, surprising his wives with their lovers, and, in a rage, orders his janissaries to slaughter the whole group. In a scene awhirl with flashing scimitars and falling bodies, Zobeida holds herself motionless, until, seeing her lover killed, she stabs herself to death. Her astonished husband bursts into tears, and the curtain falls.[1]

Diaghilev's *Scheherazade*, starring Nijinksy and Ida Rubinstein (in the role of the "unfaithful wife" Zobeida) and choreographed by Fokine, was one of the most famous premieres in an age of opening-night coups de theatre. Marcel Proust, who attended with the composer and conductor Reynaldo Hahn, his erstwhile lover, wrote afterward that the spectacle was the most beautiful he had ever seen.[2] Peter Wollen, drawing on Edward Said's *Orientalism* and related work of Perry Anderson and Arno Mayer, has deftly analyzed the implications of early-twentieth-century cultural productions such as *Scheherazade*, the fashions they inspired and the social and political attitudes they underwrote, and the fantasies that were disseminated through them.[3] These latter included racist and imperialist fantasies of white bourgeois global domination of "oriental" peoples, and depended, for the glamorous and erotic aura they exuded for many white Europeans and Americans, on other fantasies, imbricated with them, about inhabiting environments of extreme opulence in which the members of "master races" could enact with impunity "forbidden" sexual impulses on the dominated bodies of others.

Wollen focuses his analysis of *Scheherazade* on Leon Bakst's set and costume designs, which, historians of fashion agree, revolutionized consumer perceptions throughout the bourgeois world. Bakst's use of brilliant hues of blue and green and red and orange side by side was immediately imitated in cultural productions of all kinds, in painting, jewelry design, and interior decoration. Cecil Beaton, then an acute young observer of the haute monde, wrote of the Paris of 1910 in the aftermath of *Scheherazade* that "a fashion world that had been dominated by corsets, lace, feathers and pastel shades soon found itself a seraglio of vivid colours, harem skirts, beads, fringes and voluptuousness."[4] "Fringes and voluptuousness" is suggestive: in the new seraglio "look" derived from Bakst's designs, signifiers of the ostensibly trivial order of bright-colored shawls, beads, and "fringe" suddenly become ubiquitous, and included within their semiotic range a "voluptuous fringe" that lay, in a manner of speaking, just the other side of the looking glass from the wearers' ordinary lives, a phantasmagoric "oriental" margin populated by lascivious odalisques and their slave lovers, jealous masters and their terrible household executioners. When the fashionable world of 1910 donned turbans, "harem pants," oriental shawls, and beads in "shocking" quantities and color combinations, they can be seen to have been participating in a mass fantasy of joining a "voluptuous fringe" where ordinary social life took on a "barbaric splendor" and sexuality imaginarily escaped the constraints of bourgeois domestic life and took on a "savage" and many-hued intensity.

Riots did not break out at the premiere of *Scheherazade*—that famously happened to the Ballets Russes three seasons later, at the first night of *Le sacre du printemps*. Violence was largely confined to the stage in *Scheherazade*, in the general slaughter that followed the shah's vengeful entry into the scene of orgy in his own harem. In his analysis of the potent implicit political effects of the fashions—and not least of all the fashions in fantasy—a spectacle like *Scheherazade* fostered, Wollen emphasizes the enormous impact of Bakst's designs on popular perceptions and attitudes in this century. Interested as I am in the history of gay male subjectivity in the modern epoch, I want to consider another aspect of the "riot of fantasies" that converged on *Scheherazade* and that it in turn reproduced and disseminated. Besides its fosterage of colonialist, racist attitudes of the kind Wollen reads

8. Ida Rubinstein in *Scheherazade*. Reproduced by permission of the Dance Collection, the New York Public Library for the Performing Arts, Astor, Lenox and Tilden Foundations.

out of it, there are other significant ways in which the repressive violence of which I have spoken as being in one sense limited to the space of the stage in *Scheherazade* actually extended far beyond it. The ones I want to emphasize here are the misogynistic and homophobic implications of the murderous disciplinary violence the piece symbolically carried out on its "stars," Rubinstein and Nijinsky, in their respective characters of Zobeida and the Golden Slave.

In a series of performances around the time of *Scheherazade*, ranging from Saint Sebastian to Salome, Ida Rubinstein powerfully enacted a series of fin de siècle fantasies about the ostensibly "evil" potential of various modes of behavior attributed to women in some of the dominant representational regimens of the turn of the century. These ranged from phallic femininity (woman as castrator, femme fatale) to anorexic withdrawal (woman as victim, wraith). Self-styled high priestess of decadent performance in the early years of this century, Rubinstein offered to audiences sensational specularizations of some of their most resonant fantasies of gender conflict, including such complex ones as her impersonation of a "feminized" (i.e., castrated) male in her role as the protagonist of d'Annunzio and Debussy's *The Martyrdom of Saint Sebastian* (1911). *Saint Sebastian* boasted, as had *Scheherazade* the year before, not only Rubinstein's presence but also the choreography of Fokine and the set and costume designs of Bakst.[5] In his study *Idols of Perversity* Bram Dijkstra speaks of Rubinstein as having served as "an ambulant fetish expressive of the ideologically manipulated desires of [her] society." He emphasizes two of the possible bases for this fetishization of her poses on the part of male viewers: "Clearly, the fetishized emaciation of iconic figures such as Rubinstein made it possible for males to respond to them in either a sadistic or masochistic fashion, depending on whether they were seen as subjects in control of their own destinies (and hence a threat to the aggressive self-identity of the men observing them) or as ultrapassive objects of aggressive desire."[6] Although he analyzes lesbian artist Romaine Brooks's painting of Rubinstein at some length, Dijkstra limits his consideration of the possible meanings of her career almost entirely to male-centered ones. The crucial element of Rubinstein's public persona that Dijkstra fails to consider is her position as a powerful emblem for some of her lesbian admirers (these appear in his text only under the rather bland designation "her women friends") of a will to exhaust the entire repertory of binary roles through which femininity was conceived in the turn-of-the-century West. Placing predictable heterosexual male projections onto her performances to one side, one can readily imagine at least some of the ways that the more or less open secret of the lesbian sexuality she figured for some members of her audience (especially, we may assume, for lesbians themselves and for some gay male admirers) contributed to the highly charged atmosphere of her public appearances. For example, besides those aspects of her work described by Dijkstra as being in some ways compatible with contemporary male-identified fantasies of both extreme (phallic) feminine potency and no less extreme feminine passivity, the self-assertive and exhibitionistic aspects of her work also permitted her to present herself, at least liminally, as both a subject and an object of lesbian desire rendered visible to an extraordinary degree.

In her role as Zobeida in *Scheherazade* Rubinstein initially functions as a "threatening" embodiment of transgressive female heterosexual desire. But in the work's famous ending, which many members of its first audience, including Fokine, seem to have found its most overwhelming gesture, Rubinstein's motionless stance amidst the scene of massacre around her seems to have represented an almost unbearably ambiguously charged moment. For the duration of that prolonged moment Zobeida resists enacting either her rage at her husband and master or her grief over the slaughter of her lover and her other companions, and instead gathers to herself the storm of energy swirling around her by temporarily but nonetheless forcefully adopting the position and appearance of being its still center.

Only a modicum of these tensions are resolved by the abrupt gesture with which Zobeida shatters her powerful but unsustainable pose: stabbing herself to death. The performative energies of Rubinstein's repertory of symbolic roles—the male-identified potent castrator (Judith) and violated suicide (Lucrece) as well as those of possible subject and object of lesbian desire—collapse incoherently as Zobeida, the temporary imaginary embodiment of all these roles, falls dead. Similarly, the positions—of being tremendously empowered and being oppressed literally to death— between which Rubinstein rapidly oscillated in the climactic moments of *Scheherazade* are left unresolved in the case of her gay male counterpart, Nijinsky, when, after an extraordinary enactment of flight and defiance, his "slave" character is seized and executed. "How odd it is that Nijinsky should always be the slave in your ballets," Diaghilev's friend and musical adviser Walter Nouvel quipped to the impresario at the time *Scheherazade* was being planned. "I hope one day you'll emancipate him."[7] Of course, Diaghilev never did, and Nijinsky's struggle to emancipate himself was to all appearances an excruciating failure. He was to break off his relationship with Diaghilev in 1913 and to stop dancing publicly altogether by 1919, thereafter to live on in confinement, diagnosed as schizophrenic, until 1950.

At the time of Scheherazade, however, he was still successfully negotiating the powerful projections of sexual contradiction onto his performances that are as notable an aspect of the record of his career as a different set of these are of his colleague Rubinstein's.[8] Fokine, for example, praised the way the dancer's "peculiar" "lack of masculinity" made him the perfect interpreter of the role of the Golden Slave. "Now he was a half-human, half-feline animal, softly leaping great distances, now a stallion," Fokine writes in a characteristic evocation of Nijinsky's supposed resolution of highly charged contradictions in his performances, in his body, and his dancing.[9] Both subhuman and superhuman, he is simultaneously perceived as an effeminate cat and a tremendous stud, but not as "masculine" in any ordinary sense. Fokine presents his decision to eliminate ordinary "masculinity" from the expressive range of Nijinsky's dancing in Scheherazade as an inevitable consequence of what he saw as the peculiar strengths of Rubinstein's imperious appearance, and he does so with a stunning non sequitur. "Next to the very tall Rubinstein," he writes, "I felt that [Nijinsky] would have looked ridiculous had he acted in a masculine manner."[10] The astonishing success of Scheherazade no doubt had more than a little to do with the extraordinary energy with which it found terms for specularizing—rendering both visible and spectacular—the "scandals" of the sexualities of its two stars and of their respective ways of revealing and concealing these in performance. Fokine to the contrary, much more complicated relations had to be "adjusted" between the two principals in Scheherazade than Rubinstein's height in comparison with Nijinsky's relative shortness: the whole array of conflicting sexual projections that could be cast onto them and their performances had to be brought into effective relation to each other.

The main outline at least of the Scheherazade scenario as it was eventually performed by the Ballets Russes had been the idea of artist and theatrical designer Alexandre Benois, and he afterward wrote of Nijinsky's performance in terms remarkably similar to Fokine's "half-this, half-that" ones: impersonating the Golden Slave, Benois said, Nijinsky had become in rapid

9. Baron de Meyer, *Vaslav Nijinsky as the Golden Slave in "Scheherazade."* Reproduced by permission of the Dance Collection, the New York Public Library for the Performing Arts, Astor, Lenox and Tilden Foundations.

turns "half-cat, half-snake, fiendishly agile, feminine and yet wholly terrifying." [11] As with Rubinstein's performance, but in rather different terms, Nijinsky's was perceived as being both intensely phallic and no less intensely "feminine." The most significant difference between the affective ranges of Rubinstein's and Nijinsky's performances is that while her role permitted her to enact a fairly wide range of positions, including certain ones that were deemed "masculine," it was precisely these "ordinary" masculine positions that were excluded from Nijinsky's role. What Fokine calls Nijinsky's "peculiar" "lack of masculinity"—the constant interplay in his most characteristic performances of flashes of hypervirile and hyperfeminine effects, which make sensational impressions but can never be made to "add up" to "ordinary" masculinity—represents the piece's powerful negative electrical charge, at its opposite pole from the positive charge the piece locates in Rubinstein's power to enact "masculinity," at least liminally, alongside other performative modes.

Judging from available contemporary descriptions of the performance one does not get the sense that there was any moment in Nijinsky's performance in which he was permitted to signal anything like Rubinstein's "majestic" and overwhelming gesture of prolonged motionless resistance to the murderous violence that furiously manifests itself in the piece's last scene.[12] The strain of being a visible and intensely mystified embodiment of the open secret of male homosexuality in Paris and London in the decade or two after the epochal downfall and death of Oscar Wilde no doubt played a significant part in what was diagnosed as Nijinsky's schizophrenic disintegration in his late twenties, at the end of World War I. Rubinstein, as the daughter and heiress of a rich St. Petersburg family, was able to use her successes with the Ballets Russes as Cleopatra and Zobeida to launch herself as a star in subsequent productions that she herself financed; as I have said, Nijinsky's attempts to become similarly autonomous were a disastrous failure for a variety of reasons, not the least of which, I suspect, was the relation of his fame to the specularization of the imputed "lack of masculinity" that restricted him to the margins of identities of which "ordinary masculinity" was an indispensable component.

Between Diaghilev's, Nijinsky's, Rubinstein's, and Bakst's "Scheherezade party" of 1910 and Mark's and his brothers' of the early 1960s lies a half-century in which the construction of gay male subjectivity on a number of fronts has exhibited some striking—and sometimes terrible—

consistencies.[13] Some of the most effective forms of resistance to homophobic oppression that gay men have developed and practiced during the same period have shown a similar kind of consistency. One of these has been the sometimes elaborately planned, sometimes spontaneously performed "Scheherazade party," staged over and over again in this century in locations ranging from the theater of the belle epoque to, fifty years later, a suburban American living room. Rather than dismissing it as trivial, I want to insist on its having been an important aspect of the widely various repertory of political acts gay men have practiced and by means of which we have resisted this century's depradations against us. I take the "Scheherazade party"—the conspicuous energies with which it is enacted as well as the phobic violence with which it is repressed, violence of either the explosive variety that Mark experienced or the corrosive kind that gradually disabled Nijinsky—as an emblematic expression of a perilously highly charged compromise, the energies of which both "sides" in the ongoing war for and against gay visibility, homophilic and homophobic, have been effectively exploiting for most of this century.

Jack Smith, who died of AIDS-related causes on September 18, 1989, was one of the most accomplished and influential but least known producers of the extremely theatricalized, densely materialist version of urban gay male social and artistic practice that has to this point been recognized, studied, and theorized chiefly under the extremely reductive rubric of "camp." [14] In 1962 Jack Smith threw a "Scheherazade party" that has probably had more political and artistic impact, at least in the English- and French-speaking worlds, than any since the Ballets Russes's of fifty years before. Filming for seven consecutive weekends on the roof of an old movie theater, since demolished, on the Lower East Side of Manhattan, Smith and a group of friends, appareled in various kinds of drag—"harem," vampire, Marilyn Monroe—enacted for the camera a series of scenes from an imaginary transvestite orgy. They swayed to unheard music, "vamped" each other, casually and unhurriedly exposed parts of their bodies—here a female breast, there the limp penis of one reveler casually draped over the shoulder of another seated before him. Smith edited the results, added a soundtrack of old 78s of German tango bands and Latin American pop songs, and screened the film in the spring of 1963 under the title Flaming Creatures.[15] It provoked a violent response. A small coterie of admirers, including Jonas

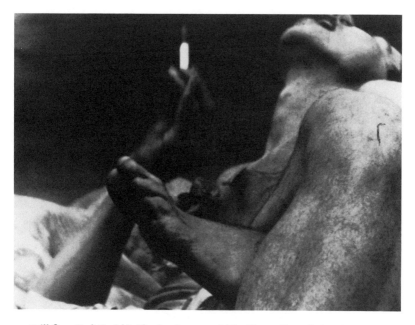

10. Still from Jack Smith's *Flaming Creatures.* © The Plaster Foundation, Inc. Reproduced by permission.

Mekas and Susan Sontag, praised Smith for helping inaugurate a new sexually and artistically radical film practice in this country. Other viewers enjoyed the film's dreamy insouciance about matters of sexuality and gender, but many hated and attacked it. Theaters that showed *Flaming Creatures* were raided, and prints of the film were seized by the New York police. A few favorable published responses aside, the history of the reception of the film has amounted in large part to a history of the effort to suppress it, both here and abroad. A print of the film was seized by U.S. customs as it was being returned from a screening in Vancouver, and showings in Ann Arbor and Austin were "busted" by local police in the late 1960s. Film scholar Karel Rowe screened the film at Northwestern University in 1972 and unexpectedly found himself the object of a mini-riot as infuriated "jock" students, disappointed in their expectations of seeing an ordinary porn film, pounded on the projection booth and demanded refunds.[16]

Smith stopped releasing films only a few years after *Flaming Creatures*, professing disgust that, as he put it, his witty and beautiful "comedy" had been reduced to a banal "sex issue of the Cocktail World."[17] Ironically, Susan Sontag became in a sense more "famous" for *Flaming Creatures*, about which she wrote a laudatory and defensive review in the *Nation* in 1964, than did its maker, Jack Smith. For every person who actually saw Smith's film, perhaps a hundred know it only from Sontag's description of it. Sontag's often cited essay "Notes on 'Camp'" appeared (in *Partisan Review*) the same year as the *Flaming Creatures* review, and from the vantage point of twenty-five years after their first appearance, one may well be struck rereading her essays by the extreme degree to which they depoliticize the sexual and artistic practices that are their subjects. For example, Sontag praises *Flaming Creatures* for its "joy and innocence" ("*Flaming Creatures* is that rare modern work of art: it is about joy and innocence"), and while I can see speaking of it as a joyous film, the other half of the formulation makes one want to paraphrase Mae West: "innocence had nothing to do with it."[18] *Flaming Creatures* not only exemplifies a remarkable range of experience and sophistication about the ways people inhabit gender and sexuality, it also manifests an acutely intelligent political awareness and engagement. The maker of *Flaming Creatures* knew how to make a cultural product "guaranteed" to explode closets, he knew where and how to detonate it, and he was aware that setting people's closets on fire is not simply a liberatory act: inevitably, some people would get burned, including, quite possibly, the incendiaries themselves.

Exploding the closet by making "outrageous" forays against the heterosexual monopoly on filmic representation was in Smith's work not unrelated to other political activities he advocated and practiced, such as his resistance to what he called "landlordism," the ruinous remaking of Manhattan in the image of real estate interests in the 1970s and 1980s, and his commitment to tending and arranging the large collection of "trash" that he assembled and used as his basic performance material. Smith tried to get theater audiences to put themselves in the place of New York City's homeless years before anyone else did: for his *Capitalism of Atlantis* (1965), he wanted spectators brought in blindfolded while a loud recorded voice exhorted them to imagine themselves passed out from exhaustion on a hot sidewalk and being assaulted by cops and dragged into custody.[19] Smith also had utopian ideas about the "trash" culture he saw us as inhabiting; he told Sylvere Lotringer in a *Semiotext(e)* interview that "in the middle of the city should be a repository of objects that people don't want anymore which they should take to this giant junkyard. . . . This center of unused objects would become a center of intellectual activity. Things would grow up around it." [20] Smith's first performance piece, a "nightclub act" he did in collaboration with filmmaker Ken Jacobs in Provincetown in 1961, was called The Human Wreckage Review. [21]

In 1967, near what was to be the end of the period of his most intense involvement with film, not only as a filmmaker but also as perhaps the most frequently featured performer in underground film during that movement's most productive decade, Smith was asked in an interview what pleasure he had taken in his film performances. "I never could afford psychoanalysis," he answered, and went on to say, "it was very brave of me to take psychoanalysis in that form." [22] The reply is in one sense instantly recognizable as a bit of period humor, but I propose to take it as more than that; I wish to affirm Smith's judgment that he "was very brave" to attempt to carry out a self-analysis—one from which I believe many other people in comparably marginal situations who have seen his work, or that of his imitators, have benefited—in a public and highly improvisatory manner, rather than the private and privileged circumstances under which analysis is normally carried out. As he treats all his other performances as opportunities for "acting out," so does Smith treat the film-journal interview as yet another venue for both enacting and examining common anxieties—common, at least, to people like him, then and since, experimenting with renegotiating their wholly or partially closeted artistic and political existences.

To a question in the same interview about his plans for the immediate future, Smith replies not with the statement about new projects in the offing that the interviewer expects, but with the wistful, pseudo-personal utterance, "Well, I have got to try to pull myself together." [23] The comedy of the director/film star who is so neurotic, so hysterically self-absorbed, that he compulsively responds to "public" interviewing with "private" psychotherapy-style answers fits the alternately glacially ironic and self-distancing but also aggressively "deviant" and exhibitionistic milieu of New York pop culture of the 1960s, a culture that first centered around Smith but soon shifted to Warhol.

It may be useful to interrogate the kinds of attributions that have generally been made to Smith and his work—"playfulness" and "innocence" as well as simple "irony" and "self-mockery"—in order better to understand how his performance career, during and after the period in which he made and/or starred in numerous films, represents an alternative to psychoanalytic theory and therapy—In some ways consonant and in other ways in strong conflict with it. However "playful" one may choose to take Smith's undeniably ironic relation to his own performances to be, I think it is also undeniable that his career represents a prolonged attempt to work out an exemplary role for himself and others like him on the sexual and artistic fringes. Asked in the interview just quoted what kind of film roles he might like to play that he had not yet done, Smith replied, "Well, I think I would like to play . . . Christ. But . . . maybe I never will—maybe the interest has all gone out of that, or maybe it would be too repetitious of Dracula" (in Andy Warhol's film version of which he had recently starred as "Batman-Dracula").[24] Smith's fleeting equation of the role of Christ with that of Dracula is an interesting one, but more interesting for my present purposes is a shift in tone at just this point in his remarks: "But anyway the world could use a new idea—a new Christ image, and it would be fun to sort of work that out." This pronouncement was no doubt made at least partly tongue in cheek, but, just kidding or not, the remark has a magniloquence of a kind that has often been associated with delusion—in the offhand manner in which Smith speaks of giving "the world . . . a new Christ image" as a secondary career goal, as something that "would be fun to sort of work . . . out," if and when he gets around to it. The extremely casual, possibly facetious, messianic intentions Smith expresses here may well remind the student of gay male subjectivity in this century of other, more fateful engagements between the "image" of Christ and gay self-identifications and self-representations. (Nijinsky, for example, engaged in extensive debate with himself as to whether he was or was not Christ in the diary he kept at the time of his breakdown, the crisis that marked the end of his performing career and the onset of his ostensible madness.)[25] Far from abandoning his public self-analysis when he ceased to make films, Smith continued in his subsequent work as a performance artist to "act out" fantasies of his imaginary identities as well as critiques of these fantasies.

One should not conclude a discussion of the imaginary identities that are most important to the performances in Flaming Creatures, as well as to Smith's performances in such other films as Warhol's Batman-Dracula, without considering the figure of the vamp and the practice of vamping. The very term vamp, which came into wide circulation around the beginning of World War I, proclaims its derivation from vampire, a word and a myth that circulated wildly through mass culture in the aftermath of the success of Bram Stoker's Dracula (1897) and its numerous stage and film versions. The reasons for the possibly strong resonance of the figure of the vampire for the young person who comes to self-awareness in the closet (as almost all young gay people probably still do) are obvious: like Dracula, gay youngsters are driven by desires they may at least initially perceive as secret, forbidden, and even monstrous in the eyes of others.[26] Reasons for the persistence of the figure of the vamp in gay subcultures long after its general disappearance from mainstream mass culture are also not far to seek. The vamp, a figure of which Theda Bara was in her brief career the prototypical performer (she enacted the vamp in some forty feature-length film vehicles between 1915 and 1919), was an exotic woman who preyed on and ruined men.[27] The socially and sexually marginal milieu that gave rise to Smith's film practice and others like it gives it marked affinities with the vamp film, from A Fool There Was (1915), which starred Bara and inaugurated the subgenre, to Blood and Sand (1922), starring Nita Naldi and Rudolph Valentino. Thierry de Duve has noted how Warhol's early films developed out of the shadow world of the Hollywood of the 1920s, in which the vamp and the drug addict were new and emblematic figures (Kenneth Anger has lovingly gathered narratives about these figures into his Hollywood Babylon books); in this respect, Warhol's films derive directly from Smith's. De Duve writes, "Warhol didn't evolve in the plastic world of stars, but in the demimonde of vamps. His cinema plays out the bland dreams of 1950s Hollywood only to materialize the terror that the Hollywood of the '20s still knew how to signal."[28] Part of the "terror" that Smith's and Warhol's films revive is the widespread fear, in a misogynistic and homophobic culture, of recognizing some women's and gay men's high level of success at the exemplary modern urban practice of "cruising," of attracting sexual attention and response from possible partners through a command of body language, especially through the direction of a powerful, desirous-looking gaze. Judging from the intensely negative reactions of many viewers of Flaming Creatures, images of Smith's face, or that of his sometime star Maria Montez, gazing out at the viewer through layers of mascara and eyeshadow, scarves and veils, elicited something of the same fascinated but phobic response that Bara's and Naldi's had fifty years before, when they first signaled for a mass audience the possibility of women's behaving in a sexually commanding manner. That there could be sexually confident and commanding gay men, rather than only disfigured and abject victims of the closet, was powerfully manifested in Smith's and Warhol's films, and the striking enactment of this possibility in some of these films may well have renewed the "terror" of vamps—this time of openly gay male ones—that had disturbed and enthralled many viewers earlier in the century, when the "ravenous" and supposedly irresistible gaze of the vamp was first brought in off the street, so to speak, and developed into a classic cinematic code.

Smith's performance practice derives in obvious ways from some of the most excessive moments of early film—the screen personalities of Bara, Naldi, and Valentino and the (to our eyes) deliciously and absurdly over-staged and overacted "orgy scenes" of which the "Babylonian" sequence of D. W. Griffith's *Intolerance* (1916) is perhaps the most notable example. Part of the success of the assault on the closet Smith's work makes is a consequence of the virtuosic fluency with which he negotiates the undulating waves of images not only across genders but also across "perversions." Successfully negotiating just such perilous performative modes—as Rubinstein in her time seems to have found ways of doing while Nijinsky did not—Smith and other featured performers in *Flaming Creatures* move insouciantly and triumphantly around and through a whole repertory of proscribed behaviors—transgressions that it would be reductive to describe as simply "transvestite," since a man's wearing feminine garb is only one of the numerous culturally enforced "police lines" Smith's performances frequently cross. Smith seems to have performed the roles of the "sheik" or the (presumably male) "vampire" at least as frequently as he did those of the "vamp" or "harem girl" in 1960s films. He played all these roles, and directed others to play them, in ways that short-circuit their relations to the heterosexualized representational regimes from which they derive. What is compelling about these figures in Smith's films is not the sheik's enactment of virility or the harem girl's of femininity; nor is it simply the reversal of these roles, as it might be if Smith's were simply another version of traditional transvestite comedy. To underestimate or dismiss the real erotic appeal Smith's "comedies" have had for many gay viewers is to ignore the primary source of their power: his films are incitements to his audience not only to play fast and loose with gender roles but also to push harder against prevailing constraints on sexuality. It therefore seems wrong to say, as Stefan Brecht does, that "Smith does not confront heterosexuality with any other kind of sexuality: sexuality is identified as heterosexuality. . . . Homosexuality is a substitute, and Smith's art is not homosexual but transvestite." [29] The problem with Brecht's formulation lies in its reductive representation of the sexual politics of the twentieth century; in this landscape, the development of behavioral and representational codes for being gay or queer in ways other than those derived from heterosexual modes of behavior and representation has been an ongoing project on a number of fronts. When commentators assert of the transgressive performance practices of the 1960s, as Brecht does, that "the queerness of queerness is that it is asexual," [30] they fail to recognize that erotic charges in a work like *Flaming Creatures* do not follow hard-wired gender lines, but move powerfully across circuits of gender and sexual identity in not altogether predictable fashions. [31]

From its inception Smith's film practice seems to have derived much of its energy from his identification with the movie star and belated vamp Maria Montez, and from what he saw as her identification with the definitively kitsch epics she acted in during her brief but stellar ten-year film career — the same length as Smith's of two decades later, as it turned out. Smith, like many other gay men of his generation, was particularly fascinated by the five Universal Studios vehicles in which Montez starred with the athletic but wooden leading-man Jon Hall: *Arabian Nights, White Savage, Ali Baba and the Forty Thieves, Sudan,* and, above all, *Cobra Woman,* in which Montez played twin "queens of the jungle," one good, one evil. [32] Smith began his career collaborating with Ken Jacobs, and their earliest joint effort appears to have been a film called *Little Cobra Dance* (the third part of *Saturday Afternoon Blood Sacrifice: TV Plug: Little Cobra Dance* [1957]), in which Smith, dressed as an "exotic" Spanish lady, launches into a wild dance, falls down, and is questioned by the police—"the last being an actual event incorporated into the film." [33] The acting-out of a pseudo-exotic transvestism, combined with a manic performance of celebration and a no less manic performance of failure ("launches into a wild dance" and "falls down"), and culminating in ritual encounters with the police, established themselves early in Smith's career as the central "business" of his performances.

The small body of writing Smith published is, however transgressive its contents, usually grammatically and syntactically conventional, so it may well be worth noting the occasional sentence that does not conform to standard, as in the following passage from his 1962–63 essay "The Perfect

11. Publicity photograph of Maria Montez. © Universal Studios.

Filmic Appositeness of Maria Montez": ". . . (Before a mirror is a place) is a place where it is possible to clown, to pose, to act out fantasies, to not be seen while one gives (Movie sets are sheltered, exclusive places where nobody who doesn't belong can go). . . ."[34] The repetition here, and the sentence's incoherent-looking movement into and out of parentheses, may seem meaningless—may, even if noticed, be easily ignored, subliminally registered as a typesetting error or at best a compositional complexity not worth puzzling out. Yet this sentence, convoluted and incomplete as it in some ways is, may be taken to be a particularly compelling statement of Smith's idea, the subject of the essay, of the "perfect appositeness" of performances like Maria Montez's and his own to what he sees as the most powerful artistic and political potentials of film. The "place" being somewhat obscurely situated in this difficult sentence is one "before a mirror," where one can see oneself without being seen by anyone else—a place somehow analogous with (or "perfectly apposite" to) the "sheltered, exclusive" movie set of Smith's fantasies, "where nobody who doesn't belong can go." One way of reading this is to imagine that these two "apposite" spaces, the one as small as a mirror and the other as large as a movie set, define the liminal horizons of the closet as Smith sees them. ("What's larger than a mirror but smaller than a movie set? The closet.") A better question may be: Is a closet as big as Universal Studios in the 1940s (home of the closed set of Smith's Montez fantasies) still a closet? Can the closet be made to cease being one if/when its bounds are extended beyond a certain point? If so, what is that point? If the closet is the place one visits or inhabits in order not "to . . . be seen while one gives," as Smith puts it, how can what is, in the space of the closet, intransitivized into objectless "giving" be retransitivized—into giving what? in? out? "head"? "the finger"? pleasure? performances? For Smith, the camera is only a more complex kind of mirror, and if the mirror is sometimes the only piece of furniture in a closet, the mirror-extended-as-camera can function as an opening onto two-way streets, onto transitivity of all kinds of officially discouraged or prohibited or persecuted varieties.

The "closed set" of Smith's Montez fantasies is, in other words, a kind of closet, but a closet with a difference: one that has been enlarged, opened, and populated with other actors, so that while it retains some of its potential for atomistic self-isolation, it has also in Smith's fantasy become a kind of palm-sheltered halfway house for 1950s queers. Smith was far too classically a paranoid New Yorker and, as an artist, a (self-) control freak to have ever actually made the move to the Montezland of sunny southern California, but a number of other queer artists of the time—especially Christopher Isherwood and Gore Vidal—have left us rich chronicles of the "life in the irony mills" that was lesbian and gay existence in the semi-sheltered gilded ghetto of postwar Hollywood.

The dream that Maria Montez's performances seem to have compelled for Smith and many other young gay men of his time was one of joy, but a joy in which screams of pain might sometimes be unpredictably mixed in with what were supposed to be screams of pleasure. The apparent wide-openness of the circuits of pleasure that energized Maria Montez's performances for herself as well as for her fans made her an exemplary figure for Smith and other gay filmmakers and filmgoers of the 1960s. Ever her own greatest fan, Montez's most oft-quoted utterance, made to an interviewer in the late 1940s, goes, "When I see myself on the screen, I look so beautiful I want to scream with joy." For me, as I suspect for many other gay men who have relished it, the charm of that remark lies not just in what a naive interpreter might call the "childlike" openness of Montez's admiration of her larger-than-life screen image, but in its intensity—signaled by the inflection upward into the hysterical register at the sentence's end: "I want to scream with joy." And one may at least partially attribute the remark's longtime currency among the many gay men for whom American popular film of the 1940s and 1950s—especially through its female stars—had been formative to the succinct way it brings "screen" and "scream" together. In her adoring self-critique, Montez demonstrates what Smith might call the relation of "perfect appositeness," the lexical as well as psychological near-mirroring, of "screen" and "scream." Smith discovers something similar in his discussion of the related political spaces of "mirror" and "movie set"; his own politics of performance exploits the appositeness of "self-indulgent" fantasy ("screen," mirror) and disruptive public enactment ("scream," movie set). Not the least of the cultural constructs shattered by the impulse to "scream with joy" at the sight of the adorable (self-)image on the movie screen is the masculine gender identity of male fans of Montez or Lana Turner or Jayne Mansfield. For how many gay men of my own and the previous generation were our earliest intimations that there might be a gap between our received gender identity and our subjective or "felt" one the consequence not of noticing our own erotic attraction to another boy or man but of enthusiastically enjoying and identifying with the performative excesses of Maria Montez rather than Jon Hall, or Lana Turner rather than Burt Lancaster, or Jayne Mansfield rather than Mickey Hargitay?

Smith, working in conjunction with Jacobs, had by 1963 articulated a full range of tentative cinematic alter egos for exploring the positions one might occupy in relation to the closet, the mirror, and the movie screen. Besides Smith's own *Flaming Creatures*, Smith and Jacobs's two most compelling collaborations, *Blonde Cobra* and *Little Stabs at Happiness*, also premiered that year. In the first of these, Smith, the "Blonde Cobra" of the title (a gesture of homage to the Brunette Cobra, Montez, as well as to the Blonde Venus of Dietrich and Sternberg) plays a character called "Jack Smith" as well as an imperious woman named Madame Nescience. In the film's central episode, the latter dreams that she is a Sadean "Mother Superior" putting down an outbreak of mass lesbian sexual activity in the girls' dormitory.

Elsewhere in the film, besides lamenting his generally degenerescent condition ("Leprosy is eating a hole in me, my teeth are falling out, my hair has turned to sauerkraut"), Smith narrates a story apparently about his childhood:

> There was once a little boy, a little tweensy, microscopic little boy. . . .
> [. . .] And . . . the little boy would . . . look for his Mother, but she was never there, and so he would finally pass out and just fall onto the floor and fall asleep just weary with loneliness and longing and frustration and frustrated longings, until, until when the shadows were lengthening and the sun was drooping he would hear the front door open and, and he would rush out into the hallway and there, and there was his Mother . . . and she always had little white bags from the ten-cent store and they always had certain kinds of chocolates in them, the brown, the droplet kind . . . and he would eat it and she would give him some but not much, just a little because she would save most of it for herself and ah so ah well ah and then, she'd go away again. Mother Mother Mother Mother Mother Mother and then, and there was a little boy that lived upstairs you see it was a two family apartment and ah and—a two family house! and then one day the little boy found the other little boy that lived upstairs the family who lived upstairs in the upstairs floor and the little boy who was less than seven, the lonely little boy, the lonely little boy was less than seven, I know that because we didn't leave Columbus until I was seven, I know it, I was under seven and I took a match and I lit it and I pulled out the other little boy's penis and burnt his penis with a match![35]

Reversing the narrative logic of the two "Scheherazade" stories recounted earlier, in which "orgy" is interrupted by "slaughter" and sexual "games" are violently broken up by an angry and vengeful parent or spouse, the mother of Smith's "lonely little boy" is represented as absent and withholding. This alternative version of the story culminates in an act that fuses the two principal roles and the two halves of the "Scheherazade party" story, the "little boy" being both the initiator of a transgressive sexual game and the figure who puts an end (in this case an immediate end) to the game—

with an act of violence against (in this case one of) its players. The whole story of "the lonely little boy" organizes itself along the manic lines of wild activity eventuating in failure (i.e., falling) and arrest that, as I have discussed, are the design of Smith and Jacobs's brief early collaboration, *Little Cobra Dance*. The little boy is said to be accustomed to "scamper[ing]" from room to room of the empty house looking for his mother, until he "would finally pass out and just fall onto the floor." There he sleeps until he is in turn awakened by the sound of his mother's arriving home, when he "rush[es] out and dart[s] out" to greet her. What is "arrested" at the end of this episode is both childhood sexuality and male-male sexual play, and what the subject, "the lonely little boy," is shown substituting for it is sadistic violence.

As an isolated anecdote, as a familiar kind of "confessional" story of childhood cruelty made "funny" by distance and by its belated avowal of antisocial behavior, as a shaggy-dog story with the unprepared-for punchline "and I pulled out the other little boy's penis and burnt [it] with a match"—as all of these formulations, the "lonely little boy" episode of *Blonde Cobra* may seem to conform in several ways to common conventions of largely straight male-identified styles of humor ("I was a wild and mean little boy, and here's a story to prove it"). But it figures as more than that in Smith's performance, and it does so by means of its engagement with other aspects of his work—and of this film performance in particular—that are different from and in some ways radically opposed to common conventions of straight male comic performance—whether we think of these performances as being carried out by professionals in clubs or on television or in films, or by nonprofessionals in the course of ordinary social life.

The Madame Nescience episode that immediately follows the "lonely little boy" part of *Blonde Cobra* is similarly potentially repugnant to many viewers, insofar as it fits into a familiar transvestite enactment of hostility toward women, toward women in positions of authority particularly, and toward lesbians and lesbian sexuality. Considered as an isolated episode, after all, Madame Nescience presents the viewer with a familiar butt of sexist comedy, the repressed and lascivious nun, here shown indulging in sadistic (homo)sexuality as she, in conformity with the "despotic" and homophobic "Scheherazade party" scenario, acts out a repressive "slaughter" of her lesbian "daughters." The rest of the film, however, provides a context in which one can think "otherwise" of Smith's Madame Nescience performance. For example, following as it does on the "lonely little boy" narrative, Madame Nescience's imaginary appearance and behavior may be read as the return of the repressed mother in that episode. And if she still seems a figure of hostile male projection when seen as a displaced version of the rejecting and withholding mother of the "lonely little boy," she may seem considerably less so if her dream of disciplinary behavior toward her "daughters"—lining them up and paddling their bare bottoms with a "silver cross"—is related to the film's ultimate image. As Smith intones a line from Baudelaire — "Life swarms with innocent monsters"—the film shows him bending forward to expose his own bared buttocks with a butcher knife thrust between them, actually held high up between his thighs but placed to look as though penetrating his anus. "Oooooooooh," Smith cries in voice-over, "Sex is a pain in the ass. Sex IS a pain in the ass."

The image has something of the violent shock value of the founding image of surrealist film, that of the bisected eye in Un chien andalou. The butcher knife driven "up the ass" of the wailing performer is the very image of the sadistic rape of one male by another, just as it is the image of the violent sexual assault that, in homophobic fantasy, gay men both desire and "deserve." Among its other possible meanings for gay male viewers, the image, in combination with the verbal utterance that accompanies it, forcefully and comically literalizes the experience of pain in anal penetration commonly felt by inexperienced men, or by men who engage in being penetrated anally who have feelings of conscious or unconscious unwillingness or anxiety toward their partner and/or toward the idea or the reality of being penetrated.

The image of the butcher knife thrust "up the ass" of the mock-lamenting "Blonde Cobra" is only secondarily an image of male-male rape or of homophobic and sadistic contempt for gay male desire for anal connection. In the economy of the film as a whole it is primarily a comic undoing of the "lonely little boy's" burning the penis of the "other little boy" in the film's first episode and of Madame Nescience's spanking her lesbian "daughters' " bottoms with a silver cross in its central episode. Horrible as it may sound, the film's climactic image of the Cobra figure's stabbed anus is, as it actually appears in the film, more an emblematic or visual metaphysical conceit than any kind of really graphic representation of physical violation. This ostensible wound sheds no blood, nor does the viewer see the knife inserted; it will be obvious to all but the most gullible viewer from the moment of the image's appearance that what one is seeing is in a significant sense not at all a realistically simulated stabbing—no fancy special effects here—but a child's trick of concealing a knife blade in a fold of the body, combined with perhaps the clown's oldest trick for mildly shocking and amusing his audience, exposing his bottom.

The titular *Little Stabs at Happiness* of Smith and Jacobs's other 1963 collaboration are some of them, too, literal, albeit recognizably theatrical, stabs. In the first episode of that film, Smith sits in an empty bathtub, his head covered with tinfoil and his nose painted blue, hectically alternating between smoking a cigarette and gnawing the crotch of a baby doll. When he subsequently grasps the doll by the head and stubs out a cigarette in its eyes, an unsympathetic viewer may respond by thinking that Smith is simply "sick," or that his particular brand of "cinema of cruelty" is puerile in the extreme. When, in the film's final sequence, he emerges onto the roof of a building, dressed in a homemade harlequin costume looking fresh from the thrift shop, to perform a rather wan balloon dance to a recording of a 1940s pop tune called "Happy Bird," it is as if for once his ritualistically alternating performances of manic energy and sodden failure have met in the hitherto unavailable psychic middle to produce simple depression. In the film, the segment is entitled "The Spirit of Listlessness."

Depression, outbursts of mania, fits of hysterical anxiety, of antisocial behavior, hostility, thoughts and memories of sadistic and masochistic desires and behavior, and fantasies of the same, moods of intensely narcissistic self-indulgence (not unrelated to what Leo Bersani has called the "grave doubt resulting from homosexual desire: the doubt about which self to adore")[36] alternating with moods of bitter despair and self-destructive impulses: the emotional weather of Smith's performances is the emotional weather of the closet. This is not to say that gay men have any kind of monopoly on these states of mind and behavior. To do so would simply be to reinscribe the homophobic discourses that for a long time deemed (in some quarters still deem) gays "disturbed" or psychically and emotionally inadequate or damaged, and blamed our sexual and social existences as gay people for the alleged damage rather than looking to the twin institutions of homophobia and the closet, which "disturb" and damage gay and straight people both, in different ways and in differing degrees.

What Jack Smith did in his film performances and "live" performance pieces during twenty historically crucial years was to keep projecting gay subjective awareness of the political and psychological realities of the closet onto the "screen" of fantasy for collective, rather than private, recognition, inspection, and analysis. He continued to do so throughout the 1970s—after Stonewall had occurred and after he himself largely stopped making and appearing in films—in a series of pieces performed in small downtown theaters or, more often, in his own loft. In sharp contrast with the spiraling trajectory of the career of his former filmmaking associate and fellow scandal-master Andy Warhol, Smith continued to seem to court and to find failure and oblivion in his post-Stonewall, post-film career. Incapacity and breakdown ceased to be alternative performative modes for him (the ritualistic "fallings" and failures of his previous work), and he made the endless deferral of performance the hallmark of his work in the 1970s. Audiences arriving at his loft for a midnight performance would regularly witness his fumblings with slides and slide projector for two and a half hours. Smith would then announce that owing to technical problems there would be no (further) performance that night. Hamlet, that most emblematically incapacitated and "blocked" of early modern young male inhabitants of the closet, became one of the predictable foci of an apparently endless series of Smith's announcing-and-deferring performances.

Around 1977 Smith effected what was perhaps his most successful compromise between performance in any ordinary sense and the kind of deferral that had largely replaced ordinary performance for him. He did this in his highly revisionary version of Ibsen's Ghosts, which Smith variously titled The Secret of Rented Island and Orchid Rot of Rented Lagoon.[37] The small group of devotees who attended the first performance were unsurprised when Smith, pleading that some of his actors had failed to appear by curtain time, invited members of the audience to "help out," and "filled in" major roles with stuffed animals from his collection. Smith played the role of Oswald, and (in the first performance) a male friend, in drag and shrouded with veils, played his mother, Mrs. Alving. Smith integrated into the production the apparently inevitable judgment that it would be an unmitigated disaster, and behaved as if he, as well as the character he was playing, were in a state of imminent mental and emotional collapse. He read his lines from the script and frequently requested help finding his place in the play from fellow cast members, who were of course most of the time as "lost" as he was. In the closing lines of the play, young Oswald's dementia, induced by a syphilitic infection inherited through his mother from his philandering but ultrarespectable father, finally manifests itself: he asks his mother to "give him the SUN," and she gazes at him with the horrified realization that he has become psychotic. In Smith's production, Oswald and Mrs. Alving continued sitting side by side in silence after this climactic moment, under an intense pinlight. Mrs. Alving slowly lowered her veil, revealing a leprous face, and Oswald opened his legs, showering a heap of brilliant glitter onto the floor from his "decaying" groin. All this was performed to the sound of Doris Day's recording of "Once I Had a Secret Love."

The camp excesses of this ending, like those of Smith's earlier film work, are palpable. What is not so readily evident in this scene are the ways in which it is consistent and continuous with the political and psychological explorations of the closet I have described Smith making in his earlier work. Young men in extremis; Doris Day's songs and screen personality; the glitter that emblematized for Smith the kind of tacky glamor Maria Montez had shored up against her ruin; secret sexual desires and afflictions; the dramatis personae and conventional apparatus of camp; the props and furniture of the closet—all are the figures and materials Smith's work tirelessly deconstructed.

Smith performed infrequently after the late 1970s. When I belatedly saw him in performance in a festival of Punk art in the early 1980s in a storefront off Times Square, he characteristically appeared late, tinkered for a long time with props and a slide projector that was never activated, and then reclined on a couch to smoke a hookah. All the while an attractive young man and woman, both garbed in "harem pajamas," read aloud in its entirety a biography of Yvonne de Carlo (star of *Song of Scheherazade* [1947]). Beyond his silent but eloquent presence onstage, Smith restricted his contributions to the rest of the performance to a few momentary interruptions of the boy and girl odalisques, to make minute adjustments to their costumes or poses, or to correct their occasional mispronunciations of words.

Later that year I saw yet another big filmic "Scheherazade party," Pasolini's *Arabian Nights*, one of his three late productions of classic literary cluster-narratives: Scheherazade's, the *Canterbury Tales*, and the *Decameron*. Pasolini subsequently repudiated the trilogy for its "liberal," optimistic "sexual pluralism," putting in its place his last completed project, the harrowing film fantasy of sexual captivity and torture under fascism called *Salo*. Although I admire some of Pasolini's films, his "Scheherazade party," the *Arabian Nights*, rehearses many of the same repugnant clichés that underlay Diaghilev's. In Pasolini's "Araby," as in so many earlier orientalizing versions of it, sex rather than survival seems to be the first priority of its denizens, and everyone except the few requisite wise old men is young, extraordinarily sexually attractive, and always available. Falling chronologically between Diaghilev's and Pasolini's deluxe productions, Smith's various versions of "Scheherazade" seem by contrast with these others to harbor real deconstructive potential in relation to the underlying sexual-political and nationalist-political agendas of almost all his big-budget predecessors and successors.

In the numerous political fables of the "harem" Smith directed and/or performed in, he privileges fantasies neither of Western nor male supremacy—as so many other orientalist fantasies do—but of what he calls "moldiness." As Madame Nescience lies on her couch, she is said to be "dreaming of old musty memories, memories that she thought that she had forgot[ten] or so she thought but you see they came up in a funky mass of ah exuding effluviums from the musty past . . . covered with moss and funk."[38] Smith calls her dream, and by extension the whole episode in which she figures, "La rêve de la purité de Madame Nescience." The manifest content of this "dream of purity," as we have seen, was one of the vigorous suppression of lesbianism in a convent by a "mother superior" who brings a suspicious degree of enthusiasm to the task. But it is not with her repressive and luridly charged "purity" that I want to close this discussion of Smith's performances, with which purity indeed had little to do, but rather with an insistence on the paradoxically "moldy," "swampy" (to use his terms) clarity with which his work pungently represents the kind of unconscious processes that have, over the past several decades, fueled innumerable small and large-scale eruptions of queer rebellion. His performances, onstage and off, galvanized many of his fellow artists and impelled careers as extraordinarily unlike each other's as Andy Warhol's and Charles Ludlam's. The "rented lagoon" of his imagination has subsided, but some of its products continue to produce astonishing effects.

the Outside: Warhol and Queer Childhood

"I was never embarrassed about asking someone, literally, 'What should I paint?' because Pop comes from the outside, and how is asking someone for ideas any different from looking for them in a magazine?" — Andy Warhol, POPISM [1]

"I was promised an improved infancy." — Hart Crane, "Passage" [2]

From early on in his career until the end of his life, Andy Warhol sketched (and later photographed or filmed) innumerable images of male nudity, ranging from models in standard "artistic" poses to men masturbating and having sex with each other. Warhol's penchant for sketching and photographing other men's bodies and especially their genitals, one of the few constants in his career as an artist from his early days as an advertising artist and magazine illustrator until late in his lifetime, seems to have been an important aspect of his ability to structure and maintain his highly productive, innovative, and influential career. During the 1950s, as Warhol became increasingly successful as a commercial artist, he repeatedly attempted to gain recognition as a "fine" artist with a series of exhibitions of his drawings. These early gallery shows, which featured images of cupids, beautiful boys' faces, and penises festooned with bows and lipsticked "kiss marks," predictably attracted little positive attention from a New York art world completely taken up with the macho heroics of abstract expressionism.

During and after the years of his first fame as a Pop artist and underground filmmaker, Warhol produced masses of hard- and soft-core images —mostly photographic ones— of male nudes, but unlike other kinds of images he made routinely, he seems never to have found a way to use his "sex pictures" (his code word for them in his diaries is "landscapes") in his artistic production; only a slight trace of them ever found any place among his exhibited works.[3] In this chapter I consider how we may understand Warhol's very early Pop paintings of cartoon and comic strip characters

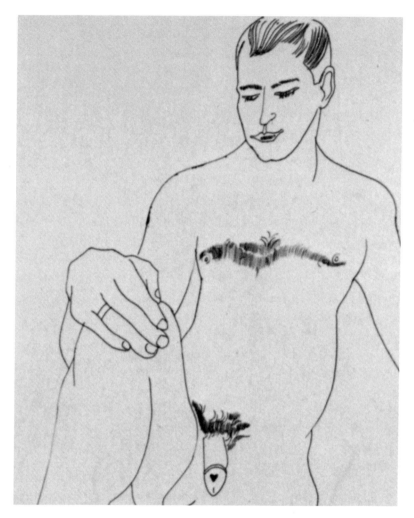

12. Andy Warhol, Untitled (male nude) (c. 1957). © 1998 Andy Warhol Foundation for the Visual Arts/ARS, New York.

(mostly produced circa 1960) as representing not a total rupture with his flagrantly homoerotic art of the fifties but rather a continuation by other means of his fey but ferocious and, in some ways, ultimately successful war against the exclusion of swishiness and fagginess from the repertory of possible gestures that could be made and recognized in visual art.[4] Recent investigations of the relation between Warhol's sexuality and his art have tended to emphasize his representations of male object-choices (for example, explicitly, in his early Pop portraits of Troy Donahue and Warren Beatty; in his 1964 film *Thirteen Most Beautiful Boys*; or, somewhat more obliquely, in his New York World's Fair installation of the same year, *Thirteen Most Wanted Men*).[5] In looking at some of the cartoon paintings that were among the key images through which Warhol established what I see as both a break with and a transformed continuation of his "fag" art of the fifties, I am concerned with his representations of a range of "queer" or "perverse" desires that include but are by no means restricted to male-male object-choice.

The third son and youngest child of Ruthenian immigrants, Andy Warhol appears to have had a difficult childhood on several counts. Perceived as being passive, effeminate, physically awkward and weak, and sometimes weird to the point of uncanniness (this last a quality that would distinguish his adult persona, too), he was frequently harassed by other children. From early on, his mother seems to have attempted to compensate him for ill treatment from others by lavishing affection and attention on him. In the first chapter of *The Philosophy of Andy Warhol*, entitled "Love (Puberty)," Warhol dispatches the subject of his difficult albeit indulged early years in a couple of highly compressed paragraphs:

> I had had three nervous breakdowns when I was a child, spaced a year apart. One when I was eight, one at nine, and one at ten. The attacks— St. Vitus Dance—always started on the first day of summer vacation. I don't know what this meant. I would spend all summer listening to the radio and lying in bed with my Charlie McCarthy doll and my uncut-out cut-out paper dolls all over the spread and under the pillow.
>
> My father was away a lot on business trips to the coal mines, so I never saw him very much. My mother would read to me in her thick Czechoslovakian accent as best she could and I would always say

"Thanks, Mom," after she finished with Dick Tracy, even if I hadn't understood a word. She'd give me a Hershey Bar every time I finished a page in my coloring book.[6]

I propose to take this little story of Warhol as a screen memory of sorts, as a scene (as Freud first theorized) that draws on actual figures and events from one's experience but that is also composed at least partly of imaginary and symbolic elements and in which the objects and events recalled become belatedly and retroactively charged with a set of meanings that simultaneously mask and reveal a network of formative perceptions and fantasies from and about one's early life. I propose at the same time to take the scene as a queered version of a "primal" one. Freud's primal scene is the traumatically anxious and frightening one of the infant's or small child's observing or hearing the sights and sounds of adults engaged in sexual acts.[7] Warhol rewrites the primal scene in the passage above to feature an all-male cast plus his mother. In this highly pastoral revision of a primal scene, anxiety and trauma are allayed so thoroughly as to raise the question of what is being held so resolutely at bay. This cartoon idyll of happy solitary play interrupted by frequent maternal attention is introduced, one must remember, as an account of what happened during what Warhol remembers as "three nervous breakdowns" he experienced between ages eight and ten. To dismiss this scene of childhood contentment as a mere wish fulfillment would be to miss what strikes me as its strong aura of aggressively suppressed and fearful defensiveness.

The peculiar version of queer-child pastoral that Warhol imagines himself performing as a little boy lying abed with his dolls and coloring book is a challenging and potentially rich site of interpretation. The presence of radio and comic strip characters as well as, on the child's part, the activity of coloring suggest that one thing we may have here is a belated and highly colored memory/fantasy about the mythical origins of the adult Warhol's having painted his way into becoming a Pop art celebrity by making numerous images of (among other subjects) comic strip and cartoon characters. Put more broadly, analyzing the elements of this scene may help us better understand the intersecting histories of gay or protogay identity and mass culture in the early to middle decades of this century.

Some of the reasons for the appeal of this scene to the adult Warhol seem obvious: consigned to recuperation in bed, temporarily "safe" from rivalry with his elder brothers and the necessity of contact with other children, his father equally, providentially (and apparently permanently) absent (being away at work in or, in Warhol's class-effacing and class-ironizing locution, "on business trips to" the coal mines), Warhol represents his child self modestly luxuriating in an ideal set of conditions of work and leisure. In the (non-)person of his Charlie McCarthy doll, he has a surrogate male partner to share his bed with him, along with a set of presiding images to guarantee the alleged unspoiledness, that is, the sexual undifferentiatedness, of the scene, the virgin pages of "un-cut-out cut-out paper dolls" that litter the spread.

The main activities represented in the scene are "listening to the radio," listening to the mother read, and "coloring." The whole scene takes place under the aegis of a woman's voice; as Warhol mentions elsewhere in his *Philosophy:* "While I was little I used to listen to The Singing Lady on the radio all the time while I was in bed coloring."[8] The fluency or uninterrupted quality of both representations of this scene ("I would spend *all summer* listening to the radio and lying in bed," and "I used to listen to The Singing Lady on the radio *all the time*"; emphasis added) is punctuated, but apparently not interrupted, by the unfluent sounds of Julia Warhola reading the comics to Andy in her (to him) incomprehensible accent.

It is perhaps the two closing references in the little anecdote, both to his mother, that are most highly charged and most densely encoded. If the child Andy claims not to "under[stand] a word" of her rendition of *Dick Tracy*, it may be because the name of the comic strip "dick" (that is, "detective") resonates obscenely in the imagined/remembered child's ear, and by extension in the mother's, not only with "dick" as the most ordinary vernacular term for "penis" but also because of the way the figure's surname resonates with what appears to have been the adult Warhol's most intensely invested mode of contact with other men's penises: photographing or drawing or "tracing" them. "Dick" is "trace-y" for Warhol in a double sense: it is a desired object to be "traced" in the sense of being detected and pursued and also in that of being captured by being drawn—and thereby kept at a safe and comfortable distance, but also still in potentially exciting proximity, in the relatively manageable form of a visual image and/or record. According to some of his early models, Warhol seems generally to have limited his own participation in many male-male "sex scenes" at which he was present from the fifties through the seventies to gazing at and "tracing," that is, visually recording, them.⁹

As with Julia Warhola's supposedly incomprehensible reading of *Dick Tracy* to her little son, her showering him with Hershey Bars can also be interpreted as fantasmatic material with its own pronounced, if encoded, erotic coloration. Like "Dick Tracy," the term "Hershey Bar" is another proper name from Warhol's childhood that is susceptible to a specifically sexual construction: at the time he was writing his *Philosophy*, "the Hershey highway" was current gay slang in Warhol's glossy disco circle and beyond it for the rectum and the sexual practices associated with it. Rather than seeing the punctuality ("regularity" is perhaps the appropriate term) with which the prized morsel (the Hershey Bar reward) is delivered up as the mother's, it may make more sense interpretively to see it as an adult's screen memory of himself as a child promptly delivering a stool to demonstrations of maternal pleasure and encouragement. Watching and photographing other men "taking the Hershey highway" (among other sexual acts) as an adult in the seventies, as Warhol was doing around the time he wrote this account of his childhood, may have contributed to his impetus to make his representative scene of early bliss close with an encoded anal exchange between himself and his mother.

Ultra Violet, in her 1988 memoir *Famous for Fifteen Minutes*, reports a conversation she had with Warhol that suggests that he himself saw this scene of his childhood as standing in some significant relation to his subsequent sexual and social history. "When Andy was a sickly eight-year-old, he was confined to bed all summer long. He listened to the radio in the company of his Charlie McCarthy doll," she begins, apparently having been given by Warhol the same cartoon-style account of his childhood he provides in *Philosophy*. The following dialogue ensues between them:

> I ask, "Did you play with dolls?"
> "Gosh, no."
> "Who were your heroes?"
> "Dick Tracy. I Scotch-taped his photograph on the bedroom wall."
> "Why Dick Tracy?"
> "Sex appeal."
> "You just stared at him?"

"I fantasized about Dick's dick."

"What?"

"I fantasized it was [a] lollipop." . . .

Andy laughs. "Yes, Dick's lollipop." He adds, "I had two sex idols—Dick Tracy and Popeye." . . .

"Did you also fantasize about Popeye?"

"My mother caught me one day playing with myself and looking at a Popeye cartoon."

"Why Popeye and Tracy?"

"They were stars. So was Charlie McCarthy. I wanted to make it with stars. I fantasized I was in bed with Dick and Popeye. Charlie would rub against me and seduce me."[10]

It might be tempting to read the "censored" version of the scene that I quoted from Warhol's *Philosophy* at the beginning of this chapter as merely a secondary version of an ontologically prior, "uncensored" scene of sexual fantasy that actually took place in the teller's childhood, as in the version Ultra Violet says Warhol told her. In my interpretation of the two versions of the scene, I prefer to maintain the tension between them rather than to dispel it by granting either some primary status. Indeed, it is the tension between the terms for the main elements of the two versions, heavily encoded in the first case and made thoroughly sexually explicit in the second, that gives the scene its powerfully ambiguous status as memory and fantasy, screen memory and primal scene. Without according either account primacy, I do want to examine more closely some of the ways in which the terms of the scene shift from one version to the other in this at least twice-told tale of Warhol. One striking change is that social and sexual differences, kept resolutely at bay in the first version, have become sharply defined in the second. In it, differences of social class register imaginarily as differences of "magnitude": the other figures are established "stars," the underclass child Andy at most an aspiring (and intensely desiring) one. Similarly, generational difference divides the quasi-adult "stars" from the child who "want[s] to make it with [them]." Finally, in this more unbuttoned account of the fantasy/memory, the virginal pages of the paper-doll books, mute guarantors of sexual undifferentiatedness, have vanished, and "Charlie McCarthy" wantonly "rub[s] against . . . and seduce[s]" the child.

The mother's voice is also silenced in this eroticized version. Rather than a voice reading in an incomprehensible accent, she has become transformed into a figure of surveillance and prohibition—but her "catching" her son "playing with [him]self and looking at a Popeye cartoon" has no apparent effects or consequences as Warhol tells the story. When Warhol tells Ultra Violet his "cartoon-orgy" story, she briefly attempts to explain the odd little scene with "pop" psychology in a double sense of the word. She asks, "Were they [Tracy and Popeye] father images to you?" According to her, Warhol replied: "Don't know. I barely knew my father. He died when I was fourteen."[11]

It is unnecessary to follow the reductive interpretive trajectory of Ultra Violet's proposal about the figures of Warhol's fantasy (that is, that they were all simply "father images" for him), but it is worth noticing that from early on in the Pop movement, Warhol was aware of—and commented on at the time—the paternal signifiers lurking in both "Pop" and "dada," the antecedent movement from which Pop—especially in its Warholian form—was commonly considered to derive: "Dada must have something to do with Pop—it's so funny, the names are really synonyms. Does anyone know what they're supposed to mean or have to do with, those names? [Jasper] Johns and [Robert] Rauschenberg—Neo-Dada for all these years, and everyone calling them derivative and unable to transform the things they use—are now called progenitors of Pop. It's funny the way things change."[12] In Warhol's reconstructions of the scene of his childhood, Tracy figures not only "dick" through his name but also "pop" through the delectable "lollipop" that Warhol claims to have fantasized was Tracy's phallus. "Popeye," whose sexual charge for the child Warhol is unspecified, also conspicuously figures "pop" through his name. "Pop" is also, of course, the name of the art movement of which Warhol became the biggest star, and in relation to which he first became famous, through being proclaimed by the mass media "the Prince of Pop" or "the Pope of Pop." Rather than reading the ubiquity of "pop" in Warhol's texts simply as a sign of his desire for his absent father, we will be able to attend to more of the meanings of those texts (both written and painted) if we also recognize the word's frequent functioning as a verb, "to pop up" or "to pop out."

Being "about to pop" was common sixties slang (among my freshman-year dorm mates and more widely, I believe) for being about to ejaculate. Part of Warhol's devotion to the term "pop" surely derived from the endless series of double entendres the use of the word made possible between his art and social milieu and the phallic and climactic character of the cycle of adult-male sexual functioning from erection to ejaculation. From the "peelable" banana Warhol designed for the jacket of a Velvet Underground album to the "unzippable" fly he designed for the jacket of a Rolling Stones album to the ecstatic face of the fellatee at the "climax" of his film Blow Job, Warhol's art is full of ritual veilings and unveilings of the phallus. Throughout his painting and filmmaking of the sixties, Warhol continues to explore phallic sexuality in two different scenes: one in which it is highly visible and highly valued, and another in which it is only one kind among many other at least equally appealing possibilities. The centrality of the term "pop" in Warhol's production during the sixties may be taken as a sign both of a hypervaluation, on Warhol's part as well as of his culture as a whole, of the climactic character of adult sexuality, especially the specifically erectile and ejaculatory character of phallic sexuality, as well as of desires for and knowledges of ways to escape or "pop out" of the culture's relentless production of heterosexual desire focused around straight men and their phallic possession of the female. Warhol's utterance, "Pop comes from the outside," betokens not only the dependence of Pop art on pop culture for its materials but also a recognition of the violently divided feelings of Warhol's version of Pop art and pop culture about "Pop's" (that is, Dad's) explosively phallic sexuality.

Warhol's early Pop art derives much of its energies from its contradictory emphases: one a fascinated devotion to sexuality at its most flagrantly phallic, and the other a no less marked concern with "marginal," nonphallic erotics (for example, the infantile erotics of withholding and releasing urine and feces, which I shall discuss a little further on in relation to two of Warhol's early Pop paintings). The revisionary queer power of much of his Pop cartoon work proceeds from its ability both to evoke and to a considerable degree to celebrate the phallic and also to subvert it comically and to disperse it across the range of abjected erotics I shall discuss in relation to a number of his early Pop paintings of cartoon characters.

Dick Tracy and Popeye (not to mention Charlie McCarthy) may seem odd or at least unexpected erotic choices for a child, but given the novelty and ubiquity of comic strip characters in U.S. culture of the thirties, the kind of fantasy attachments to such figures that Warhol had was probably quite common. Besides their extremely wide availability—as well as the never-to-be-underestimated vagaries of desire—other, more specific factors no

13. Andy Warhol, *Dick Tracy* (1960). © 1998 Andy Warhol
Foundation for the Visual Arts/ARS, New York.

doubt played a part in Warhol's early fantasy-choices and his adult memories or fantasies about them. Consider, for example, that the graphic signature of Chester Gould's image of Dick Tracy is the literally "clean-cut,"
razor-sharp appearance of his facial profile—in (again, literally) clear-cut
contrast with the "villains" of the strip and their "blank," disintegrative, or

104   *Warhol and Queer Childhood*

otherwise disfigured, repellent, and grotesque facial features. The potential of such a graphic schema is, of course, high for generating invidious narratives about the supposedly inevitably authoritarian, violent, and punitive relations of "clean-cut" men to other men; one can read out of Warhol's subsequent biography the complicated effects the general cathexis of "movie star good looks" on a mass scale in the thirties and thereafter had on his attitudes toward himself and other people and on his choices of erotic objects as an adult.

Yet Warhol seems to have gotten more out of *Dick Tracy* than unmitigated reinforcement for his self-hating attachment to conventional good looks. In having fantasized as a child that "Dick's dick" was a "lollipop," Warhol proved himself able to find a fantasmatically sweet and pleasurable organ on the Tracy character's otherwise hard and sharply contoured body. The erotic appeal of Popeye to the boy Warhol provides another instance of a possible kind of resistance on the child's part to the brand of "hard and sharp" male good looks and behavior promoted by Dick Tracy and his Crimestoppers' Club and in some ways internalized by the child Warhol. No one is movie star handsome in *Popeye*; all the characters are drawn as grotesques, but (in contrast with Gould's practice in *Dick Tracy*) affectionately so. Popeye's facial profile, from sailor's cap to pipe clutched firmly in prognathous jaw, is repeated in the profile of his whole body, with its outsize forearms visually echoing the pugnacious curve of his chin. The appearance of his face and body mark him not only as working class but even within that general category as a transgressive outsider: in one sense, he's the "one-eyed sailor," the rapacious phallus of male folklore. Popeye and his friends are cheerfully and aggressively lower class, their cartoon careers one long celebration of their ability to enjoy their "low appetites" — for each other, for food and drink, and, most of all, for spectacular brawling.

Yet within this carnivalesque milieu, Popeye is in one way an anomalous character, that is, in his relation to work and to technology in the industrial workplace of the earlier twentieth century. Indeed, Popeye's "sexiness" for the young Warhol may have inhered in part in his magical relation to physical strength and capacity for work, especially as these could be maximized by technology, as much as it did in Popeye's potentially queer (because he is the antithesis of a "proper" bourgeois male such as Dick Tracy) and pro-lie insouciance. One can readily imagine how appealing this combination of characteristics in a single figure might have been to a child with Warhol's anxious and ambitious relations to work, social class, and gender.

14. Andy Warhol, *Saturday's Popeye* (1960). © 1998 Andy Warhol Foundation for the Visual Arts/ARS, New York.

The artist who famously proclaimed, "I want to be a machine," as Warhol did in the early sixties, may well have found a major, early fantasy-model for himself in the figure of Popeye, who, as Michael Wassenaar has argued, played a uniquely complex role in mass culture representations of "man and machine" and specifically "man as machine" in the thirties and thereafter. Of the *Popeye* cartoons of Warhol's childhood in the thirties, Wassenaar writes: "Much like a metaphorical engineer, Popeye transforms himself in each of the Fleischer cartoons into the engine through which energy is transformed into work. As both regulator and regulated, engineer and machine, Popeye is a popular hero of the cybernetic." [13]

Dick Tracy and Popeye are the subjects of several of Warhol's first Pop experiments, as are Superman and Batman. Warhol embellished several versions of each of these images of his early Pop practice with repetitive crayon-stroke patterns, as if to signal that the two classes of figures (comic strip character and costumed comic-book superhero) constituted one class of objects to the desiring child whose first art was "coloring." As we have seen, according to Warhol's own testimony, Dick Tracy and Popeye were both "sex symbols" to his child self. In recovering his memories of the sexiness that comic strip characters had had for him in childhood, Warhol assumed an attitude less marked by a coy and defensive knowingness than many of his contemporaries in the sixties, who affected to relish the kinky, fetishistic, and queer effects that the exploits of (for example) Batman and Robin continually produced while in many cases remaining committed to some version of a "liberated" heterosexuality for themselves.[14]

It is through the potential links that exist between the images of costumed superheroes and their potential erotic-fantasy value for children and adults that Warhol found one of his principal ways of radically refiguring the male-homoerotic in his earliest Pop paintings. In contrast with his numerous overtly erotic drawings of male friends and models in the pre-Pop work, his portrayals of a figure such as Superman complicate the questions of what is erotically appealing about such a figure and how many kinds of desires can be served by a single, supposedly simple, cartoon image. Warhol and his fellow innovators of Pop had been among the first generation of children to participate in the early-childhood practice of fashioning "capes" and "disguises" out of towels and bathrobes and "flying" around the house with arms outstretched. (As I have discussed in the previous chapter, underground films such as Warhol's *Batman-Dracula* and Jack Smith's *Flaming Creatures* retain some of this charge of childhood "make-believe" that can blur superhero drag with such a supposedly different style as a Sternbergian "exotic-lady" drag of veils and hyperfemininity.)

Although a superficial look at Warhol's *Superman* (1960) might suggest that it was merely a careful, uninflected copy of an image of the figure chosen at random, further inspection reveals numerous links between this work and the kinds of transformative labor the figure of Popeye represented in the popular culture of the 1930s. The figure of Superman hovers in the upper left-hand corner of the image, emitting a blast of air that fills the lower right-hand corner. Superman's "thought," "Good! A mighty puff of my super-breath extinguished the forest fire!" is recorded in a bal-

15. Andy Warhol, *Superman* (1960). © 1998 Andy Warhol
Foundation for the Visual Arts/ARS, New York.

loon that Warhol has carefully copied and then partially obscured with
white paint; the only immediately legible word in the picture is the great
red "PUFF!" across its center. One set of gay male subcultural meanings in
which the painting may participate links it with *Blow Job*, the early film of
Warhol made only about three years after this painting, which shows only
the face and upper torso of a young man being fellated. Reversing the ver-
tical visual logic of the film, the object of Superman's titanic "blow job"
is below the lower border of the image, which is itself approximately six
inches above the lower edge of the canvas, which is blank, except for a

couple of paint drips. Although the figure of Superman is raised above the spectator's gaze and the lower back of his body is turned toward us, the picture does not represent the cleft of the buttocks, one of the conventional foci of male-homoerotic visual representation and one of the features of the male anatomy Warhol would have been most likely to emphasize in his pre-Pop homoerotic work. Indeed, Superman's trunks seem ovoid, even in-flated, in a way that hardly conforms even to the loosely cartoony anatomy of the figure as ordinarily drawn; the trunks look more like a diaper or in-fant's rubber pants than like tight-fitting briefs over muscular adult-male buttocks.

Although in actual comic-book art characters' body parts are gener-ally indicated in only the most stylized manner, the depiction of the "superhero" body costumed in alternately flowing and fitted fabrics (cape and tights), conspicuously demarcated into separate regions, has its own strongly sexualizing implications, as it does in this image by alternating red and blue garments, which highlight the chest, hips, buttocks, genital region, and feet. Despite (or perhaps because of) the way the figure's geni-tal area and buttocks look somehow "diapered," concealed, and sealed off from the rest of the picture, its lower half is dominated by several massive columns of heavy "smoke" that look phallic and fecal at the same time; that the great flood of breath with which Superman extinguishes the for-est fire is painted in a way that could also represent a great blast of water (the more usual way of putting out large fires) makes the image potentially one of urethral eroticism, too—so that several kinds of infantile erotic pleasure, available to so-called adult sexuality, too, although officially pro-scribed for it, are figured in the painting. In a way, the painting simulta-neously fulfills and dismisses the fearful prophecies of Fredric Wertham and other moralizing critics of comic books in the 1950s who feared (and so testified before government investigating bodies) that the early cathexis of costumed superheroes by child readers might produce a mass "pervert" culture of sadomasochistic fetishism.[15]

I was in junior high school during the years Warhol produced his early Pop paintings and can testify that pubescent boys were at the time still passing around their own crude cartoon drawings of Superman doing his superphallic thing, so to speak, usually to a prone and not quite recogniz-able Lois Lane. The hyperpotency of Superman and the literal defacement of Lois Lane in these drawings spoke volumes about both the phallic focus

16. Andy Warhol, *Nancy* (1960). © 1998 Andy Warhol
Foundation for the Visual Arts/ARS, New York.

of our own newly imperative sexual desires and our collective although entirely unvoiced inability to imagine our desires inspiring any feelings in
others besides fear and disgust. The image was one of many around which
boys my age inducted ourselves with varying degrees of unwillingness into
a scene of heterosexuality based on a restaging of the primal scene in which
the imaginary object of our desires was at best faceless and at worst a victim of rape. I suspect that such fantasies and images had been formative
for at least a generation at the time Warhol produced his revisionary image
of a "superhero" of perverse, infantile pleasures.

Infantile eroticism bodes large in another of Warhol's initial Pop experiments: *Nancy* (1960) shows approximately a frame and a quarter of
(presumably) a three- or four-frame sequence of the Ernie Bushmiller cartoon character. In the upper, "full" frame, Nancy, standing in front of
her house, holds herself and shivers, "BRR MY SNOW SUIT ISNT WARM

ENOUGH—ILL PUT ON A SWEATER TOO." In the lower partial frame, all that is visible are the words "BRR IM STILL." To understand the relation of this early Pop painting to the process of gay male encoding I have been analyzing, one might begin by recalling that "nancy" was (along with "fairy") one of the most common terms in circulation at the time of the painting's production, both inside and outside gay culture, for an effeminate and therefore presumptively homosexual man. In considering the range of sexualities the painting might represent, we should bear in mind the prevailing climate of homophobia and misogyny manifest in some of the dominant psychoanalytic and psychiatric discourse of the 1950s and 1960s. Take, for example, the widely cited work of such a prominent New York psychoanalyst of the period as Edmund Bergler, whose insistence on vaginal orgasm in heterosexual intercourse as an index of mental health in women ("Under frigidity we understand the incapacity of a woman to have a vaginal orgasm during intercourse," Bergler writes in his characteristically now-hear-this manner; a few lines later he foments, "The sole criterion of frigidity is absence of vaginal orgasm") [16] was as vehement as his parallel insistence on the necessity of psychiatric cure (what he calls "destruction of the perversion") for homosexuals.[17] Bergler and other "medical authorities" of his time took on what they saw as "sexual neurotics" in single groups in some of their books and articles and across the board, as it were, in other publications, as the title of a book of Bergler attests: Neurotic Counterfeit-Sex: Homosexuality, Impotence, and Frigidity. The book's procedure, accurately articulated in the title, is to equate with each other the members of various groups of men and women who fail to achieve what Bergler and his colleagues see as a "healthy" and affirmative relation to heterosexual-male dominance. To deviate from this absolute standard is by definition to occupy one of the other positions, all of which are stigmatized as not only "neurotic" but also "counterfeit" (criminally false and deceptive) in the same gesture.

Besides those of the infantile pleasures we have already noticed, one of the other abjected positions Warhol explores in his early work—especially, perhaps, in Nancy—is that of the "frigid" woman; in this image he represents a transitional scene of thawing between her position and that of the similarly abjected gay male "nancy" and raises the question of whether there might not be strategic advantages in a gay man's energetically taking up the position of what may be the most misogynistic of twentieth-century psychiatric constructions, the frigid woman. "Frigid people really make it" became one of Warhol's favorite mottos, and although "frigidity" certainly admits of a wider range of meanings than simply "sexual unresponsiveness" (such as "habitually indifferent behavior" or "frostiness of manner"), there is a sense in which this putatively feminine sexual characteristic remains the "core" of the "frigid" identity he embraced as one of his chief public personae.[18]

Nancy was one of the first of Warhol's early Pop works to attract the attention and admiration of Ivan Karp of the Castelli Gallery. According to David Bourdon, what "grabbed" Karp about it on his first viewing was its "interrupted narrative sequence and its implication that Nancy remains out in the cold indefinitely."[19] Karp later spoke of the powerfully "chilling" effect of Warhol's early cartoon paintings, praising them for their "cold," "bleak," and "brutish" aspects—effects particularly conspicuous in Nancy, where the "frigid" effects the artist was producing in much of his work of the period are literally thematized: "outsider" Nancy tries to "warm up" but fails to and "stays frigid."[20]

Karp became an instrumental figure in explaining and defending Warhol's Pop work to art dealers and collectors as well as to the media, but considerations of gender and sexuality played no part in his or, to my knowledge, any other critic's theory of Pop until years afterward. Yet what Karp immediately recognized as some of the most notable qualities of a painting like Nancy—its "chilling" and "brutish" appearance, its "interrupted[ness]," its "freeze-frame" visual construction—all these characteristics require consideration in relation to the pathologized representations of feminine and gay male identity described above. As several lesbian and gay historians have amply demonstrated, gay people began "coming in from the cold" in large numbers in the fifties and sixties, began banding together socially and politically to reject the collective position that had been imposed on them of being officially "frozen out" of common life.[21] In the figure of Warhol's "Nancy," "STILL" freezing or frigid no matter how many garments she puts on, we have not only a picture of a frigid woman starting to thaw or melt but also an emblem of sorts for a strategic repudiation of "warm" models of gay male desire (of which the "warm" nudes of Warhol's late-fifties sketches could be said to represent literal exemplars) and gay male "community" and a similarly strategic embrace of an attributive femininity (or effeminacy) in its extremest (frigid) form (see this chapter's first illustration, one of Warhol's conventionally homoerotic male nudes of the 1950s).

In a note to one of his major discussions of screen memories and memories of childhood, Freud interprets "frozenness" as a sign of the phallus. "From a dream of P.'s," he writes, "it appears that ice is in fact a symbol by antithesis for an erection: i.e. something that becomes hard in the cold instead of like a penis—in heat (in excitation)."[22] Warhol, too, attributed phallic significance to some of his more famously static or "frozen" Pop productions, such as his eight-hour film of the top section of the Empire State Building, which he reportedly referred to as "an eight-hour hard-on," predictably linking its subject to one of the hunky costumed cartoon and serial heroes of his childhood: "The Empire State Building is a star. . . . It's so beautiful. The lights come on and the stars come out and it sways. It's like Flash Gordon riding into space."[23] We may recall from his narration of his memory of his childhood illness to Ultra Violet that "star" seems to have served him as a term both for the phallic object of desire ("dick," Dick Tracy, and so forth) and for the paradoxically "cold" source of light and identification. "Frozen" by their stardom into an imaginarily permanent state of "erection" or elevation above the field of desire, Warhol's cartoon "stars" are the symbolically saturated figures of his childhood to whom he ritualistically—and productively—returned when he undertook to produce a break between his identity and his work, as well as in his own relations to these phenomena.

Again, we may look to *Nancy* for a complex representation of some of the signs of infantile erotic desire and pleasure that I have discussed in relation to Warhol's *Superman*. Most of the left three-quarters of the painting (showing the exterior of Nancy's house) is what one might call a "muddy" or "urine" yellow, while the upper right-hand quarter of it is a cool "ice blue." This dual color scheme is interrupted two-thirds of the way down the canvas by the horizontal bank of "snow" in which Nancy stands, a patch of paint that extends from one side of the painting to the other and ranges in color from off-white to a dingy brownish white (significantly, the two speech balloons are painted in the same way the snowbank is). The three large patches of color that make up the painting are brought into particularly tense relation to each other in the figure of Nancy herself, who stands hunched stiffly forward from the shoulders, her knees flexed and held tightly together in a way that suggests she not only might be cold but also might have to pee; the ice-blue pants of her snowsuit heighten the subliminal effect of the pose of "frozen" discomfort, and their "puffy" and "stuffed" appearance suggest—as the similar appearance of the trunks did in *Superman*—that an infantile urethral erotics may be in play here. *Superman* is energized by the "mighty puff" of "super-breath" that also looks like a flood of water (or urine) loosed from on high; the energy of *Nancy* is withheld or held in through the crouching figure of Nancy, although the field of "urine" yellow that surrounds her hints at a release of energy and tension—from urethral retention—of a kind that doesn't do any "work" (as the "mighty puff" of "super-breath" does). I have been arguing that the cartoon figures in Warhol's early Pop paintings are "symbolically saturated" ones, and here in a sense is a picture that is on one level all about saturation, of the literal kind everyone experiences in infancy and early childhood (and sometimes later, although the experience of "wetting oneself" as an adult is so highly stigmatized that it hardly makes it into discourse except as a sign of intense abjection).[24] In the mid- to late seventies, Warhol made what he informally called "Piss Paintings"—later exhibited and sold as *Oxidation Paintings*—on canvases that had been specially prepared to register permanently the streams of urine directed onto them by the artist and some of his assistants, but an early Pop painting like *Nancy* experiments with literalizing urination in less direct fashion.

Nancy's boots are a blur of bright red, the same color as the bow in her hair; these are two of the painting's "hot spots," suggesting that Nancy is "hot" from head to toe at the same time that she's "STILL" (the painting's enacted but unspoken—because interrupted—words) "COLD" or even "FREEZING." The blurry, undelineated appearance of Nancy's boots marks them as a particularly highly liminal space in the painting, between heat and cold, frozen and liquid, body and landscape. The push-panel on the door behind her, the point of possible escape for her from the frigid scene she inhabits, is the painting's other bright red hot spot. Nancy's flesh-colored face, fiercely punctuated by her black porcupine hairdo, is the only small area of what one might call tonal neutrality in the little "war" among the red, blue, and yellow physical states (heat, cold, and urine or urination) that the painting depicts. It is notable that the way the painting represents the expression of intense concentration and resolve on Nancy's face is through a configuration of punctuation marks: her brows, the wrinkles of concentration between them, her eyes, nose, and mouth form a kind of typographical pun on a determined face, composed entirely of parentheses, quotation marks, hyphens, and periods. It is as if the missing punctuation from the sentence in the speech balloon over her head had migrated to her face, which registers for the viewer as a kind of complex exclamation mark.

This figure of a child's body, eroticized in terms of an infantile erotics that is subliminally represented as potentially dissipating its energies in a puddle of urine and/or thawing slush, is instead arrested, "frozen," and focused at a threshold moment of increasingly intolerable discomfort. The painting as a whole, like others of the early Pop work, itself functions as a kind of complex, hypergraphic punctuation mark, like the stars-inducing "punch" of the mighty fist in Saturday's Popeye (1960) and Popeye (1961) or in the aforementioned cyclonic "PUFF!" of Superman. The affective burst that Nancy enacts is perhaps more rather than less powerful than Popeye's or Superman's supervirile actions because it is deferred indefinitely ("IM STILL"), represented as simultaneously being contained and becoming uncontained, like the thawed water emerging from the snow or the urine (already coloring most of the scene) threatening to escape from the body.

As we have seen him doing in the painting Nancy and as I believe we see him doing in much of the Pop painting of the early sixties and in his writing and other kinds of production most closely related to it (for example, his films), Warhol derived—from the most hieratic and highly stylized gestural moments ("the frozen moment") of operatic and balletic performance, of highbrow and middlebrow tragedy, of middlebrow melodrama and lowbrow cartoons—a cool, mechanical, antitragic, antigrandiose, anti-self-sacrificial moment of a kind that had a powerfully disruptive effect on the cultural pieties that underwrote much female and gay-male oppression and self-oppression in postwar culture.[25]

If "feelings" and "styles" of some kinds do get eliminated from Warhol's early Pop work, other kinds of "feelings"—commonly despised ones, infantile and other kinds of proscribed ones—play lambently around the margins and, as we have just seen, sometimes at the center of his transformed practice. What Warhol spoke of at the time as the total elimination of "style" from his work is rather an elimination of what was generally considered to constitute style in the midcentury United States: carefully cultivated technique employed in the painstaking transmission of a highly refined body of artistic conventions. In attempting, beginning around 1960, to rid his art of all conventional signs of the "piss-elegant" style he had pursued so fervently and single-mindedly in his pre-Pop art, Warhol discovered in the process of reengaging with the comic-strip style and the comic-strip erotics of his childhood a field of representation that, however far removed from the explicit pre-Pop drawings of male nudes, is nonetheless valuable precisely for the ways in which it complicates and enriches notions of what constitutes queer artistic production.

FIVE ✦ *Outlaw Sex and the "Search for America":*

Representing Male Prostitution and Perverse Desire in

Sixties Film (My Hustler and Midnight Cowboy)

One of the most notable developments in U.S. culture in the 1960s was the increasing visibility and audibility of gay men and lesbians and of the social institutions of same-sex desire, especially those of the urban underground, the neighborhoods, streets, parks, bars, and theaters where gay people mingled with each other and with other denizens of the underground: hustlers and their clients, female and drag prostitutes, drug users and dealers.[1] The emergence of this underground into representation in books and films of that decade made the urban sexual-outlaw figure a staple of both avant-garde and mainstream writing and filmmaking for the first time. The publication of Jean Genet's novels in English translation and the great critical acclaim with which they were received in the United States, along with other important and controversial fiction like James Baldwin's, John Rechy's, and Hubert Selby's, made such figures as the "promiscuous" (i.e., sexually active) gay man, the hustler and his johns, and the drag queen objects of unprecedented public attention, "concern," and, in some quarters, sympathetic interest and identification. Film treatments of homosexuality in the broader context of the urban underground followed, and the figure of the male prostitute and the subcultures through which he moved became central preoccupations of films as various as Andy Warhol's underground *My Hustler* (1965), John Schlesinger's mainstream *Midnight Cowboy* (which won the Oscar for Best Picture of 1969), and the Warhol-produced, Paul Morrissey–directed trilogy *Flesh, Trash,* and *Heat* (1968, 1970, and 1972, respectively).

While it is true that such spectacular and influential film representations of male-male sexuality as Kenneth Anger's *Fireworks* and Genet's *Un chant d'amour* had been available since a few years after the end of World War II, the audience for these short experimental films had been relatively small. In the course of a series of *succès de scandale*—Anger's *Scor-*

pio Rising (1963), Jack Smith's *Flaming Creatures* (1964), and Warhol's *My Hustler, Chelsea Girls* (1966), and *Lonesome Cowboys* (1967)—films representing gay/drag/drug/hustler subcultures began to command a substantially larger and broader audience. By the end of the decade and just after, the representation of male-male sexuality had expanded enormously, and filmgoers in many U.S. cities could see work ranging from Broadway-style "identity-crisis" comedy-melodrama about gay men (*Boys in the Band*) to no-holes-barred gay porn (*Boys in the Sand*)—in much of which the figure of the hustler and the practices of hustling were key elements. The histories of these changes are by no means the simple stories of "progress" and "increased understanding" on the parts of either producers or audiences, as they sometimes have been heralded by liberal "sympathizers" and apologists for Hollywood's treatment of lesbians and gays. In the discussion that follows, I want to explore some of the political complexities of some of these changes.

The young man who plays the title role in *My Hustler* adopted the screen name "Paul America" for the film. The name is interesting in relation to comments such as Richard Dyer's on the emergence of the male prostitute as an important symbol for some (supposedly) specifically American characteristics or problems of the early sixties. In "the novels of urban alienation" that Dyer briefly discusses (Baldwin's *Another Country*, Rechy's *City of Night*, Selby's *Last Exit to Brooklyn*, James Leo Herlihy's *Midnight Cowboy*), "poverty, prostitution, drugs and street life are represented as the condition of America."[2] Dyer contrasts the depiction of the hustler in this new, gritty mode with the previously dominant way of representing male-male desire, which featured young male characters whose most marked characteristics were their sensitivity and vulnerability:

> If the sad young man of earlier novels is in search of his "self" and his "true nature," the hustler is by contrast testing himself; if he is in search of anything, it is "America." The structure of the earlier novels hinges on discovery and revelation: the character discovers "what he is." There is no such introspection with the hustler. The tension derives more from the uncertainty about his masculinity and heterosexuality. It is not that he wants to find out if he is gay or what that means, but that he wants to prove that he is masculine. He does this by making it with women and only having sex with men for money.

Heterosexuality proves he is a man, and manliness has not to do with inner feeling but with performance, acting like a man.[3]

Dyer's basic perception here is a valuable one. The change in focus from earlier fictions of young-male sexual exploration to sixties hustler novels was a change from inward-looking melodramas of "self-discovery," the politics of which was liberal and the sexual charge vanilla, to a less psychologized and privatized form in which the toughness and powers of resistance of the protagonist are represented as high values. The politics of these hustler fictions tends to be anti-liberal, angry rather than consolatory and affirmative, and the sexual charge intense and often non-vanilla.

In the United States at the beginning of the sixties, it seemed not only right and fitting but inevitable to many people that questions about "what it means to be a man" could be answered only by a widespread set of assumptions about "what it means to be a [male] American": a good boy (scout), soldier, husband, father, worker, citizen. The refraction of these questions through the figure of the hustler made some of the most glaring contradictions inherent in this interlocking set of assumptions about male identity particularly salient.[4] One of the primary beliefs these hustler fictions challenged was that "manhood"/"masculinity" is both a "natural" trait of "normal" men and (contradictorily) a moral achievement won through struggle in war or some metaphorical equivalent thereof. Looking at how the figure of the hustler works in representation, or at how the complementary figure of the drag queen does, reveals that performance precedes (or exceeds) essence, that one ultimately cannot permanently and stably "be a man" (or a woman), that "acting the part" is as much as anyone does or can do.[5] However, in making his brief general description of this innovative and critical subgenre, Dyer oversimplifies considerably the period's representations of hustlers. The hustler in *Another Country* or *City of Night*, or in *My Hustler* or *Midnight Cowboy*, far from lacking inwardness, is a well of imputed subjectivity and also an active and sometimes even articulate participant in the complex social scenes whose strong fears and desires he by turns enacts and embodies. The stereotype of the silent, nonintrospective hustler that Dyer evokes gets fractured in a multitude of ways in books like Baldwin's and Rechy's and films like Warhol's and Schlesinger's. The nationalistic model of male citizenship that equates "manhood" with being an actual or potential "good soldier" ("stoic, isolate, and a killer" was D. H. Lawrence's memorable formulation of this American-male ideal) does not simply get "proven" or "disproven" in any of the works under consideration. Indeed, it is interesting to notice, for example, how much more politically critical and subversive Rechy's hustler's-eye view of "America" is in *City of Night* (long sections of the book are set in San Antonio, New York, Los Angeles, and New Orleans) than a representative post-Stonewall, pre-AIDS tour of gay America like Edmund White's *States of Desire* (1979).

One of the ways the urgency of the prolonged political crisis brought on by the involvement of the United States in Vietnam manifests itself in sixties culture is in the regularity with which both prose and film fictions of the time turn into allegories about a "search for America." Besides the question of who the "real men" were, the question of where the "real America" was became a central preoccupation: was it in the (at the time) booming metropolitan centers, where the whole range of increasingly visible subcultures had long been proliferating, or in the small towns and countryside, which were widely perceived as being intolerant of any but "traditional values"? Was it on the "sophisticated" and "decadent" East coast, epitomized by rich and swinging Manhattan, or in the still countrified West, where the pop-culture ideal of the "quiet," manly, "ruggedly individual" cowboy/soldier supposedly still predominated? Films like *My Hustler* and *Midnight Cowboy* situate themselves at different points of social and political collision between highly symbolically charged places and populations like Warhol's New York and John Wayne's "America." *Midnight Cowboy* takes the boy out of the country (which can mean both the West and the "whole country," the nation) by setting him down on the streets of New York, and then plays with the idea, frightening to many Americans of the time, that you actually can take the country (the supposedly inbred nationalism) out of the boy.

My Hustler, the kind of sixties gay film long typified as apolitical, also situates itself, in less obvious but no less provocative ways, in relation to the signs of the times for the acrimonious public debates about the character of "real" manhood and "real" Americanness. The film takes the boy out of the city, but only as far as Fire Island: faggy, sybaritic Manhattan raised to exponential heights. The viewer of *My Hustler* never sees Paul America outside the very limited spaces of a stretch of beach and a beach-house bathroom, but the limits of the physical world he inhabits should not blind us to the various ironic relations to a nationalized masculinity that his name signifies. He is, like successive "Mr. Americas," a bodybuilder, a group whose membership overlaps with that of hustlers. Unlike the generally more disaffected hustlers, however, bodybuilders have an organized, competitive institution that names annually the "outstanding individual" whose physical strength and skill at muscle-posing entitles him to national prominence—literally entitles him to embody "Mr. America." But the tensions in "being a man" are exacerbated, rather than reduced, for the would-be occupant of the position of national-allegorical man: is the Mr. America candidate's physical strength to be taken as a "real" sign of his "moral" strength—that is, can it guarantee his "proper" heterosexuality? Only to the degree that this is not undermined by his penchant for and skill at exhibiting his body and his muscles for an audience—a practice that inevitably raises questions about "how heterosexual" a chorus line of bikinied beefcake can "really" be.[6]

The hustler who, like Paul America, poses as "trade" (a straight male who is "only in it for the money") has to negotiate an even further intensified version of this double bind between looking and acting hypermasculine without seeming to overact at any point in a way that undermines the ostensibly desired effects of the performance ("what a man"). He has to engage in sex—that is, minimally, get an erection, and, desirably in most instances, ejaculate—with other men regularly while maintaining the fiction that these bodily phenomena are disjunct from the physical and emotional satisfactions of the "real" sex life he supposedly carries on elsewhere. There is a particularly complex kind of epistemology of the closet in play when a "straight-acting" hustler and a trade-seeking john confront each other: the john wants a virile youth and consequently (to his mind) a straight-identified one, but what he really requires is a youth who will at least pretend to be straight.[7] The supposedly spoiled and stigmatized role of john may be recuperated for some johns by making a kind of imaginary straightness of his own depend on the performed straightness of the hustler: a john's not descending to (in his mind) the depths of being queer while continuing to have sex with young men may depend on his success at maintaining the pretense that he does not have sex with queer men or boys and is consequently "not really queer." These interactions are not merely a prologue to or desperate rationalization of what ensues, they are themselves a sexual activity, in which the two men strip down and simultaneously imaginarily reclothe themselves in the fantasmatic bodies of two straight guys who "mess around" with each other a little on the side because they like each other. "Only a miserable slave or a bourgeois has sex completely naked," Charles Ludlam once wrote unforgettably.[8] Many hustlers and johns of the sixties, otherwise untroubled by exposing their bodies to each other, might have felt intolerably "naked" having sex without first putting on this ragged pretense.

Both partners to this transaction, voluble john and taciturn hustler, have a stake in perpetuating this erotic fiction that they both from their different positions believe and disbelieve. This latter (il)logical condition of simultaneous recognition and denial of what is (and at the same time is not) the case is of course the classic condition of fetishism in psychoanalytic theory: the fetish both is and is not the magically invested erotic object of the fetishist's desires.[9] In the case of hustler and john, the "fetish," rather than (or in addition to) being a pair of underpants or socks or a jockstrap or whatever, gets partially dematerialized and deliteralized from a material object into the pretense that neither partner to their sexual interactions is "really" queer. Both men "never feel straighter" than when they are having sex with each other, the hustler's (imaginary) straightness (at least partially) ensured for him by his desired virility (desired enough to be paid for), and the john's by his (paradoxical) insistence on having sex only with males who claim to be straight, who (according to the shared fiction) wouldn't have sex with another man under any other conditions. But no one is more aware of the impossibility of securing this highly unstable, intricately interdependent fiction of the hustler's unproblematic straightness and the john's consequent and dependent nonqueerness than the queens who often play the role of mock-Greek-chorus in representations of hustler-john dynamics. According to City of Night, it is the time-honored saying of queens on the topic of straight-identified hustlers that "today's trade is tomorrow's competition."[10] Thirty years after Rechy's novel, in some ways little has changed in this formation, and in other ways much has; the greatly increased possibility of "gay" and more recently "queer" self-identification on the part of many hustlers has transformed that side of the relation for many male prostitutes, as evidenced by the comments of the queer-identified hustler from Los Angeles ("Chad") whom Film Threat magazine invited to review Gus Van Sant's My Own Private Idaho: "If a hustler tells you he's 'straight,' he means 'straight to bed.' I bet half the guys I've tricked have been 'straight' in their regular lives—husbands, fathers, boy-friends. But everybody's got a little queer in them. [Laughs] And for the right money, they can have this little queer in them." [11]

Students of Warhol's career as a producer and director of films tend to agree that My Hustler represents a, perhaps the, transitional moment in the evolution of his work in film, from the early, supposedly "unmoving pic-tures" (Sleep, Empire, Eat, etc.), in which the film consisted of a single, some-times very prolonged, shot of one object, to the later, relatively conven-tional and "commercial" Morrissey-directed films starring Joe Dallesandro (Flesh, Trash, Heat, etc.). Although My Hustler was nominally directed by Chuck Wein—an aspiring young filmmaker who, with his friend Edie Sedg-wick, had come to New York from Cambridge, Massachusetts, only months before the film was made—Wein, Warhol, and Morrissey all seem to have had significant input into the shape and direction of the film. It derives in some obvious ways from Warhol's earlier portrait films and the compila-tion films made from them like Thirteen Most Beautiful Boys (1964 or 1965).

In the opening scene of the film, while the young hustler played by Paul America suns himself on the beach, an upper-class, middle-aged, bitchy queen (Ed Hood), in voice-over, begins to discuss the young man's charms with two visitors, a slightly older, still comely hustler named Joe (John Mac-dermott, known in Warhol's circle as the Sugar Plum Fairy), and a young woman neighbor (Genevieve Charbon).[12] The older queen self-defeatingly bets his two visitors that neither of them can take Paul America away from him. Paul Morrissey, who was working on sound on the film, asserts that it was he who urged Warhol not to keep the camera on the young hustler alone but to show Ed Hood, too, "who was extremely funny to watch as well as hear," doing his virtuoso evil-queen act. According to Morrissey, Warhol at first resisted the idea, but the finished version of the film includes a version of the opening scene that repeatedly pans back and forth between the image of the hustler on the beach and his admirers on a nearby deck.[13]

It has been an article of Lacanian-feminist film theory that the gaze, and the film shot, that frames the object-of-the-gaze as if there were no space or materiality intervening between gazer and object, represents the phal-lic gaze that seeks and finds only reassuring images of the phallus in all its imaginary invulnerability and impenetrability. Yet, as we have seen, the fractural epistemology that links and sunders the performances and desires of hustler-and-john does not permit us or either of them "really" to believe in either this stable phallus or the "unproblematic" masculinity it is supposed symbolically to secure. When the camera (and by extension the audience) "worships" Paul America in the long opening shot of *My Hustler*, and then when it cuts away to reveal his lusty crew of admirers, and then again sweeps back out to the beach to focus on him and his body, what Stephen Koch calls the "shock" of these transitions has not only to do with their disruption of Warhol's previously "motionless" style of filmmaking, but also with shattering the highly hypostatized dyads of gazer and object of the gaze, "stud" and "queen," hustler and john.[14] The introduction into the minimal plot of *My Hustler* (which of the three contenders will "get" Paul America?) of the second hustler has further shattering effects on this set of dyadic interdependencies.

A primary liability of theoretical paradigms of the spectator and of the phallic vision has been their tendency to blind the theorist to the kinds of internal differences that palpably manifest themselves in film practices such as Warhol's, in which the image of the object of the gaze (often a beautiful "boy" or woman) seems to disintegrate or shatter itself. The performer in the object-position usually accomplishes this either by expressing strong emotion (often in the form of discomfort and rage) or by filling the space of exposure and potential humiliation opened by the unblinking camera with a performance of "narcissistic" self-pleasuring. Among Warhol's superstars, it was probably Eric Emerson who took this latter alternative farthest, as when he addresses the spectator directly in his solo scene in *Chelsea Girls*: "I don't have anything to say so I'll just sit and groove on myself. . . . Do you ever just groove on your body?"[15] Emerson grins sunnily, plays with his lips and hair, gazes into and drools on a small hand mirror, and finally, inevitably, takes off his clothes, in a performance of narcissism so knowing about its own supposed unself-awareness as to shatter some viewers' moralistic preconceptions about it.[16] Under the combined gazes of his would-be seducer(s) and the audience for whom he (they) stand(s), Paul America exudes a similarly self-shattering "narcissism,"[17] theatrically self-conscious in its studied unself-consciousness, an attitude that oscillates between the reflective mirror before him, in which he butchly preens, and the "two-way" mirror of the camera behind him, for which he also quietly but artfully struts his stuff.

The second half of the film, set in a tiny beach-house bathroom, presents this intense and intermittent erotics with uncommon thoroughness, as Paul America and Joe, the older hustler, chat, shower, urinate, stand at the sink shaving, patting on aftershave, combing their hair—continually moving around each other, frequently almost touching each other, executing an electrically charged and elegantly paced dance of seduction, all in the name of "sharing the mirror." The two hustlers who sniff and scope each other out for half an hour while pretending to carry on a "casual" business conversation about whether young Paul might be interested in becoming a hustler emblematize some of the ways in which Warhol was innovatively bringing the contradictions and paradoxes that link sex and business in our culture into productive and sometimes explosive relation to each other.[18] Men can do business and have sex at the same time, the second half of My Hustler languorously suggests. When are the two men merely having a "business" conversation and when are they involved in a dance of mutual seduction? When is business being negotiated and when is pleasure? When is either man pleasuring himself and when is he (also) pleasuring the other? These are the kinds of questions that the dual performance in the second half of My Hustler makes thoroughly undecidable.

By showing the supposedly one-way mirror of the hustler's ("narcissistic") desire turning on another such supposedly one-way mirror (hustler to hustler) and in the process producing a range of other perverse desires and pleasures, My Hustler complicates not only the questions of what a hustler is and what he wants, and what a john is and what he wants, but also those of what an adequate model of same-sex desire would be, and what one might look like that has as much space for the differentials as for the equations between and within persons in relations of same-sex desire. (Here, the problematics of the closet and of the "closed set" of Jack Smith's fantasies, discussed in chapter 3, are pertinent.) It is clear from the film that "simple narcissism," the stereotypical form of feminine and gay-male and hustler desire, is not adequate to the case. One of the first films to take male prostitution as its subject, My Hustler is in some ways the least metaphorical, least displaced representation of the intersections of hustling, perverse pleasures, and same-sex desires of the lot.

Midnight Cowboy was British director John Schlesinger's first American film —and first film "about America." Reminding ourselves of this may help clarify the particular ways in which the film participates in the national imaginary (what does it mean to be a man? an American?) that was being so violently contested at the time. The fairly simple story John Leo Herlihy's modest novel tells about the problems of two down-and-out young men from contrasting backgrounds in the big, mean city is in Schlesinger's re-telling transformed into another allegorical "search for America." Looking more closely at the film's terms for what it's representing may also help us rethink one of the major assumptions that commentators have made about the film, that the love-relationship that develops between the two male protagonists is entirely nonsexual. This insistence on the nonerotic quality of the undeniably erotic bonds that circulate around and between the two characters has tended to obscure the film's notable, if only partial, suc-cess at representing a range of sexualities that most commentators have failed either to recognize or to find significant or valuable. It is my conten-tion that in its representations of male-homoerotic and other "perverse" desires Midnight Cowboy deserves comparison with such highly successful experiments of the time as My Hustler, and that in the former film these representations are richer and more complex than either gay- or straight-identified critics have tended to see.

Joe Buck, a very-dumb-but-decent hustler from Texas (Jon Voight) whose very name evokes his double status as virile male animal and male prosti-tute (he is a buck for a buck), and Ratso Rizzo, a sickly and disabled small-time con man (Dustin Hoffman), are the two characters whose evolving relationship with each other is the primary subject of Midnight Cowboy. The film has been highly regarded by some critics — and apparently, by many viewers — for, as Joan Mellen put it, "separat[ing] sensitive homosexual feeling from the stereotype [of gay-male sexuality as predatory and jadedly promiscuous] and . . . expos[ing] the repressed and latent homosexuality in male bravado" — or, as Schlesinger himself put it more economically in an interview with the press, showing "how two men can have a meaning-ful relationship without being homosexual." [19] According to much of its mainstream reception, the film shows Buck and Rizzo ultimately succeed-ing at establishing an intimate but nonsexual relationship with each other, but only at the point of Rizzo's death and only to the degree that they are finally able to escape the "fags" who pursue hustler Joe Buck, as well as the "castrating bitches" who are his female clients. A minority of crit-ics, most of them gay and "out," have criticized the film from the time of its appearance for the way Schlesinger and his stars apparently jointly decided during production to keep the relationship between Buck and Rizzo "untainted" by sex or even signs of desire, and to keep Rizzo's sexuality "vague"—nearly to the point of nonexistence.[20] Gay commentary from Parker Tyler to Vito Russo has been especially critical of a climactic scene of the film in which Buck, previously an almost entirely peaceable street person, violently beats and perhaps murders an older john named Towny (Barnard Hughes) as he steals the money from him that enables Buck and Rizzo to take off for Florida together in the film's closing sequence. Tyler, Russo, and others have taken Joe Buck's burst of violence and his immediately subsequent "heroization" at the end of the film (when he cares for the dying Rizzo on the bus) as a sign of the film's endorsement of queer-bashing. When British reviewer Jan Dawson writes of the end of the film, "Joe may forget about the telephone he has rammed into the mouth of the badly bleeding queer, but surely we are not expected to forget as well," the word "surely" functions to cast doubt rather than to reassure readers that the film is, at this crucial point, in control of its representations of violence and kindness, gratuitous cruelty and heroism.[21]

A scene early in Midnight Cowboy, which sets up some of the film's key terms and images, may help us in reconsidering the dynamics of the later scene in which Joe Buck bludgeons one of his johns. This earlier scene occurs when Buck picks up his first sex client on the streets of Manhattan. The film seems to begin literally undoing representational conventions when Cass (Sylvia Miles), a brassy "older woman" who has brought Joe upstairs to her apartment, carries on a phone conversation with her boyfriend while she turns around and emphatically unzips Joe's fly. Soon thereafter, there is a brief shot across the room of Cass retreating into her bedroom, followed by Joe Buck, his pants down around his ankles and his buns bouncing as he hops after her. The sex scene that ensues is well summarized in Dawson's review of the film: "Shots of [Buck's] bare and vigorously bouncing buttocks alternate with flashes of TV programs (the couple are of course copulating on top of a remote control channel changer), and the orgasmic moment is registered by a shot of coins spurting from the mouth of a fruit [i.e., slot] machine."[22]

In its movement from shots of phones and trouser-flies to ones of Joe's perky buns, then to images of fruits, showers of coins, and, finally, a transfer of cash, this scene makes a rapid and thorough survey of the film's basic image-repertory, the principal elements of which recur in various charged combinations in the film. Rather than abstracting (in a manner of speaking) what it presents as the "essence" of hustling to the figure of two nearly naked hustlers slowly and steadily cruising each other before a camera and a bathroom mirror, as *My Hustler* does, *Midnight Cowboy* presents a rich—perhaps an overrich—play of metaphors for what hustlers do and are. Essentially, the images presented in this scene suggest, hustlers are those young men who make the luscious fruits of their bodies (their buns, their genitals) available to fruits (fags, johns, and overripe female fruits like Cass) for coins, for cash. In doing so, they experience mixed feelings of desire and undesire, pleasure and unpleasure (the coins pour out of the slot, but the cash gets paid out by the hustler rather than paid to him, as it "properly" should be, as at the scene's end, when Joe Buck gets manipulated into giving Cass money instead of the reverse).

The other image of Joe Buck's exposed buns in the film is, in contrast, quite a fleeting one, and it bears an affective load quite different from the earlier, "follow-the-bouncing-buns" shots. It is, in fact, so fleeting as almost to qualify as "subliminal," but, as I shall try to demonstrate, it is an image not to be overlooked or dismissed lightly by anyone who is seeking, as I am, some of the sources of the film's compelling and disturbing power in trying to work out the visual (il)logic of some of its key images.[23] This image occurs in one of Buck's flashback memories of the sad fate of his adolescent girlfriend "Crazy Annie," who was a "slut"—that is, she had (in the judgment of the boys besides Joe who had sex with her) "too much" sex with "too many" boys, sometimes in groups. This second shot of Buck's bare bottom flashes across the screen as he is violently spread over the back of a car by a gang of teenage boys, who are shown in a series of very rapid, disjointed shots apparently raping both him and "Crazy Annie." Given the brevity and fragmentariness of the shots showing teenage Joe Buck being (or about to be) anally raped, it seems to me impossible to say what their function in the film is supposed to be, or to adjudicate whether the shots are supposed to provide some kind of explanation or motivation for Joe's demeanor or behavior, or whether they are only the incoherently fragmentary residue of a scene for which the narrative links may have been edited out of the final version. This momentary shot of Joe Buck about to be raped may have been dropped into the sequence in order simply to pump up the intensity of the audience's (homophobic) anxieties about all the attention the film and other new films of the time like it are paying to male bodies and male-male sexuality.

Midnight Cowboy anticipates later films like William Friedkin's Cruising (1980) in the way it allows, and to some degree exploits, audience confusion and anxiety about so-called random urban violence and the urban institutions and venues of male-male sex and of S-M sex. Midnight Cowboy makes no explicit references to or representations of urban S-M scenes, but its concern with representing, albeit incoherently, the relation between Joe Buck's memories, including his memory of being raped and seeing his girlfriend raped, and the possible relation of this past to his career as a hustler, to his complicated relationship with Rizzo, and, especially, to his outburst of violence toward Towny all suggest that pleasure and pain may not be as easily separable as common sense would have it.

Given the ubiquity of S-M imagery and situations in high-fashion design and photography, art photography, and popular film over the past decade and more, it may be hard to recall how largely invisible S-M was in mainstream representation of the sixties. It was not until what one might call "The Joy of Sex Moment" at the very end of the sixties and the beginning of the seventies that S-M became at all familiar to large numbers of readers or filmgoers, when Oh! Calcutta, with its knowing send-ups of S-M and other kinks, was for a time the hottest ticket on Broadway, and when Alex Comfort's The Joy of Sex, a self-proclaimed guide to the full menu of gourmet sex, brought S-M into America's living rooms and bedrooms.[24] Although Warhol was commonly perceived as simply being effeminate, a nelly queen, much of his public persona during his main filmmaking years (1963–68) derived from S-M subculture—his silent but demanding demeanor, his position as "boss" to a stable of performers of various styles of social and sexual perversity, the assaultive character of his filming methods, his habitual wearing of "shades" and black-leather trousers.

It is this inability to represent S-M desires or practices in any but a highly incoherent and uncomprehending form that makes Joe Buck's beating of Towny in Midnight Cowboy so hard to account for in relation to the rest of the film. James Leo Herlihy's novel, however, which incorporates a fair amount of the discourse of the sociology and psychiatry of "deviancy" current in the fifties and sixties, makes explicit the S-M overtones of the beating for both Towny and Joe Buck. In the novel, the narrative makes it clear that

Towny is masturbating while Joe beats him and that when he ejaculates he breaks off the stream of verbal self-abuse he has been delivering ("Joe did not at first understand what had taken place. He hadn't struck the man, and yet [Towny] Locke had given up the battle. Then Joe looked down and saw the evidence of the gratification Locke had received").[25] What the novel goes on to suggest that is entirely missing from the film, where no perceptible sex takes place or has taken place between Towny and Joe, is that in shoving the phone receiver into Towny's toothless mouth Joe is performing an act so intensely satisfying for himself that it qualifies as a sexual act. The novel describes it in these words: "Joe still held in his mind the image of the man and the telephone, the telephone and the man, and in his confusion he still felt it necessary to subdue the two of them. He therefore pushed Locke to the floor, sat astride his chest, and shoved the telephone's receiver into the toothless mouth."[26] Less invested than the novel in pathologizing narratives of perversion, the film presents no ready way of understanding the meaning of this last grotesque image. The film's insistence early on on the image of Joe's blooming bare backside as "sign of sex" gets refigured— but only incoherently so—in his bloody oral rape of Towny.[27]

Ratso Rizzo and Joe Buck have their own sexual exchanges, including S-M ones, but they are for the most part—at least the ones that get articulated verbally—highly encoded. At one point in the film, Rizzo angrily tells Buck, "You're never gonna make it with women in that cowboy getup. That look's strictly for fags," and although he is supposedly just offering some frank, street-smart advice to his very naive friend, there is a way in which utterances like these, of which Rizzo makes a number, may be loaded with overtones beyond their literal ones—for example, the remark just quoted does not or does not only convey "neutral information" from Rizzo to Buck; it may also be taken to signal that Rizzo himself may be a fag, or at least "knows what fags like," and also that Rizzo recognizes that Buck is (also) a fag, or at least shows potential. In other words, Rizzo's taunts and advice and Buck's interested responses can be understood as functioning as flirtation, courtship, and would-be seduction between the two men, in much the same way that the older man in My Hustler keeps up his line of chat about showing Paul America the ropes of hustling while they cruise each other at the same time. This kind of exchange in Midnight Cowboy sometimes also looks strikingly like the complex games of "playing it straight" between hustlers and johns that abound in hustler texts of the period.

In Herlihy's novel Rizzo goes on in the same conversation (about why Buck should shed his cowboy costume) to tell Buck that it is only the allegedly "very small masochistic element" among male homosexuals who will be attracted to his western pose. "Never mind what that [i.e., masochism] is," Rizzo says, "You wouldn't believe it if I told you."[28] Buck may be entirely clueless about what sadomasochism is or how it might be a source of sexual pleasure and excitement, and Rizzo's only relation to S-M desire may be some properly incredulous attitude he's picked up from popularizations of contemporary psychiatry—yet assumptions about the near-complete "innocence" of both men tend to collapse in the course of the film as they do in the novel under a burden of mounting irony. We need supplement Schlesinger's bland description of the film quoted earlier only slightly in order to arrive at an accurate-enough working description of its sexual politics: *Midnight Cowboy* is a film about how two men can have a meaningful S-M relationship without admitting to being homosexuals. Or perhaps it would be more accurate to say that the film is about the anguish of two men trying to establish a meaningful S-M relationship despite their both being Ms in relation to each other, and finally having to settle for fiction's stock resolution to the M-M crisis: the death of one partner and the permanent bereavement of the other.

When Rizzo gets sick and wets his pants on the bus to Florida, Joe Buck buys them both new, clean "vacation" clothes, discarding Rizzo's grimy "city" rags and his own cowboy hustling outfit. The last sequence of the film begins with a shot of Joe and Ratso sitting side by side on the bus as Joe finishes dressing his friend in his new clothes. As he finishes doing so, he zips up the fly of the sleeping Ratso's new pants with something of the same emphatic quality with which Cass had unzipped Joe's own pants at the beginning of his brief but eventful hustling career. A little later, Joe realizes Ratso is dead, and with another emphatic gesture reaches over and takes hold of his friend's body, drawing it gently toward him, as if both to embrace and to protect it. This strong closing image of the film resonates powerfully against—does anything but erase or obscure—the terrible preceding image of the bleeding man lying with a phone jammed into his mouth and Joe Buck looming over him. I take the tension between these two images to be an index of the intensity of Midnight Cowboy's engagement with the "dark" side of relations between men, unsuccessful as the film is in most ways in getting more than the most tenuous grip on its representations of these relations. Buck's final gesture of dressing himself and Rizzo in new, clean clothes—"signed" with the gesture of his zipping up Rizzo's new pants—also recalls the way in which (as I have discussed above) hustler and john "invest themselves," fantasmatically dress each other, in their provisionally "straight" identities. When Joe Buck performs this fantasy on himself and Rizzo, he is unwittingly performing an act of (eroticized) mourning, undressing and dressing Rizzo not for sex but for burial. The mourning the scene evokes is not only a specific act of mourning for Rizzo but a more general one for the losses and emptinesses enshrined in the game of the straight-acting hustler and the trade-seeking john. In the years since the film's appearance, many commentators have taken this ending as yet another act of ritual mourning for the death of straight-white-American-male "innocence" in the face of successive waves of black, antiwar, feminist, and gay and lesbian political activism. Despite its apparent concession to the desire of many of its viewers to believe that Joe Buck, despite his hustling and his violence, and Ratso Rizzo, despite his con games and his sexual knowingness, are "really" and ultimately "innocent," Midnight Cowboy suggests something much more complicated, and much more perverse, about its protagonists and the masses of men they represent.

Joseph Cornell started making his assemblages, or "boxes," as they're commonly known, in the 1930s and continued making them until his death in 1972. Living in Queens all his adult life, Cornell's chief diversion for many years was going into Manhattan and browsing in the used book stores that used to line lower Fourth Avenue. He also haunted thrift shops and five-and-dime stores, and his boxes contain a rich mixture of his acquisitions from these outings: pages and lines cut out of nineteenth-century French books, ballet and opera programs and posters, deluxe European travel books, reproductions of Italian Renaissance portraits; but also fan photos from movie magazines, little toy lobsters made of red plastic, color lithographs of parrots and rabbits, soap-bubble pipes, jacks, balls, and marbles. The first Cornell box I ever saw was one of the series called "Medici Slot Machine," and I remember being shocked and delighted at the way it fused the glamor and prestige of the museum, of quattrocento portraiture and tales of the Medici, with the pungently American vulgarity of the slot machine, the peep show, and the schlocky toy.

The longer Cornell's work sits in the museums and the more routinely reproductions of it appear in textbook histories of modern art, the more likely it is to lose its power to surprise viewers with its recastings of history and high culture as penny arcade. The bulk of the critical literature on Cornell's work, with a few happy exceptions, is of little help to those of us who would like to continue to cultivate our sense of what seems striking or original about his work. Most commentators on Cornell's work—ranging from John Ashbery to Hilton Kramer—have uncharacteristically spoken with almost one voice in praise of its allegedly "innocent" and "enchanting" qualities. The downside of these terms of reception is of course the unavoidable implication that Cornell's boxes are simple, "magical"—that is, we can't understand how their effects work, they "just do"—and,

17. Joseph Cornell, Untitled (Medici Boy) (1953). © The Joseph and Robert Cornell Memorial Foundation. Collection of the Modern Art Museum of Fort Worth, Museum Purchase, The Benjamin J. Tillar Memorial Trust.

furthermore, that they are to be appreciated uncritically—that is, there really isn't much to say about them, just "enjoy what's there." One of the more or less unspoken assumptions of this response is that, unlike, for example, much of the surrealist art to which Cornell's is in some ways clearly related, which takes the representation of bodies, body parts, and erotic desire and especially prohibited or transgressive erotic desire as one of its primary focuses, Cornell's work is contrastingly "free" of such concerns.

Limited as it is, this "enchanting innocence" line of criticism has provided until quite recently the only terms available for discussing our pleasure in Cornell's work. Aside from it, criticism of Cornell's art has strongly tended to emphasize its alleged austerity, its silence, the meticulous precision of its gestures, and the ineluctability and otherworldliness of its effects. It has concentrated on the connections of Cornell's work with such high-modernist and protomodernist movements as European symbolist and surrealist poetry and painting. The reception of Cornell's work has had the effect of relegating it to the airless jewelry-store ambience of the renovated Museum of Modern Art and the Madison Avenue gallery.

In reducing Cornell's boxes to high-modernist high art we have almost entirely lost the funky, sexy, and witty mode of engaging with a wide range of bodies and sexual desires that animates Cornell's massive project from beginning to end. In these pages, I want to explore some of the many ways in which Cornell's work represents and refers to bodies and the bodily in ways that until recently have been almost entirely ignored or overlooked. Bodies and bodily desire have tended to get ignored in the reception of Cornell's work not because of their alleged general absence, I would argue, but, indeed, because there are "too many bodies" and bodily desires circulating in his work for the comfort of many of his critics and even for many of his professed admirers. The overdetermined stereotype of the ascetic, inscrutable and elegantly absent and thoroughly disembodied Cornell that they have tended to emphasize not only tends to impoverish our understanding of the richness and complexity and erotic power of his achievements; it also has the effect of occluding our vision of the many commonalities that his work and working methods share with many of his contemporaries with whose work his own has the strongest affinities, such as that of Andy Warhol, Kenneth Anger, and Jack Smith. To reclaim a ubiquitous and various sexuality in Cornell's work is important not only for its sake alone but also for the sake of our understanding the role of sexuality in much of the most powerful art that has in various ways followed the example of Cornell's work.

Mary Ann Caws's generous 1993 selection of writing from Cornell's archives, entitled *Joseph Cornell's Theater of the Mind*,[1] constitutes a crucial intervention in the artist's legend, providing as it does abundant material in Cornell's own words on what one might call the messier or juicier aspects of his biography: his obsessions with female stars of opera, ballet, and movies; his love of wandering around Manhattan shopping for materials for his art while simultaneously indulging his ancillary passions for scoping out and consuming junk-food desserts and for discovering new nymphets to visit at their work places and to fantasize and write about back home (Caws speculates that Cornell saw the girl he christened the *fée aux lapins* selling stuffed bunnies at a five-and-dime; "the apricot fairy" was named after her orange dress — but also, perhaps, after a favorite flavor of danish).

One of the things that has intrigued me most in reading Caws's collection of Cornell's writings is the way this artist complicates our understandings of sexuality in its relations to representation and artistic production by asserting supposedly unrelated and even mutually exclusive patterns of desire and taste. For example, Cornell's personal cults of ballerinas and female opera and movie stars are something he had in common with many gay men his age and younger, especially many gay men in the New York and a few other metropolitan areas. However, his avowed and densely represented desire for young girls complicates any assumptions we might make on the basis of his (to some minds) stereotypically urban gay male taste in performers and performance. To add to the complications, one may note that for every glamorous "Medici Princess" box in which Cornell represents a very young girl as ideal object of desire, there is a corresponding "Medici Prince" box that seems to render the question of the gender of this ideal object practically moot; that is, Cornell's work in some instances seems as capable of positing a boy-child as ideal object of desire as readily as a girl-child. Let me turn this screw of "contradictory" and multifold desire one more time by noting the intensity of erotic desire for adult women that Cornell's boxes register more and more directly as he began to include photographs or portions of photographs of female nudes in his work of the 1960s, as graphic erotic representation became more and more widely available and accepted during that decade. Yet, given the wide range of desires that Cornell's art encapsulates, one should hesitate, I believe, in thinking of or calling Cornell's desire for women simply "heterosexual." In advancing the umbrella word of our sexual moment, "queer," for the sexuality of Cornell's work, I hope I will by this point be understood to be saying other things rather than simply, "Cornell secretly desired other men." As I have suggested above, erotic desire is "all over the place" in Cornell's work, which is not to say it does not in specific instances locate itself on particular erotic terrains and orient itself in relation to particular persons, bodies, types of bodies, or body parts. But object choice is not definitive of the desires Cornell represents in his boxes. Cornell represents many desires; even when they seem to collect around similar types of objects, it would be a mistake, I think, to reduce them all to one or to a small class. In looking at a wide range of writings ancillary to many of his boxes that concern themselves with women and women's performances, I want to consider some of the ways in which Cornell through his boxes discriminates, proliferates, and disperses desire(s).

I want to begin my examination of this Cornellian eros at the level of the oral, with the artist's passion for sugary treats, of which he made no secret. When other famous artists visited him at home, he exuberantly served them store-bought jelly roll and Kool Aid. He seems to have been nearly as forthright about his strong attraction to and vivid desires for the sweet "sylphide" daughters of various of his friends. His avowed (or would the litotes "undisavowed" be more accurate?) yearnings for the lives and bodies of sweet young women and girls and boys, living and dead, are acknowledged and enshrined in many of his boxes. Caws's publication of five hundred pages of Cornell's diaries and working notes (she mentions that thirty times as much of his writing still remains unpublished) makes it quite evident that it has become necessary to rethink Cornell as an artist who was not only the maker of the supposedly "silent" and inscrutable boxes but also a writer of daunting prolixity *and* extraordinary dedication and articulacy. I believe it is urgently necessary, at least as much for our sake as for his, to recognize the courage and rare self-knowledge with which he explored his own supposedly forbidden desires for a wide array of sweet objects of many different types. Whatever Cornell's personal relation to his erotic yearnings may have been, his work represents and explores several kinds of (sweetly) devouring desires with a minimum of anxiety and self-censorship.

The glimpses one gets of Joseph Cornell through the memories of his friends and acquaintances often suggest a personality — or perhaps several of them — not just at variance with the legend of his work as austere, remote, and unearthly, but in aggressive combat with such notions. To visitors from the international art world who came expecting to encounter a mandarin master-modernist on the model of the urbane and cosmopolitan Marcel Duchamp, Cornell and his milieu sometimes came as a shock, pleasant or unpleasant. The artist lived all his adult life with his mother and his brother, who suffered from cerebral palsy, in a modest 1920s frame house on Utopia Parkway in Flushing, Queens. The house was strewn with piles of papers and decorated with what were known at the time as "knick-knacks," some of which were fine and others junk, to some visitors' eyes. There was a small and scrappy garden in back that gave Cornell great pleasure; there is a photograph of him showing off some painted plaster squirrels he had installed there. After a walk through the house and a look at the garden, sweets would be served and Cornell would talk, thereby satisfying at least two of his apparently inexhaustible urges to eat sweets and to produce language through speaking and writing — these great impulses that I am calling his "oralia."

The artist might or might not then show his visitors some of his new work. Many people found the combination of the rarified and the banal in Cornell's home life magical; others decided after a visit to revert to admiring him and his work from afar. Some were fascinated and some appalled with the scene of the maker of the elegant and elusive boxes at home amidst the litter of his gleanings from Flushing's dimestores and his brother's train sets. Having made a pilgrimage to meet a surrealist wizard, some visitors were understandably perplexed to encounter someone who collected plaster squirrels and served jelly doughnuts.

Cornell seems to have accepted people's responses to him and his milieu with equanimity. Strong impulses toward intimacy and countervailing impulses toward distance and formal restraint structured his relationships, powerfully if not always coherently; he recognized that many of these bonds were better served by the exchange of letters, phone calls, "found objects," gifts, or artwork than by routine social contact. Given the breadth of his acquaintance and the even greater scope of his correspondence, Cornell's reputation as a hermit among people who did not know him both puzzled and amused him. His widespread reputation for reclusiveness had little basis in fact, but the combination in his life of what are commonly regarded as incompatible and incommensurable tastes and affinities did disturb and even repel some people—not only some who actually visited him but many more people who knew him only through the highly mixed medium of his work. Anecdotes about visitors' surprise at and discomfort with Cornell's home life interest me because of the way they seem to me to figure, often in sharp relief, a more general and less clearly articulated kind of resistance to the mixture of materials and meanings in his art and writing.

Visitors who spoke or wrote about having found Cornell and his ambience off-putting sometimes mention the kitschy surroundings and refreshments, but mostly they complain about his noninteractive and monologic conversational style, a characteristic that drove some people (e.g., Mark Rothko) away, while others (e.g., Duchamp, Robert Motherwell) accepted it, albeit often with considerable reservations. Cornell seems to have cultivated his most intense conversational style on the telephone with his chosen confidantes (performance artist Carolee Schneeman, editor Leila Hadley, curator and art critic Diane Waldman, among others), with whom he reportedly held four- or five-hour sessions in which they interpreted dreams and discussed other matters relating to their emotional and spiritual states.

Given how obviously lonely, eccentric, and self-absorbed Cornell seems to have been, it is easy to overlook not only how actively social, and even, in his somewhat strange way, gregarious, he was, but also to ignore or underestimate the range and extent of his eros, diffused as it was across a broad and full spectrum of friends, acquaintances, and *princesses lointaines* of the upper, middle, and lower classes. He formed close relationships of various kinds with friends and their children as well as with a number of his "helpers" (as he called his assistants), male and female. Women colleagues with whom he exchanged ideas, work, and support for work ranged over time and temperament from Marianne Moore and Dorothea Tanning to Carolee Schneeman and Susan Sontag. Besides his many infatuations with the various "sylphides" he encountered in his daily wanderings around Main Street, Flushing, and into Manhattan (as late as 1966, he was per-

18. Joseph Cornell, American, 1903–1972, Untitled (Penny Arcade Portrait of Lauren Bacall). © The Joseph and Robert Cornell Memorial Foundation. Mixed-media construction, 1945/46, 52.1 × 40.6 × 8.9 cm., Collection of Lindy Bergman, 292.1983, Photograph © 1997, The Art Institute of Chicago, All Rights Reserved.

ceiving a romantically "dark Coppelia" in the "Courtesy Drugs check-out girl—seen in Food Shop" [340]), and besides the nineteenth-century divas he maintained voluminous files on, dedicated boxes to, and occasionally wrote about (the ballerina Fanny Cerrito, the legendary singer Maria Malibran, and others), Cornell also intensely admired and made boxes and collages of the starlets of the forties, fifties, and sixties, from Hedy Lamarr and Lauren Bacall to Marilyn Monroe, Joan Collins, Yvette Mimieux, and Sheree North (an early "Marilyn clone"). Many entries in his diary make clear that Cornell did not consider his imaginative engagements with the reigning pop divas of the day a trivial matter or a form of imaginary slumming for him. As in the cases of female contemporaries of theirs who wielded considerably more cultural authority (e.g., the prima donnas Maria Callas and Kathleen Ferrier), Cornell cultivated intense imaginary communications with selected girl pop stars, often in conjunction with sublime music; witness a diary entry for April 1, 1963: "in the evening Patty Duke was here via Mahler [Symphony] #3." The "sylphides" of Woolworth's and Courtesy Drugs trailed clouds of glory in his visions of them, too; the diary passage just quoted continues, "of course it was so much more than the usual . . . but there are no words *at the moment* for life experience such as this . . ." (302; my ellipses)—but the appearance or arrival of the necessary words seems imminent at many such points in Cornell's diary.

A chain of association that Cornell produced for *New York Times* reporter Grace Glueck at an exhibition at the Cooper Union in 1972, the last year of his life, brings starlet, "sweet," and successes and failures of reciprocal communication together in a characteristically Cornellian way. The exhibit had been announced as being "for children only," and brownies and cherry Cokes were served at the opening. When asked by Glueck if he liked cherry soda, Cornell replied: "In a very mystical way. They have them in the underground in those big conveying machines—it brings back memories . . . cherry and lime also remind me of Sheree North—a starlet they were going to build up to Marilyn Monroe roles, but it didn't happen. I sent her a small box once, but never heard from her." [2]

Caws argues in her introductory essay to *Joseph Cornell's Theater of the Mind* that there is a close parallel between Cornell's motives for making his boxes and his lust for sweets:

> Many of his boxes were made for the starlets and models whose charms he sought to salute and capture—as if imprisoning them in

boxes were his sole way of partaking of the experience he was never to have. This whole sensuality of voyeurism extends to the sweet rolls he consumed, even as he gazed longingly at the orange glaze on a layer cake in Horn and Hardart's automat, the chocolate icing on another, and the pink icing on yet another cake in the window, which he regrets not purchasing. There is a strong parallel between his sensuality connected with food and his unattainable starlets; both are associated with sweetness and a sort of hovering delight, but also with a cloying abundance the desire for which he found reprehensible in himself. (34–35)

While I find myself in general agreement with Caws about seeing a parallel between Cornell's desires for young female "stars" and for dessert pastries, there are several points about the terms in which she draws the parallel that I would want to question. Why, one may wonder, does she not consider the enormous excess of language that Cornell produces—his relentless writing and speaking styles—alongside his supposedly excessive visual appetites? Caws tends to leave Cornell's outpouring of language out of her analysis of his consuming passions, and her understanding of the analytical category she does propose—"voyeurism"—sometimes seems limited and conventional, as in the passage just quoted, where her "imprisoning" metaphor seems reductive of what must be or have been a more complex process. Here, Caws seems to me to overemphasize the importance of Cornell's motive for capturing and confining his models in his artwork. When she writes, "as if imprisoning them in boxes were his sole way of partaking of the experience he was never to have," her own term for at least one of the other things Cornell may have been about in making some of his boxes—"salut[ing]" as well as capturing a starlet—gets left out of the account. And one might be mystified by the sense of her phrase, "his sole way of partaking of the experience he was never to have," were it not clear enough that the implication of her phrasing is that she supposed that "impossible" experience to be one of Cornell's actually sexually possessing the object(s) of desire. I want to argue to the contrary that the repressive hypothesis (which in this case one might state as, because Cornell couldn't sexually possess these young women, he therefore made works of art in their images, dedicated to them) has little to tell us about the transformations of pleasures available to the maker and/or the beholder of Cornell's boxes. The dichotomy Caws introduces into her discussion of the fate of Cornell's desires admits of only two possibilities: "consummation" versus "sublimation." Before considering "sublimation" as a possible analytical term for describing the course of Cornell's desires, I would at least want to reintroduce some sense of the processual and multi-phasal back into the term; "sublimation," we know from Freud as well as from various theories of the sublime that long antedate his work, is not a one-step transformation, nor is it a unidirectional one.

I would want to question further Caws's use of the term "voyeurism" in this passage to describe the parallel between desiring starlets and desiring pastry. While (as she asserts) the two phenomena do share a powerful imaginary visual lure for Cornell (starlets and iced cakes look extremely sweet and luscious), calling his pleasure in them and his means for sustaining and/or transforming it simply "voyeuristic" begs the question of how to understand such a process outside either a traditional moralistic explanation (i.e., lusty gazing is simply evil in itself) or a pathologizing psychiatric one ("visual sex" is a partial, unsatisfactory, and unhealthy substitute for "real" and/or "mature," i.e., "genital," sexuality). As "sublimation" is a complex process, so is voyeurism, but there is a way that accounts like Caws's reduce such processes to pre- or nontheoretical labels. But if we consider voyeurism to be an at least partially autonomous sexual practice, not just an inadequate substitute for some "other" whole or healthy sexuality, then some theory of voyeurism might be more helpful to us in thinking about Cornell's work and other work like his.

I would also want to supplement any account of the role of voyeurism in understanding the pleasures of looking at Cornell's boxes and of his other works with a couple of other questions I want to pursue. What does voyeurism have to do with oral desire in his work, oral desire understood broadly enough to comprehend his intense pleasure in certain kinds of verbal articulation (trying faithfully to record his changing emotional states in his diary day by day, often almost hour by hour; monologuizing and engaging in marathon-length, séance-like phone conversations with intimates)? Also, what may Cornell's allegedly "chaste," "pristine," "austere" boxes have to do with the long-established (even, in some European cultures, apparently ancient) vernacular practice of thinking of and referring to female genitals as "boxes"? Let me consider this latter question first.

In his 1913 essay "The Theme of the Three Caskets," Freud surveys a wide range of literary and folk materials (the myth of the Judgment of Paris, *The Merchant of Venice*, etc.) about a man's choosing among three "caskets," which Freud interprets as a metonymic reference to three women by way of a symbol for their genitals. Boxes, baskets, caskets, etcetera, Freud writes in this essay, can all symbolize female sexual organs.[3] Freud had made several similar observations in the first edition of *The Interpretation of Dreams* (1900), and he had supplemented this list in 1909 by adding cases, chests, cupboards, and ovens, and supplemented it again in the 1919 edition by adding hollow objects, ships, and vessels of all kinds.[4] Earlier, a woman patient of Freud had, as part of their work on a dream of hers in an analytic session, recalled for him a conversation she had heard at a party "about the English word 'box' and the various ways in which it could be translated into German—such as *Schachtel* (case), *Loge* (box at the theater), *Kasten* (chest), *Ohrfeige* (box on the ear), and so on. Other portions of the same dream enabled us [Freud writes] to discover further that she had guessed that the English 'box' was related to the German *Büchse* (receptacle), and that she had then been plagued by a recollection that *Büchse* is used as a vulgar term for the female genitals."[5]

Cornell, who was as close a student of Freud as his surrealist contemporaries were, could hardly have been unaware of the discussions scattered throughout Freud's writing not only of the box or case as unconscious dream symbol for female genitals but also of the similar symbolic meanings of jewels, watches, etcetera—the kinds of objects and mechanisms that Cornell placed in many of his most celebrated box-constructions—for example, *Métaphysique d'éphémère: Nordis* (1941), *Homage to the Romantic Ballet* ("Taglioni jewel casket") (1942), *Medici Slot Machine (Bernardino Pinturicchio)* (1943). Since Cornell was also a lifelong collector of nineteenth-century books and a haunter of the used and antiquarian bookstores on Fourth Avenue, neither could he have been unaware of the so-called ladies' gift books that sold in large numbers in the mid-nineteenth century United States. Hawthorne, Longfellow, Elizabeth Oakes Smith, and many other writers published in them; they featured verse, tales, engravings, and tunes for the parlor harmonium. Some of the most popular series were entitled the *Casket*, the *Gem*, the *Lady's Repository*—terms that anticipate Freud's association of such objects and spaces with a highly metaphorized femininity that by Cornell's time may well have come to seem exaggerated, commodified, and fetishized. Cornell, as well as some of the women and gay men

(Parker Tyler, John Ashbery) who admired him or his art, may have taken pleasure in his work partly because of the ways in which it reproduced such a version of femininity in some ways at the same time that it articulated an ironic distance from it in others. For viewers such as Marianne Moore or Dore Ashton, Parker Tyler or John Ashbery—or Cornell himself—who were as thoroughly versed in early-to-mid-nineteenth-century modes of representation as with modernist ones, it was possible to enjoy Cornell's assemblages with one desirous and appreciative eye, so to speak, firmly focused in the nineteenth century and the other in the twentieth. "(Seen through the stereoscope)" is the subtitle that Cornell gave his important early film scenario, *Monsieur Phot* (short for "Photographer," one of its main characters), and one of the chief pleasures of his work resides in the way it juxtaposes Romantic and modernist images and modes of perception, continually uncovering striking consonances and dissonances between them.[6] In contemplating much of his work, one can stylistically have one's cake and eat it too (a fantasy with a particularly strong appeal for Cornell).

Cornell was not only passively aware of Freud's interpretative schemas; he applied them to the interpretation of his dreams and other intriguing mental phenomena. Cornell's friend Dore Ashton records that "many [of his] acquaintances were tentatively questioned [by him] about their dreams, and some were directed to Freud, or rather to [a section of] chapter 6 in *The Interpretation of Dreams*, which deals specifically with 'condensation' in dreams. . . ."[7] The idea of "condensation" fascinated Cornell because it arose in Freud's thinking in response to a kind of discrepancy that was for Cornell constitutive of his practice as a writer and an artist: this was the discrepancy (as Freud describes it) between the content of a dream (often "brief, meagre, and laconic," he writes)[8] and the thoughts the dream-symbols represent, which may run to the equivalent of dozens of pages of writing but nevertheless leave the analysand feeling that he or she still has much more to say about thoughts associated with the dream. Cornell was struck by the way the discrepancy noted by Freud between the apparently meager content of a dream and the massive amount of thinking that it might turn out on reflection to represent spoke to his own experience of a discrepancy between moments of exaltation that he experienced in daily waking life—unexpected, momentary, flickering, intense—and the inadequacy of even the most elaborate and painstaking efforts on his part to understand or to give an account of them—in his diary, in his collecting and archiving activities, in his artwork, or in his marathon phone conversations. Such moments might come unbidden to Cornell as he enjoyed a dessert and hot drink at an automat or cafeteria and gazed desultorily out the window at passersby or at a sylphide behind the counter; as he bicycled around Bayside; as he caught a glimpse of graffiti on a sunny brick wall as the subway disappeared into the tunnel on the way to Manhattan (yes, Cornell was a dedicated reader of Proust). "*Garden Center 44,*" Caws writes in an editorial note, "Cornell's most extensive file, is named after a nursery in Flushing . . . where Cornell did some selling and handiwork in 1944. For more than twenty-nine years, Cornell built up this file of 'explorations and extensions' associated with an 'Arcadian atmosphere' " he had experienced there (106). Though he might often revisit the scenes of his enchantment, in person or in memory, there was never any guarantee that the precious moment of "upsurge" or "illumination" (his terms) would ensue: on January 12, 1960, he wrote of a visit to a favorite cafeteria on Eighth Avenue, "fruit tart but no capture of that mood that has come in this spot with such transcendency" (271). On April 27, 1958, he had written, "Endless marveling at the way in which routine experience suddenly becomes magically imbued and transformed with a joy too elusive to catch in words" (235). Unserenely, he wrote on March 6, 1967, "now penning in Flushing Main St. library pondering *life* the ever maddening[ ] elusiveness of satisfactory recording" (355). Rather than seeing Cornell's boxes as monuments to silence, reading his diaries and other personal papers may incline one to see them as participating in an endless, two-sided, never resolved dialogue between a set of (in Freud's terms) apparently "brief, meagre and laconic" contents and the torrents of thinking, reading, writing, and conversation they absorbed and could, with effort, release.

Ashton links Cornell's fascination with psychoanalytic condensation theory to his lifelong devotion to the writing of one of Freud's principal romantic precursors in working out a dynamic theory of dream and desire, Gérard de Nerval and his "*roman personnel,*" *Aurelia* (1855). *Aurelia* is a narrative of blissful amorous longing that is also an excruciating record of the lover-narrator's ongoing psychotic disintegration. What Freud calls "condensation," Ashton writes in her memoir of Cornell, is "the very process described with such meticulous attention to detail"[9] in Nerval's late novellas *Aurelia* and *Sylvie*. Proust preferred *Sylvie*, but Cornell's dedication to both the matter and "method" of *Aurelia* seems never to have wavered since his early reading of the book as a schoolboy at Andover.

The narrator's "method" in *Aurelia* is to proliferate figures on different ontological levels for an actress with whom he has been passionately in love, who has rejected him and subsequently died. His female beloved partially ceases to be a particular person and becomes a succession of avatars — "Divas," "Peris," "Undines," and "Salamanders" [10] (these are of course all types of female fairy-characters in the Romantic writing and ballet that Cornell loved: *Giselle, Ondine, La Sylphide, Swan Lake*). "Lying on a cot," the narrator says early on in *Aurelia*, "I seemed to see the heavens unveiled and opened, revealing a thousand vistas of unparalleled magnificence." In his vision, he says, "a female deity, always the same one, smilingly removed, one after another, the fleeting masks of her various incarnations. . . ." [11] Different elements of his waking experience and his intense hallucinations are condensed into the composite figure of "Aurelia," a negative and sublated figure for the possibility of the dispensation or refusal of love, and of the survival or death of the beloved and, by extension, of nature itself.

Late in the book, the narrator is residing in an asylum where he continues to have visions. After he manages to coax a word from a fellow inmate who has long refused to speak, he dreams again of a smiling goddess who visits and encourages him. "The joy which this dream diffused within my spirit afforded me a rapturous awakening," he says. "I wanted to have some material evidence of the apparition which had so comforted me, and I wrote on the wall these words: 'You visited me last night.'" [12] Cornell noted in his diary that "the intensity of consolation" that a dream about a very young and beautiful dancer ("Italian peasant type") had given him had "evoked a sympathetic feeling of kinship for Gérard de Nerval who scribbled on the walls of his asylum cell 'tu m'as visité cette nuit'" (115).

It is easy to understand the long-lasting appeal Nerval and *Aurelia* exerted over Cornell as he produced his own pantheon of vaguely but powerfully eroticized female avatars of a set of longings toward which he felt language could only gesture—although he never gave up trying to extend what he considered its limits. Cornell, who converted to Christian Science at the age of twenty-one and remained committed to its teachings and principles throughout his life (although he did not hesitate to consult doctors or undergo hospitalization when he judged he needed to), predictably found

Nerval's evocations of a matriarchal polytheism highly agreeable; over fifty years after his conversion Cornell wrote in his diary, "Long Junipero of Christian Science recalled noted now 1st time—the warm hospitality—'wine or coffee'—(Mother—God; divine & eternal Principle; Life, Truth, & Love)" (331).

The narrative of *Aurelia* shuttles back and forth between noting the narrator's waking activities and recording his various dreams and hallucinations. The two terminuses of the narrative, never far distant from each other in any case, begin blurring with each other a few pages into the text; the third of the text's sixteen sections famously opens:

> Here began for me what I shall call the overflowing of the dream into real life [*l'épanchement du rêve dans la réalité*]. From this moment on, everything took on at times a dual aspect, and this without the reasoning process ever lacking logic, without memory losing the slightest detail of what was happening to me. But my actions, apparently those of a madman, were subject to what human reason would call illusion.[13]

Robert Motherwell has referred Nerval's phrase, "the overflowing of the dream into real life" to Cornell's work,[14] without specifying how he understands these terms to signify in that context. I am struck by the way the phrase resonates in relation to Cornell's "overflow" or "outpouring" of speech, of writing, of energy, of desire, as reported by his acquaintances and friends and by himself in his voluminous diaries, letters, and files—especially as this excess arises in response to the endless, impossible but also irresistible task of attempting to render in writing the occasional irruptions of magical atmospheres and feelings of joy and "warmth" he experiences in the course of his most routine activities. One of Cornell's primary terms for this irreducible gap or ratio is "aurelian"; he writes at different times of an " 'aurelian' image," of "the 'aurelian' world" (78–79), of "the total 'aurelian' drama" (313) manifest in various overflowings between certain "real-life" experiences and the wealth of affect-laden if partial perceptions that sometimes attend them in unpredictable and elusive ways.

In Cornell's case the fragmentariness of some of his most powerful perceptions may be attributable to the "overflow" or "outpouring" in his experience between oral and visual routes of desire, and the way this *épanchement* of one into the other both blurs and revivifies the differences and incommensurabilities between them. I have asked above of Cornell's work what the relationship may be in it between voyeurism and oral desire, and without wishing to produce a functionalist account of what this relationship may be, I would adduce the fertile and intensely pleasurable confusion near the center of Whitman's "Song of Myself" as seeming to evoke a similar kind of productive albeit often painful conflict between vision and speech that Cornell found codified in other terms in Freud's discussion of the meagerness of dream content versus the inevitable prolixity of dream interpretation. I am thinking of such lines from Whitman as, "Something I cannot see puts upward libidinous prongs, / Seas of bright juice suffuse heaven" ("Song of Myself," section 24); "My voice goes after what my eyes cannot reach, / With the twirl of my tongue I encompass worlds and volumes of worlds"; and "Speech is the twin of my vision, it is unequal to measure itself . . ." (both "Song of Myself," section 25).[15]

Perhaps part of the reason that the austerity and taciturnity of Cornell's boxes has been exaggerated is because some critics have been loath to confront the volubility with which many of them articulate romantic and sentimental scenarios of lost or doomed love or fugitive pleasures—scenarios that have long been regarded as embarrassing, hokey, kitsch. Cornell's former assistant Larry Jordan addresses this omission or suppression in the reception of Cornell's work directly when he says, "People love the austerity of his boxes, and are afraid of the sentiment."[16] Actually, I believe, the sentimental side of Cornell's work has a lot to do with its popularity as well as with its generally high critical standing, but its concern with lost or forgotten childhood or children, with the pastimes of other days, with unrequited love, with the fleetingness of youthful beauty and of life itself, is treated as an open secret, something that many viewers may enjoy but that tends to get slighted in our accounts of this work. The boxes should be understood not simply as terminuses of signification, erotic or otherwise, but as indices of the always high ratio of possible articulations in relationship to elusive and momentary but nonetheless transformative overflows of perception and feeling.

With this in mind, let us consider a text of Cornell's that definitively exceeds and eludes the myth of the romantic artist or romantic subject as pathetic sufferer, loser, or victim of loss, prisoner of or martyr to impossible desires. Cornell records in his diary that he spent the morning of March 1, 1947, at the library doing research for one of the special issues of Lincoln Kirstein's journal *Dance Index* that Cornell edited on the culture of ballet in the Romantic period. Coming across a reference to Malibran in Poe's *Marginalia* surprised and delighted him. He writes:

> The finding of the Poe transcended the occasion of locating material for Dance Index in the way in which other parts of the MARGINALIA, "fancies of fancies, etc." filled my preoccupations with the display in the baker across the street—before going into library a pink icinged vanilla cream-filled rolled cake had been observed—later when stopping by to purchase some things its disappearance from its plate glass pedestal in the window brought a real kind of regret of a delicacy that went beyond the mere regret—lunch in a diner, banana creme pie, doughnut, and drink. (141)

What is notable about this passage is not that Cornell regretted not having bought the scrumptious-looking pink cake before someone else did—anyone might have felt that banal response—but his assertion that there is a parallel between the excess of pleasure he had taken in discovering the Poe passage about Malibran and the similar surge of feeling that "went beyond mere regret" at the discovery of the cake's "disappearance from its plate glass pedestal in the window." But the cake's is not the only disappearing act that occurs in this passage. Cornell's syntax works overtime to dissociate the surge of feeling of regret "beyond . . . regret" from himself, or, indeed, from any perceiving subject whatsoever. Looking back at the passage, one notices that no one in particular is said to have *found* the Poe, and the perceiving subject is also missing from the initial observation that there is a delicious-looking cake in the window across the street: a combination of passive-voice construction and a dangling modifier eliminates the observer from the scene altogether, almost as if the cake itself were walking into the library: "before going into the library a pink icinged vanilla cream-filled rolled cake had been observed." Similarly, "later when stopping by to purchase some things its disappearance from its plate glass pedestal in the window brought a real kind of regret of a delicacy that went beyond the mere regret"; who might we understand to be "stopping by to purchase some things"? and to whom did "its disappearance" bring "a real kind of regret . . . beyond the mere regret"? Again, the cake itself is so intensely present *and* absent in the scene, so acutely observed and then so delicately regretted, or, rather, meta-regretted, it seems almost as though the cake itself is the sole agent of the scene, noticing its presence in the window, then regretting its mysterious disappearance. Poe's reference to Malibran is the kind of little discovery that often served as the nucleus of one of Cornell's boxes, but the scene of the window with the plate glass pedestal with the cake missing from it *is* one of Cornell's boxes; it requires no further development than the full syntactical elaboration he has already given it. The little anecdote enthrones the cake's disappearance (on its empty pedestal) as it focuses the refined, doubled, "transcendent" regret that a dislocated and unidentified phantom is said to have felt for a pink cake that seems to have absconded with (or from) itself.

Such a scene cannot be said to be simply one of absence or silence. Jacques Derrida's reading of the text *Mimique* of another of Cornell's talismanic authors, Stéphane Mallarmé, suggests some of the ways in which the kind of Cornellian/"aurelian" "drama" I have just rehearsed can be understood as a performance and as mimetic—or at least as a manifestation of performativity and as a special kind of mimetic practice. Derrida writes, in a famous passage from "The Double Session" of 1970:

> *There is* mimicry [in Mallarmé's *Mimique*, where it seems to reach a kind of vanishing point]. . . . We are faced then with mimicry imitating nothing; faced, so to speak, with a double that doubles no simple, a double that nothing anticipates, nothing at least that is not itself already double. There is no simple reference. It is in this that the mime's operation does allude, but alludes to nothing, alludes without breaking the mirror, without reaching beyond the looking-glass.
> . . . In this speculum with no reality, in this mirror of a mirror, a difference or dyad does exist, since there are mimes and phantoms. But it is a difference without reference, or rather a reference without a referent, without any first or last unit, a ghost that is the phantom of no flesh, wandering about without a past, without any death, birth, or presence.[17]

"Mallarmé thus preserves the differential structure of mimicry or *mimesis*," Derrida goes on, "but without its Platonic or metaphysical interpretation, which implies that somewhere the being of something that *is*, is being imitated. Mallarmé even maintains (and maintains himself in) the structure of the *phantasma* as it is defined by Plato: the simulacrum as the copy of a copy. With the exception that there is no longer any model, and hence, no copy. . . ."[18] "*There is* mimicry," Derrida begins; unlocatable "in" Mallarme's text, the text nevertheless (some would say) "performs" the very mimicry it declines to maintain on conventional premises—that is, as supposedly grounded in a metaphysically guaranteed separation of imitation from original, of copy from model. Derrida cannot point directly to "mimicry" at any point in the text or at the text as a whole in order to locate it, but he can and does make an emphatic deictic gesture in its direction, as if he were seeing a ghost that the reader had not yet spotted.

Judith Butler has discussed Derrida's reading of *Mimique* in her essay, "Imitation and Gender Insubordination," in which she makes a kind of congruent argument that "*gender is a kind of imitation for which there is no original.*"[19] Butler thereby refutes the charges that homosexuality is a deficient or inadequate imitation of heterosexuality, that gay men and women are degraded versions of straight men and women, that queens, butches, or femmes are aping (with the pejorative force of that term intact) straight male-female relations and roles. Released from a metaphysics of meaning that supposedly secures some (different) authentic essence for every referent, the gender hierarchy begins to break down, no longer underwriting the supposed naturalness, superiority, or inevitability of heterosexuality. Mallarmé and Derrida, and Butler after them, unsettle the has-been/would-be-foundational notion that mimicry can only occur under circumstances in which the question of who and what are originals (primary) and who and what are copies (secondary) is never really at issue or in contest.

In his essay "Ballets," Mallarmé makes the similarly unsettling observation that "the ballerina *is not a girl dancing*"; the famous passage begins, "*Here* is a judgment, *here* is an axiom for the ballet!" with the kind of deictic frenzy Derrida may be imitating when he insistently writes, "*There is* mimicry." The rest of the passage reads:

> I mean that the ballerina *is not a girl dancing;* that, considering the juxtaposition of those group motifs, *she is not a girl,* but rather a metaphor which symbolizes some elemental aspect of earthly form: sword, cup, flower, etc., and that *she does not dance* but rather, with miraculous lunges and abbreviations, writing with her body, she *suggests* things which the written work could *express* only in several paragraphs of dialogue or descriptive prose. Her poem is written without the writer's tools.[20]

Like the mime, the ballerina figures a performativity whose ties to a meta-physically secured world of referents and originals have snapped; her gender identity (she "is not a girl") and her actions (she "is not . . . dancing") are transformed by the disjunction. She is said to pass through being an open-ended series of metaphors ("sword, cup, flower, etc.") that suggests something like the inventories of the contents of many of Cornell's boxes (they also suggest some of the elements of the Tarot, with which Nerval and other Romantics were fascinated). Rather than dancing, she is said "with miraculous lunges and abbreviations, writing with her body," to "*suggest*[ ] things which the written work could *express* only in several paragraphs of dialogue or descriptive prose"—that is, she condenses meanings with her body that, like the saturated metaphors of dreams, generate large amounts of verbiage while still exceeding and in some sense eluding such articulation. The "suggest[ive]," rather than the more directly "express[ive]," quality of the "miraculous lunges and abbreviations" with which she does her writing produces the kinds of shocks of sudden, strange, unexpected juxtaposition that the collage method of composition does, and collage is where Cornell's art started. I believe I am following Cornell's and Mallarmé's lead when I find myself wanting to read the ballerina as not only a figure of gender performativity but also as one of sexuality. According to Mallarmé the ballerina performs her "miracles" with her feet and legs, her steps, and the way she uses them to "writ[e] with her body." Cornell supplements this account, this articulation of the ballerina's writing with her body that both demands and eludes full verbal articulation, by suggesting in a highly overdetermined manner that she does it with her "box," not only with her genitals but with the sexuality of which they are both a locus and a sign—but not a sign with a stable referent. Like the mime who (as Judith Butler puts it) "constitutes . . . the phantasm of the original in and through the mime,"[21] the ballerina constitutes her "box" and the sexuality it fails to contain in and through her dance; there is no metaphysically secured femininity of natural and inevitable womanhood and motherhood to which the sign of her genitals refers.

The performance Cornell accomplishes with each of his boxes is that he, too, performs a miracle with the "box" of the figure, the diffraction and indeed the constitution of that figure's sexuality through her performances of her gender, her sexuality, her particular mode of writing with her body—through dance or opera singing or movie acting. Cornell re-presents, re-performs, and thereby may be said to "ghost" (i.e., to inhabit fantasmatically) each of his boxes and invites the viewer to do so, too; anyone can temporarily inhabit a given box and absorb and transmit the performative energies it enshrines, erotic and otherwise. Cornell's boxes do not simply imprison the women whom they salute, as some critics have suggested; of course, they do not simply liberate them, either. Rather, they produce virtual space in which women performers and their admirers can fantasmatically interact in a public sphere that is otherwise accessible to a relative few. Understanding that this public space is also a scene of performance of female sexualities goes a considerable way in helping us understand why there has been so much resistance to recognizing the complex eroticism of Cornell's boxes—why many interpreters of these eloquent provocations to thought and desire have felt compelled to render them mute and immobile.

Not knowing whether to laugh or cry is a classic affective dilemma. The mixed sense of pain, absurdity, and ridiculousness that has been the common emotional lot of protoqueer children and adolescents over the past century has probably made many queer adults less patient than we might otherwise be with neat academic distinctions between the comic and the tragic. The intensity and unpredictability with which these two supposedly discrete dramatic modes can interact with each other is a primary concern of the following exploration of relations between two theatrical renaissances in New York, that of the Yiddish theater of the turn of the century and the queer theater of the 1960s and after.

"The accent of the very ultimate future, in the States, may be destined to become the most beautiful on the globe and the very music of humanity," Henry James writes in The American Scene, "but whatever we shall know it for," he goes on, "certainly, we shall not know it for English. . . ."[1] James rarely indulged in science fiction, so his speculation here about the transformation or supersession of English in the United States by some other language or languages in "the very ultimate future" strikes an odd note in a text primarily devoted to the author's impressions of America on his return to it after a twenty-year absence. However, a context can be provided for this by noting that James made this remark apropos of the English he heard being spoken as he sat in the Cafe Royal, on the Lower East Side, a favorite resort at the time of Jewish journalists, artists, playwrights, and actors. What was James hearing, and how did he come to be in this place?

It would be wrong to assume—as readers probably have often done— that the languages James was hearing that moved him to make this prediction were primarily Yiddish and Yiddish-accented English. According to Nahma Sandrow, the leading English-language historian of the Yiddish theater, the Cafe Royal at the turn of the century was a principal social headquarters of New York's Russian Jewish intelligentsia, and the dominant languages spoken there were Russian and Russian-accented English. "These intellectuals respected Russian as the language of the Russian people and as the vehicle of a great literature," she writes; "they sweated to learn English: but they scorned Yiddish as the *jargón* of pietism, lullabies, and *shund* [Yiddish for "trash"]."[2]

James's host on his visit to the Lower East Side was Jacob Gordin, who had made himself into the Yiddish theater's leading playwright in the preceding decade.[3] Growing up in the Ukraine, Gordin spoke and wrote Russian more comfortably than Yiddish, and as a teenager began publishing articles and other writings in Russian newspapers. Arriving in New York in 1891 at the age of thirty-eight, a refugee from the czarist police with a wife and eight children, Gordin still found writing in Yiddish hard work, but writing for one of the new Yiddish newspapers on the Lower East Side was the job he found available, so he took it.

Gordin and his fellow Russian Jewish intellectuals were contemptuous of the popular Yiddish theater, which at the time was only in its second decade, and still consisted primarily of slapdash adaptations of old and new theatrical classics, clunky operettas set in a vague romantic past, and creaky domestic melodramas. This theater, which had a large and fervent audience composed of both lettered and unlettered working folk, shamelessly mixed elements from the theatrical grab-bag: high tragedy and low comedy, stagey heroics and patter songs, ritualized "business" and antic improvisation.

Gordin saw his first Yiddish play the year he arrived in New York. Both repulsed and excited by the spectacle, he set to work on his first contribution to the theater, which was produced later that year. Subsequent plays of his—*God, Man, and Devil, The Jewish King Lear, Mirele Efros*—became the backbone of the Yiddish repertory and the signature roles of some of its most popular stars: Jacob P. Adler, Sigmund Feinman, Bertha Kalish, Esther Rokhl Kaminska ("the mother of the Yiddish theater"), David Kessler, Keni Liptzin, Sigmund Mogulesko.

Gordin's struggles to reform the Yiddish theater are legendary. Performers commonly "raised the tone" of language they found too plain, delivered stirring speeches or crowd-pleasing wisecracks *ad libitum*, and eked out their roles by interpolating songs and dances at what were supposed to be moments of gravity.[4] In a marked departure from tradition, Gordin forbade all these practices. He rebuked some of the stars of his plays during performance for reverting to what he saw as their old bad habits, even breaking out of character if he was also in the cast, or railing at them from his box in the theater (thereby at least momentarily contributing to the chaos on which he was otherwise dedicated to imposing order). In 1904, around the time he escorted Henry James through the Lower East Side, Gordin had attempted to establish a theater that would perform his plays in repertory and had seen the venture fail financially. Five years later he was dead, at the age of fifty-six. Actors in the Yiddish theater mourned that without him to show the way, it was "back to the wooden swords and paper crowns" of the Purim plays in which Yiddish theater had had its long gestation.[5]

James appears to have attended two performances of the Yiddish theater during his time in New York. Leon Edel mentions his visiting "a Bowery theatre with the cosmopolite name of Windsor" where, Edel writes, the audience was, to James's eye, full of "alien faces, Moldavian, Galician, Hebraic."[6] Actually, although James mentions "the hue of the Galician cheek, [and] the light of the Moldavian eye" in his account of the occasion in The American Scene, the term "Hebraic" in Edel's list seems to be his own addition; James leaves it at the vaguer and perhaps more euphemistic "Oriental."[7] Edel seems not to realize that the Windsor was a major Yiddish theater at the turn of the century. Hutchins Hapgood, in his classic account of the Lower East Side in his 1902 The Spirit of the Ghetto, mentions in passing that at that time (two or three years before James's visit), the Windsor was under lease to "Professor" Moyshe Hurwitz, known to history as one of the early Yiddish theater's two leading schlockmeisters (the other was Jacob Lateiner).[8]

James describes his attendance at the Windsor at some length in the fifth chapter of The American Scene, "The Bowery and Thereabouts"; he introduces the episode by mentioning "the accident of a visit, one afternoon of the dire mid-winter, to a theatre in the Bowery at which a young actor in whom I was interested had found for the moment a fine melodramatic opportunity."[9] James represents himself as feeling distinctly an outsider, and recalling the native Yankee audiences that had filled the theater when he was a child. His response to the performance itself as he recalls it takes the form of bemusement at the contradiction he sees between the "Oriental public" that now fills the theater and the "superior Yankee machinery" that provides the play with what little point it seems to have: "a wonderful folding bed in which the villain of the piece, pursuing the virtuous heroine round and round the room and trying to leap over it after her, is, at the young lady's touch of a hidden spring, engulfed as in the jaws of a crocodile." What James took away from the occasion was a lingering sense of "a queer, clumsy, wasteful social chemistry." [10]

Apparently on the occasion of his visit to the Lower East Side, Jacob Gordin escorted him to the Yiddish theater as well as to the Cafe Royal. What he saw on that occasion he recalls as "some broad passage of a Yiddish comedy of manners." James again finds himself disturbed, as he had been listening to the languages of the Cafe Royal. Once again, his unease arose from what he perceived as the threat of linguistic mixture and transformation: the stars of the Yiddish theater were beginning to appear in productions in other languages, or, as James puts it, "in a language only definable as not in intention Yiddish—not otherwise definable." This fault, if it was one, was not that of the Yiddish theater performers themselves so much, James claims, as a reflection of turn-of-the-century New York audiences in general, where "auditors seem[ ] to know as little as care to what idiom they suppose[ ] themselves to be listening." "Marked in New York," James concludes, "by many indications, this vagueness of ear as to differences, as to identities, of idiom." [11]

It seems strange that when Gordin escorted James, a major celebrity of the Anglo-American literary world, on a visit to the Yiddish theater, he took him to see a characteristic piece of shund—"trash," vulgar pop theater—rather than to one of his own plays or some other worthy, "artistic" production of some realist Yiddish drama. James soon expressed a desire to depart from the theater. Edel writes, embroidering James's laconic account of the event, "The place was convivial; the ventilation left much to be desired, and after looking at some broad passage of a Yiddish comedy of manners he walked out—'it was a scent, literally, not further to be followed.' " [12] Did the theater and/or the comedy James and Gordin dropped in on actually stink, or did James's unease conduce him to respond with his own "broad" display of airy anti-Semitism? James's views of life in New York and in the United States as a whole in 1904–5 are fairly uniformly pessimistic, especially with regard to the emergence of mass culture in this country, but his recurrent negative responses to New York's Jewish masses are notably more visceral than his responses to any other group—except perhaps the sharp disgust he had privately professed with Oscar Wilde ("a tenth-rate cad") at the time of his arrest and trial ten years earlier.

James was in some ways very much a product of New York's antebellum Anglo patriciate, and his often patronizing and stereotyping remarks about Jews, in his published and private writings, were echoed by Edith Wharton and others of his fellow expatriate New Yorkers. Leon Edel in his familiar role as James's principal apologist has defended James against the charge of anti-Semitism with regard to his extended characterization of the "swarms" of Jews he unhappily observes on the Lower East Side; while this matter deserves closer attention than Edel gives it, other narratives Edel makes available in the course of his biography of James, such as James's disagreement with his friend Paul Bourget over what he saw as Bourget's indefensible attitude toward the Dreyfus affair, do suggest that while James shared some of the unexamined anti-Semitism of his class, he was quite capable of thinking otherwise—at least about goings-on in countries other than the United States and cities other than his native New York.[13]

However deplorable—and typical—James's attitudes toward Jews and Jewish culture may have been, what he thought of as his "artist's" curiosity about the world and its ways led him sometimes beyond such limitations; one can hardly imagine Henry Adams's or Edith Wharton's making such a visit to the Lower East Side or seeking out Yiddish plays and playwrights. Perhaps also his fascination with theater and actors contributed to his interest in the newly emergent Yiddish stage. And we should not ignore James's professed motive in making his visit to the Windsor Theater: to see "a young actor in whom [he] was interested." Although James is not one of the many authors whom Daniel Itzkovitz analyzes in his groundbreaking study of relations between Jewishness and queerness in twentieth-century American literature and culture, it was Itzkovitz's work on these imbrications that first suggested to me that James's relation of attraction-repulsion to the Lower East Side might be connected with his complex and conflicted relation to male-male homoerotic desire and the subcultural formations through which such desire began to be articulated and publicized in the closing decades of the nineteenth century.[14]

Absent from The American Scene, as it is from any history of the Yiddish theater that I have seen, is any consideration of the matter with which historian George Chauncey opens his book Gay New York: the Bowery in particular and the Lower East Side in general were, at the time of James's visit and during the early decades of peak activity in the Yiddish theater, also the city's chief (in Chauncey's phrase) "haven and spectacle" for male "degenerates" and male prostitutes. "Paresis Hall" and "Little Bucks," located across the street from each other on the Bowery at Fifth Street, were among the half-dozen saloons or dance halls in the area singled out by an investigator in 1899, along with Manilla Hall, the Palm Club, the Black Rabbit, and Samuel Bickard's Artistic Club, where men gathered who "act[ed] effeminately; most of them are painted and powdered; they are called Princess this and Lady So and So and the Duchess of Marlboro, and get up and sing as women, and dance; ape the female character; call each other sisters and take people out for immoral purposes." [15] The full range of such performances occurred not only in these half-dozen notorious resorts, but, by the turn of the century, had gone on for years in the heart of the Jewish tenement world. Chauncey writes:

> Billy McGlory had realized as early as the late 1870s that he could further the infamy of Armory Hall, his enormous dance hall on Hester Street at the corner of Elizabeth, by hiring fairies — powdered, rouged, and sometimes even dressed in women's clothes — as entertainers. Circulating through the crowd, they sang, danced, and sometimes joined the best-paying customers in their curtained booths to thrill or disgust them with the sort of private sexual exhibitions (or "circuses") normally offered only by female prostitutes. [16]

It is of course doubtful that anyone would have escorted Henry James, and probably equally doubtful that he would have found his own way, to such "low dives," but they were only one particularly pungent set of sites of possible male-male erotic interaction, the lower range of what was no doubt a larger network of public and semipublic spaces — streets, parks, clubs, bars, theater and hotel lobbies, public baths, waiting rooms in train stations — where men cruised each other, sometimes with a mind to finding sex, sometimes just for the pleasure of seeing one's interested and appreciative gaze returned.

According to Edel and subsequent chroniclers of his life, James seems in later middle age — that is, at the turn of the century, at the very time he revisited New York — to have lost most if not all of his earlier circumspection about expressing (in letters, in physical gestures) his strong affection and desire for a number of his young male friends and admirers (Hendrik Andersen, Jocelyn Persse, Rupert Brooke, Hugh Walpole). But, as I shall discuss below, James manifested at many points in his writing, some of it published long before the turn of the century, a highly developed and fairly outspoken appreciation of male good looks and erotic desirability. Part of the effect of Edel's influential representation of James as having "discovered" the possibility of having romantic relationships with other men only late in life has been to divert attention away from the considerable variety of kinds of male-male eros that impel much of James's writing from well before the turn of the century.[17]

While James's biographers and critics have for the most part become increasingly open to considering how same-sex desire may have circulated in his milieu and informed much of his writing, no such opening has yet been made with respect to the performers or playwrights of the Yiddish theater.[18] Almost every account rehearses classic smoking-room stories about male sexual prowess and promiscuity applied to the legends of the theater's most popular leading men—Jacob Adler and Boris Thomashefsky. Still, it seems appropriate to assume that queer desire between men and between women on the Yiddish stage occurred with its usual high frequency among a social group with significant numbers of young members, many of them recently arrived in the big city, who were often alienated and in flight from their biological families and religious and cultural traditions.

However, rather than outing this or that star of the Yiddish theater, it would be productive to consider one of them as an example of the kind of erotics of spectatorship, stardom, and fandom that Richard Dyer, Miriam Hansen, and other historians of film culture and female and/or queer spectatorship have taught us to recognize.[19] The aforementioned Boris Thomashefsky participated in the founding of Yiddish theater, first in Eastern Europe and then in its earliest days in New York, while still a boy soprano playing female parts (women were not at first permitted onto the Yiddish stage, and boys played their roles). As the theater itself rapidly developed into a going concern, Thomashefsky became its first matinee idol, specializing in the princely heroic roles in low-budget musical-historical extravaganzas that were *shund* at its most intense. In the early years of the theater, the problem of how to stand out from the other leading actors seemed to have simple solutions—or so Thomashefsky recalls: "If Kessler wore a big hat with a long feather . . . Adler wore a bigger hat with three feathers and a gold scarf. . . . I piled on colored stockings, coats, crowns, swords, shields, bracelets, earrings, turbans. Next to me they looked like common soldiers. . . . If they rode in on a real horse, I had a golden chariot drawn by two horses. If they killed an enemy, I killed an army." [20] Thomashefsky soon distinguished himself not only by his propensity for piling on the costumes but also for tossing them off—this latter move apparently enthralling his legions of fans even more deeply. Heavy but shapely in his youth, he played many of his big scenes (and posed for photographs and posters) stripped to the waist and clad in flesh-colored tights. Passing on the theatrical lore of the time, Sandrow says "respectable people" worried about the effect of the spectacle of his "luscious calves" and "his soft and luxuriant masculinity" on "the modesty of American Jewish womanhood." [21] But Thomashefsky no doubt had his male fans, too, some of them devouring his very bodily performances with no less avidity and fervor than their female relatives and friends. Not all the preening, peacocking, desiring, and admiring that was going on among males on the Lower East Side was confined to Paresis Hall.

In 1898, James had seen his first film, seventy minutes of the Corbett-Fitzsimmons world championship prizefight, and he had "quite revelled" in it, by his own testimony.[22] So we need not assume that he was insusceptible to the beefy charms exhibited by performers like Thomashefsky. And James was disarmingly forthright in his theater reviews about the frank appraisals he and his fellow theatergoers made of the physical appearance of such actors as young H. B. Conway, whose "first claim to distinction is his remarkably good looks, which may be admired, along with those of other professional beauties, at half the photograph shops in London." [23] As for the male stars of the French stage themselves, James writes, "manly beauty is but scantily represented at the Théâtre Français. . . ." Only Jean Mounet-Sully (who had been Bernhardt's lover a few years earlier) "may be positively commended for his fine person"; indeed, James goes farther, to say that the young actor is "from the scenic point of view, an Adonis of the first magnitude" (73).

James, it would seem, was capable of enjoying a wide range of kinds of performances of male prowess and beauty, from Corbett and Fitzsimmons to Mounet-Sully. We may not be able to discover at this point the identity of the actor James went out one "dire midwinter" afternoon to see on the Lower East Side, but it is clear from James's account of the young man's performance that whatever pleasures he may have taken in it were far from unalloyed in this instance. James's elaborate indications in *The American Scene* of his impressions of the (to him) strange meeting of "Yankee" mechanical efficiency onstage with the exotically "Oriental" appearance and demeanor of the audience raise the possibility that it was perhaps not only linguistic crossings, mixings, and passings that may have troubled James on his visits to the Lower East Side. The "queer, clumsy, wasteful social chemistry" that bothered him about the audience at the Windsor Theater, or the "vagueness of ear as to the difference, as to identities, of idiom" that disturbed him about New York audiences in general: both these phrases suggest that somewhere in James's attraction toward and repulsion from these scenes there is a sense of uneconomical, nonreproductive social relations between persons insufficiently attuned to a precise knowledge of, and commitment to maintaining, separate and distinct "identities" and "idiom[s]." "Queer, clumsy, wasteful" are James's anxious terms for the Yiddish theater, betraying a depth of disturbance on his part that may make us wonder if James's violently mixed response to it may not have been more genuinely and powerfully an erotic response than were the relatively straightforward pleasures he took in watching a prizefight or the handsome young leading man of the *Comédie Française.*

James's professed unhappiness about the supersession of English by other languages in New York or in the United States sits oddly with the rich and complicated relations of his own writing to any monolingual or monocultural model of language, English in particular. In his private correspondence, and to a lesser but still substantial degree in his published fiction, a host of (mostly) French terms perform such a crucial expressive function that the reader devoid of a knowledge of upper-class French and English slang of the turn of the century may often be "left hanging fire" as to what a sentence or a passage in James's writing is about, or what its exact tone may be; indeed, many students of late-nineteenth-century Franco- and Anglo-American cultural hybridity have picked up as much of this long since vanished argot as we have principally from reading James.

Nor was James's visit to the Cafe Royal by any means his first or only experience of polyglossia. Reviewing a performance by the Italian tragedian Tommaso Salvini in the March 1883 *Atlantic Monthly*, James deplored — in an otherwise admiring review — that the great actor had performed the respective title roles of *Macbeth*, *Othello*, and *King Lear* in Italian while the entire supporting cast "answered him in a language which was foreign only in that it sometimes failed to be English" (169). James's formulation here anticipates his criticism of the Yiddish performers twenty years later for performing "in a language only definable as not in *intention* Yiddish." Interestingly, some years earlier, in a review he wrote for the *Nation*, James had mentioned without negative comment that when Madame Ristori appeared in the United States in 1875, she performed (excerpts from?) her most famous roles (Medea, and Schiller's Mary Stuart) in her native Italian (29). Four years later, reviewing for the same journal a series of performances by Sarah Bernhardt and the *Comédie Française*, then making a short visit to London, James writes: "The appeal has been made to a foreign audience, an audience whose artistic perceptions are the reverse of lively, whose ear does not respond quickly to the magic French utterance, and whose mind does not easily find its way among the intricacies of French sentiment; and yet the triumph has been perfect, and the Comédie Française and the London public have been thoroughly pleased with each other" (125). Unlike the "Oriental public" and the "wonderful folding bed" onstage at the Windsor Theater, which join to produce what James calls "a queer, clumsy, wasteful social chemistry," this time the theater and its imperfectly comprehending audience form a perfect match.

At least, that is what James begins his extensive review by announcing. But a troubling excess soon manifests itself in his account of the success of the *Comédie*. That is "the extraordinary vogue of Mademoiselle Sarah Bernhardt." James had first reviewed Bernhardt's acting in 1876, in a letter from Paris to the *New York Tribune*, when he saw her play a mixed-blood heroine ("the daughter of a mulatto slave-girl and a Carolinian planter") in *L'Etrangère* by Alexandre Dumas *fils*. James frequently mentions Bernhardt's performances at the *Comédie* over the next several years, and his comments are extremely mixed: she possesses "extraordinary talent" (63) and "extraordinary intelligence and versatility" (64), but she is "rather weak" in some aspects of her art (78), which is itself only "small art" in comparison with an older and greater actress, Madame Plessy (63). In his review of her performances in London, he seems finally to articulate the reason for his strong reservations about the actress: while she is an "artist" in James's view, she has also become a "celebrity," but not of the ordinary sort. She has a positive genius for generating publicity about herself; "she may, indeed, be called the muse of the newspaper" (129). Her most recent publicity concerns her decision to resign her official membership in the Comédie Française and to begin planning what would turn out to be the first of her tours of the United States. James predicted for her, with blinding accuracy, a "triumphant career" in the States exceeding anything she had previously done: "She is too American," he wrote, "not to succeed in America" (129).[24]

As Sander L. Gilman and Carol Ockman have recently reminded us, in separate articles, Bernhardt was widely regarded as the most notorious and sensational embodiment of the contradictory meanings imputed to Jewish femininity throughout the fin de siècle.[25] Regarded as being in some ways a reincarnation of Rachel, the Jewish superstar tragedienne of the first half of the nineteenth century, the two women held a uniquely charged place in misogynistic and anti-Semitic discourse: tubercular and otherwise "diseased," ruthless manipulators and exploiters of male lust and gullibility, these celebrated actresses look in the lurid light of these representations astonishingly like the "fairie" prostitutes who flounced through the Bowery taverns and allegedly performed "live sex acts" in the curtained booths of a Hester Street dance hall. The intensely mixed feelings James expressed toward Bernhardt's persona are of a piece with his interested but essentially unhappy response to the powerful Jewish presence in his childhood neighborhood around and below East Fourteenth Street in Manhattan, and his similarly "mixed" (intensely confused) relation to the publicization of erotic desire between men in the 1880s and 1890s.

Bernhardt made her American debut in New York the year after she left the Comédie. She and her company performed an entire repertory of plays in French. As we have seen, visiting European actresses like Madame Ristori had given programs in foreign languages in the United States before then. What is different about Bernhardt's relation to her American audiences is that she immediately became a mass phenomenon; the Europhiles and connoisseurs of acting who attended Ristori's American performances were supplemented in Bernhardt's case by tens of thousands of people who would never otherwise have attended a performance in French. One can imagine how James would have responded to the audiences who flocked to vast auditoriums and circus tents to see Bernhardt on her successive American tours. The majority of them could not follow whatever Bernhardt was saying in her beautiful and extraordinarily expressive voice, but they seem to have been thrilled by the spectacle of her grandly intimate acting style, the music of her declamation, the gorgeous and fashion-setting costumes and sets. For many of them, going to see this notorious French actress may have seemed slightly transgressive and adventurous, so they might have had the unusual experience of going slumming and attending a glittering social event at the same time. A Hartford audience, handed a synopsis of Phèdre by inattentive ushers as they entered the theater, thought they were sitting through Racine's masterpiece while Bernhardt was actually performing a new vehicle written for herself entitled Froufrou. No one complained.[26]

It was not only the peanut-crunching crowd that seems to have felt that something precious was being transmitted to them through Bernhardt's performance, through her voice and person, even (or especially) if they did not know enough French to follow her lines or the plot of the play. On her own American (lecture) tour about forty years after the event, Gertrude Stein recalled having seen Bernhardt perform in San Francisco:

> I must have been about sixteen years old when Bernhardt came to San Francisco and stayed two months. I knew a little french of course but really it did not matter, it was all so foreign and her voice being so varied and it all being so french I could rest in it untroubled. And I did.
>
> It was better than opera because it went on. It was better than the theatre because you did not have to get acquainted. The manners and customs of the french theatre created a thing in itself and it existed in and for itself as the poetical plays had that I used so much to read, there were so many characters just as there were in those plays and you did not have to know them they were so foreign, and the foreign scenery and actuality replaced the poetry and the voices replaced the portraits. It was for me a very simple direct and moving pleasure.[27]

Typical as Stein's decision to relax and enjoy, to go with the flow of, Bernhardt's performances apparently was, few playgoers could have had as much at stake as the young Stein may have had in the spectacle of Bernhardt's being acclaimed as a genius despite, or even perhaps in part because of, the incomprehensibility of her performances to her American audiences. Stein would herself come to constitute the limit case of how incomprehensible an artist could be and still attain major celebrity in the United States and Paris in the years after Bernhardt's death in 1923. Fascinated with the writing and career of Henry James, Stein nonetheless did not at all share his defensive and protective attitudes toward the "purity" of the English language.

The spectre and spectral voice of Bernhardt also haunt at least two of the formative, crystallizing moments in the recent history of queer theater. In the early 1970s, James Roy Eichelberger, a young gay actor, the son of Amish Mennonite parents, who was paying a brief visit to New York from the regional repertory theater in Providence, Rhode Island, where he was then employed, wandered into the Lincoln Center Library for the Performing Arts. There, as part of an exhibition of historical theatrical materials, a gramophone had been set up to play a wax-cylinder recording of Bernhardt performing a *tirade* from Racine's *Phèdre*—which was, along with *La Dame aux camélias*, her greatest role. Eichelberger later recalled being electrified by the expressive powers of Bernhardt's voice and vocal performance: "It changed my life. I listened to it over and over. Every time it stopped I pressed the button again. . . . I figured it was time to go in another direction. I tried to go back to the nineteenth century, to that 'declaiming,' to where you take human speech . . . one step further." [28] Deciding to abandon his career in more conventional theater, Eichelberger began to perform a solo version of a script he had cut and pasted from Robert Lowell's translation of *Phèdre*, first back in Providence and then in New York, where he soon settled. He renamed himself "Ethyl" Eichelberger, earned a cosmetologist's license, and began to support himself by doing hair and makeup for downtown theatrical companies. Over the next twenty years, he would perform a long series of "Strong Women of History," ranging from Medea and Jocasta and Nefertiti to Elizabeth I, Lucrezia Borgia, and Carlotta, Empress of Mexico. He also appeared in a number of productions at Charles Ludlam's Theatre of the Ridiculous. He was for some years Ludlam's partner and lover.

A decade before Eichelberger's discovery, Ludlam had himself experienced a transformation from a mediocre undergraduate student of theater at Hofstra University to a full-blown *tragédienne*. This life-altering change he attributed to having seen by chance on television a broadcast of Greta Garbo's *Camille*, while he himself was bedridden and semidelirious owing to a passing illness. As soon as he was recovered, according to his own account, he began to collect photographs and recordings of great actresses in the role, including Bernhardt, who was perhaps the most celebrated of all its exponents. Within ten years or so, Ludlam would himself become New York's favorite *dame aux camélias*, playing the role hundreds of times.[29]

Following in the traces of the heroic and mock-heroic playwrights and performers of the classic Yiddish theater, Ludlam was perhaps the most accomplished and inspired *pasticheur* and *bricoleur* of the theater in our day (the Yiddish theater spoke of pulling plays together from an implausibly various set of sources, high, low, and "out there," as "baking" a play; the baking tended to be done rapidly at a high heat). Ludlam's work as playwright, performer, and (as he was sometimes called) "the last of the great Victorian actor-managers" might have often recalled, for anyone who knew of them, the practices of the divo-impresarios of Second Avenue. It manifests many ties to the Yiddish theater and its performance traditions, explicitly, as in his 1977 mock-homage to Wagner, *Der Ring Gott Farblonjet*, or more implicitly in his general practice of creating shows by "collaging" an outrageous assortment of theatrical texts and modes—Marlowe, Molière, and Ibsen colliding with "blue" burlesque-house humor, silent-movie and vaudeville shtick, and the stylistic tics of film noir, Russian ballet, and late-night-TV commercials:

> CHESTER: [Dressed in leopard skin] (*Lets out a Tarzan cry then speaks in an almost expressionless voice. He is no actor*) This is The Artificial Jungle. Bring love into your home with a cuddly pet or add a touch of the exotic with a home aquarium, tropical fish, a snake, lizard, or even a tarantula. We have everything you need to bring adventure into your living room. Or take home a cuddly hamster, rat, mouse, or gerbil. Whatever your choice we have all the accessories to turn your home into an artificial jungle too. Open six days a week except Sunday. Conveniently located at 966 Rivington Street in lower Manhattan.[30]

Interviewed by Neil Bartlett around 1988, Eichelberger called himself "a tragedienne" working in "the American tradition"—by which he meant he considered himself a daughter of Rachel and Bernhardt, but one who had come up as a performer through a full range of the vernacular performing traditions in this country: "When I was a kid I was a tapdancer, and I used to see (God this is showing my age) the travelling minstrel shows. I come out of a really grassroots performing tradition, and it is a living tradition, it's only the academics that give us trouble." [31]

"It's vaudeville, it's burlesque and it's Yiddish theater," Eichelberger goes on to say of the main components of this "living tradition" he saw himself as embodying and transmitting. Of the Yiddish theater in particular, he says:

> those actors are especially important to me, you know that down here [Eichelberger was speaking to Bartlett in the building where the Theatre of the Ridiculous was then located, near Sheridan Square, in the Village] was Yiddish Broadway, especially their tragedy, that was an important tradition here in the East Village, on Second Avenue. People do view me more now as comedy, well if people think of me like that then that's fine, I've found that if they laugh then that gives me a chance to go on and perform. Let them laugh, it's fine.[32]

Ludlam made similar remarks about playing roles like Marguerite Gautier in *Camille:* "When the audience laughed at my pain, the play seemed more tragic to me than when they took it seriously."[33]

When Eichelberger and Ludlam make these observations they are taking up—as they often did—a matter with its own long performance tradition. The trope of the audience's mistaking tragedy for comedy or vice versa, or of the author or actor's willfully combining or confusing the two, is a constant in Western theories of spectatorship, authorship, and performance. At the very end of Plato's *Symposium,* when everyone else has passed out or gone home, Socrates begins to argue "that the same man might be capable of writing both comedy and tragedy—that the tragic poet might be a comedian as well." Marx's correction of Hegel in the opening lines of the *Eighteenth Brumaire* ("Hegel remarks somewhere that all great, world-historical facts and personages occur, as it were, twice. He has forgotten to add: the first time as tragedy, the second as farce") famously gave the old generic distinction/confusion renewed dynamism as markers of historical repetitions with a difference (or with a vengeance).

Marx was not the only stagestruck nineteenth-century writer to ponder the relations between tragedy, comedy (or farce), and various histories. Charles Lamb, in his essay, "My First Play," recalls as a small boy sitting at Congreve's comedy *The Way of the World* "as grave as a judge," mistaking "the hysteric affectations" of Lady Wishfort for "some solemn tragic passion," apparently oblivious, or at least indifferent, to the laughter of the rest of the audience. He remembers sitting through the "clownery and pantaloonery" of a pantomime he was taken to see during the same season with similarly fascinated gravity. I have already, in the opening pages of this book, alluded to the aged Henry James's account of his memory of himself as a small child seeing a production of *Uncle Tom's Cabin*. He remembers the event as "a brave beginning for a consciousness that was to be nothing if not mixed." The most significant part of the mixture is for him his sense of enjoying above all "the fun, the real fun" of his and his companions' unwillingness to discriminate between "the tragedy, the drollery, the beauty" of a crude but nevertheless powerful performance. The great pathos of the story *and* the clunky mechanical creaking of the "ice floes" over which Eliza escapes are both indispensable elements of the full effect of the experience for James.[34]

Like James, Ludlam and Eichelberger had been fascinated with the effects of theatricality in its many modes from early childhood. Ludlam saw a Punch and Judy show at the Mineola (Long Island) Fair in 1949, when he was six years old, and set up his own puppet theater at home soon thereafter. The following year he appeared in his first school play, *Santa in Blunderland*. Puppets, animated cartoons, comic books, Hollywood movies of the 1940s, and dressing up as a girl for Halloween were all formative of his theatrical sensibility, but so also was a voracious appetite for the classical dramatic literature of the past four centuries. Shakespeare, Molière, Punch and Judy, Tom and Jerry, Norma Desmond, and Maria Montez: the young Ludlam channeled them all. "Classics seemed to be the alternative to theatre as 'show business,' " he wrote, "although I did have a kind of show business fantasy, too." [35] Similarly, as a child in Pekin, Illinois, in the 1950s, Eichelberger studied piano and tap dancing, composed music, formed a song-and-dance team with a friend, and, in the fifth grade, played the witch in the class play, *Hansel and Gretel*. "My mother made me a big black crepe paper dress and a big black pointed hat. She put pink yarn on it for hair." "I've never recovered," he commented as an adult after telling Neil Bartlett the story.[36] When I saw his production of *Medea* at the S.N.A.F.U. bar in New York circa 1980, the aggressive versatility of his performance was nearly overwhelming: his Medea combined elements of Kabuki with old-fashioned hoofing and accordion-playing. When her rival in love attempted to reason with her, Medea bombarded her with small but deafening charges of live explosives (cherry bombs), sending patrons seated in the front half of the performance space scurrying for cover, hands over ears.

This kind of devotion to a literally volatile "theater of mixed means" has generally not found favor with theorists of drama and performance. Practitioners since Plautus (who called his *Amphitryon* a tragicomedy) have been eager to establish the indispensability of the notion of an unproblematically "mixed" genre called "tragicomedy." Consider this exemplarily academic commentary on the matter:

> What has tragicomedy actually contributed to the modern drama since the Renaissance? Tragicomedy, whether actually so called or not, has always been the backbone of the modern drama, which has always been a compromise between classical tradition and the modern way of life, and a compromise between classical tragedy and classical comedy. . . . The term is now antiquated . . . but most of the significant modern dramas still occupy a middle ground between tragedy and comedy.[37]

In this simple academic equation, tragedy + comedy = tragicomedy; "compromise" and "a middle ground" punctually present themselves as needed, and there is no contradiction remaining anywhere in the process. Introducing Marsden Hartley's *Adventures in the Arts* (1921), Waldo Frank complicates the matter by mapping tragedy, comedy, and tragicomedy back onto the kind of child-adult distinction dear to the heart of a first-generation Romantic like Lamb: "Tragedy and Comedy are adult. The child's world is tragicomic." In doing so, Frank finesses the issue in a way I want to resist. The standard edition of the classic script of puppet-theater farce, first published in 1828, seems to me to get something right that writers like Frank may tend to reduce to a simple "fusion" too quickly: the book in question is entitled—take your pick—*The Tragical Comedy or Comical Tragedy of Punch and Judy*. Not tragicomedy *tout simple*, but the unresolved contradiction "tragical comedy or comical tragedy" seems richly evocative to me of a crucially important aspect of the epistemology of queer childhood, the recognition of how thoroughly permeated with each other these two performative modes—one associated with loss, psychic pain, mourning and grieving, and the other with the powers of wit, laughter, and ridicule—can be.

The anecdotal history of the Yiddish theater is predictably rife with such tragedy-comedy confusions. When, for example, Adler made his much-heralded theatrical debut in New York, he declined to appear in Gutskov's *Uriel Acosta*, which would soon become one of his signature roles, and appeared instead in a comedy called *The Ragpicker*. But the audience, primed to see a great new tragedian, took the play seriously (as Lamb had done at his first plays), leaving themselves and their would-be new star performatively stranded at evening's end. On other occasions, the "confusion" functioned as part of the compact between artists and audience; Carl Van Vechten recalled in 1920 having seen, years before, a fine production of Gorky's *The Lower Depths*, a "sordid tragedy, unredeemed by a single ray of humour . . . played for comedy" at the popular actor David Kessler's theater.[38]

More often, it seems, the "confusion" was the consequence of neither a special understanding nor a misunderstanding on the audience's part, but of a general, although by no means universal, appreciation—shared by audiences, playwrights, and performers alike—of the intensely "mixed" and fertile origins of the Yiddish theater in the popular hybrid theatrical mode of *shund*, "trashy," "rubbishy," "something-for-everybody" theater. Theater historians offer various folk-etymologies for the term *shund*; some say the term is related to *shande*, Yiddish for "shame," while others trace the word back to *shindn*, "to flay a horse."[39] Unqualified to judge the merits of these, I want to hold onto shame and horse-flaying while adding a third possible etymology: Nahum Stutchkoff suggests that the word *shund* may be related to the phrase *miesse meshina*, "ugly or unfortunate fate or death."[40] Leo Rosten writes, "The phrase is widely used by Jews either as a lament ('What a *miesse meshina* befell him!') or as a curse ('May he suffer a *miesse meshina!* ')."[41]

What the great tragic *and* comic performance traditions of Yiddish and queer theaters remind us is that in this rapidly passing century, impulses to curse and lament and impulses to laugh and play do not necessarily arise at any safe distance from each other. Impulses toward grief and toward mockery and self-mockery disorient our ordinary sense of distance and difference between the playhouse (an archaic term for theater) and scenes of death and loss—between the house of mirth and the house of mourning.

Rosten notes that the Yiddish *meshina* ("ugly or unfortunate") derives from Hebrew *meshuna*, meaning "unusual, abnormal." Weird, wicked—queer? "Ah, what queer fates befell them." "May I (you, s/he) die a queer death." At the end of the twentieth century, Jews and queers of all kinds are (un)fortunately richly well-equipped to understand the varied performative valences of that utterance—as curse, as lament, as blessing, as wish.

NOTES

Introduction

1 The theoretical literature on various aspects of visual representation is massive, extending from Jacques Lacan's work on vision as a function of language, specularity, and the
gaze to Maurice Merleau-Ponty's on vision and perception, Roland Barthes's on photography, and Jacques Derrida's on painting, the parergon, and the cartouche. Even a
very partial bibliography of recent American work on these topics must include Michael
Fried, *Absorption and Theatricality: Painting and Beholder in the Age of Diderot* (Berkeley: University of California Press, 1980); Susan Buck-Morss, *The Dialectics of Seeing: Walter Benjamin
and the Arcades Project* (Cambridge, Mass.: MIT Press, 1989); Jonathan Crary, *Techniques of
the Observer: On Vision and Modernity in the Nineteenth Century* (Cambridge, Mass.: MIT Press,
1990); Mieke Bal, *Reading "Rembrandt": Beyond the Word-Image Opposition* (Cambridge: Cambridge University Press, 1991); Rosalind E. Krauss, *The Optical Unconscious* (Cambridge,
Mass.: MIT Press, 1993). Three important recent collections of theoretical work are
Visual Culture: Images and Interpretations, ed. Norman Bryson, Michael Ann Holly, and Keith
Moxey (Hanover, N.H.: University Press of New England, 1994); Lucien Taylor, ed., *Visu-
alizing Theory* (New York: Routledge, 1994); *Vision and Textuality,* ed. Stephen Melville and
Bill Readings (Durham, N.C.: Duke University Press, 1995). Linda Williams has gathered
a selection of recent work on visual representation, subjectivity, and film spectatorship
in *Viewing Positions: Ways of Seeing Film* (New Brunswick, N.J.: Rutgers University Press,
1995). Queer theory, queer practice, and visual culture intersect in *Queer Looks: Perspectives
on Lesbian and Gay Film and Video,* ed. Martha Gever, John Greyson, and Pratibha Parmar
(New York: Routledge, 1993). Thomas Waugh explores the histories of gay-male sexuality and visual culture in *Hard to Imagine: Gay-Male Eroticism in Photography and Film from
Their Beginnings to Stonewall* (New York: Columbia University Press, 1996).

2 Roland Barthes, "Ravishment," *A Lover's Discourse,* trans. Richard Howard (New York: Hill
& Wang, 1978; Paris, 1977), p. 192.

3 Henry James, *A Small Boy and Others* (New York: Scribner's, 1913), p. 104. Hereafter cited
parenthetically in the text.

4 Deborah Solomon tells the story of Cornell's boyhood fascination with Houdini in *Utopia Parkway: The Life and Work of Joseph Cornell* (New York: Farrar, Straus, and Giroux, 1997), pp. 27–28.

5 See Ruth Brandon, *The Life and Many Deaths of Harry Houdini* (New York: Kodansha, 1995), p. 7, and illustrations 13, 20, and 21.

6 Besides widespread feminist critique of the fantasy of the invulnerable male body, a number of critics and theorists have launched critiques of the presumed whiteness of the "desirable" male body, and of the representational appropriation of the bodies of men of color in elite and popular culture. For the latter, see, for example, Richard Fung, "Looking for My Penis: The Eroticized Asian in Gay Video Porn," and Kobena Mercer, "Skin Head Sex Thing: Racial Difference and the Homoerotic Imaginary," both in *How Do I Look?: Queer Film and Video*, ed. Bad Object-Choices (Seattle: Bay Press, 1991).

7 Esther Newton, *Mother Camp: Female Impersonators in America* (Chicago: University of Chicago Press, 1972); Severo Sarduy, *Written on a Body*, trans. Carol Maier (New York: Lumen Books, 1989); Judith Butler, *Gender Trouble: Feminism and the Subversion of Identity* (New York: Routledge, 1990), and "Imitation and Gender Insubordination," in *Inside/Out: Lesbian Theories, Gay Theories*, ed. Diana Fuss (New York: Routledge, 1991), pp. 13–31.

8 *Aurelia*, p. 824, in *Gérard de Nerval: Oeuvres*, ed. Henri Lemaitre, vol. 1 (Paris: Garnier, n.d.).

9 John Preston, "The Theatre of Sexual Initiation," in *Gender in Performance: The Presentation of Difference in the Performing Arts*, ed. Laurence Senelick (Hanover, N.H.: University Press of New England, 1992), pp. 324–35.

ONE A Small Boy and Others

1 For Girard's major formulations of his theory, see "Triangular Desire," the first chapter of *Deceit, Desire, and the Novel: Self and Other in Literary Structure*, trans. Yvonne Freccero (Baltimore: Johns Hopkins University Press, 1965), pp. 1–52; "From Mimetic Desire to the Monstrous Double," in *Violence and the Sacred*, trans. Patrick Gregory (Baltimore: Johns Hopkins University Press, 1977), pp. 143–68; "Mimetic Desire," in *Things Hidden Since the Foundation of the World*, trans. Stephen Bann and Michael Metteer (Stanford: Stanford University Press, 1987), pp. 283–347; and Walter Burkert, René Girard, and Jonathan Z. Smith, *Violent Origins: Ritual Killing and Cultural Formation*, ed. Roger G. Hamerton Kelly (Stanford: Stanford Univ. Press, 1987), esp. pp. 7–20 and 121–29. See also Eve Kosofsky Sedgwick's reformulation of Girard in the opening pages of *Between Men: English Literature and Male Homosocial Desire* (New York: Columbia University Press, 1985), esp. pp. 21–25.

2 Mikkel Borch-Jacobsen, *The Freudian Subject*, trans. Catherine Porter (Stanford: Stanford University Press, 1988), p. 26. Hereafter cited parenthetically in the text.

3 Sigmund Freud, "The 'Uncanny'," in Philip Rieff, ed., *Studies in Parapsychology* (New York: Collier, 1963), pp. 19–60.

4 "The Sandman," in E. T. A. Hoffmann, *Tales of Hoffmann* (Harmondsworth: Penguin, 1982), p. 282. Hereafter cited parenthetically in the text.

5 Lacan equates the phallus with the "copula" in "The signification of the phallus," *Ecrits: A Selection*, trans. Alan Sheridan (New York: Norton, 1977), p. 287.

6   Kyle MacLachlan plays Jeffrey in *Blue Velvet*; Laura Dern, Sandy; Dennis Hopper, Frank; and Isabella Rossellini, Dorothy.

7   Andy Warhol's diary entry for December 15, 1986, reads in part: ". . . Dennis [Hopper] told me the other night that they cut the scene out of *Blue Velvet* where he rapes Dean Stockwell or Dean Stockwell rapes him and there's lipstick on somebody's ass" (*The Andy Warhol Diaries*, ed. Pat Hackett [New York: Warner, 1989], p. 784). Warhol's account of this is obviously somewhat garbled, but it does suggest that Lynch had planned (and he and his actors had perhaps filmed) a more literal male-male rape scene than the "symbolic" one that appears in the film.

8   *The Independent*, 5 January 1899, p. 73; rpt. in *Henry James: The Turn of the Screw*, ed. Robert Kimbrough (New York: Norton, 1966), p. 175. Shoshana Felman discusses this review in *Writing and Madness: Literature/Philosophy/Psychoanalysis*, trans. Martha Noel Evans and the author with the assistance of Brian Massumi (Ithaca: Cornell University Press, 1985), pp. 143–44.

9   Walter Benjamin, *Charles Baudelaire: A Lyric Poet in the Era of High Capitalism*, trans. Harry Zohn (London: Verso, 1983), pp. 46–47.

10 William Thackeray, *Vanity Fair* (New York: New American Library, 1962), p. 257.

11 Citations to the text of "The Pupil" are to Leon Edel's edition of the tale in *The Complete Tales of Henry James*, Vol. 7, 1888–1891 (Philadelphia: Lippincott, 1963). The passage quoted here occurs on p. 409.

12 Joshua Wilner has urged me to consider that it may be more proper to think of the young man Pemberton as the initiate in James's story, rather than the boy Morgan. Yet even if one grants this, James's practice remains radical: if we take Pemberton to be James's initiate, and he is roughly as old as Lynch's Jeffrey (i.e., no longer a boy, definitely a young man), it is nevertheless true of James's two "initiators" (Morgan and his mother) that one of them is hardly more than a child. Frank and Dorothy, the primary initiators in Lynch's film, are by contrast represented as being emphatically no longer young, while Jeffrey's young girlfriend Sandy is conventionally represented as someone who is just outgrowing the role of being an innocent child.

TWO *Initiation into Style*

1   James's relation to homosexual possibility was neither of the high-ethical type advocated by Symonds ("a queer place to plant the standard of duty," James privately commented on one of Symonds's pamphlets in defense of sexual love between men), nor of the blatantly public-performative type embodied and enacted by Wilde. Henry James, letter to Edmund Gosse, 7 January 1893, in *Selected Letters of Henry James to Edmund Gosse, 1882–1915*, ed. Rayburn S. Moore (Baton Rouge: Louisiana State University Press, 1988), p. 90.

2   Recent work in art history by, among others, Thomas Crow, Whitney Davis, Carol Ockman, Alex Potts, and Abigail Solomon-Godeau has very productively reexamined the history of French painting from David to Géricault and Delacroix to tell a story—many stories—that had long fallen into relative obscurity about the uses of the image of the heroic male nude.

3　I quote from Alex Potts, *Flesh and the Ideal: Winckelmann and the Origins of Art History* (New Haven: Yale University Press, 1994), p. 127.

4　Letter of 7 November 1869, in *Henry James: Letters*, ed. Leon Edel (Cambridge: Harvard University Press, 1974), vol. 1, p. 166.

5　Leon Edel, *Henry James: A Life* (New York: Harper and Row, 1985), p. 73.

6　Whitney Davis writes about this in his Winckelmann article (see note 8 below).

7　For an account of some of the roles of classical sculpture in neoclassical art and aesthetic theory, see Francis Haskell and Nicholas Penny, *Taste and the Antique: The Lure of Classical Sculpture 1500–1900* (New Haven: Yale University Press, 1981).

8　Whitney Davis, "Winckelmann's 'Homosexual' Teleologies," in Natalie Boymel Kampen, ed., *Sexuality in Ancient Art* (Cambridge: Cambridge University Press, 1996), pp. 262–76.

9　The dandies of the nineteenth-century metropolises and a few of the elite military corps were two of the small numbers of men who had not acceded to what psychoanalytic theorist J. C. Flugel called "The Great Masculine Renunciation," which he placed at the end of the eighteenth century, in which "men gave up their right to all the brighter, gayer, more elaborate, and more varied forms of ornamentation, leaving these entirely to the use of women. . . . Man abandoned his claim to be considered beautiful." J. C. Flugel, *The Psychology of Clothes* (London: Hogarth Press, 1930), pp. 110–113. The passage quoted occurs on p. 111.

10　Quoted in Leon Edel, *Henry James: The Master* (New York: Lippincott, 1972), p. 57.

11　Quoted in Simon Nowell-Smith, *The Legend of the Master* (New York: Scribner's, 1948), pp. 5 (Sedgwick), 3 (Millar), and 5 (Conrad).

12　Henry James, *A Small Boy and Others* (New York: Scribner's, 1913), pp. 347, 350. Hereafter cited parenthetically in the text.

13　Gautier's description of *Romans of the Decadence* is quoted by Michael Fried in his article, "Thomas Couture and the Theatricalization of Action in Nineteenth-Century French Painting," *Artforum* 13, no. 10 (June 1970): 44.

14　Albert Boime, *Thomas Couture and the Eclectic Vision* (New Haven: Yale University Press, 1980), p. 188.

15　For "power of the wing": Walter Pater, *The Renaissance: Studies in Art and Poetry* (Oxford: Basil Blackwell, 1967), p. 202.

16　Boime, *Thomas Couture and the Eclectic Vision*, p. 111.

17　See, for example, Alex Potts, *Flesh and the Ideal*, p. 118.

18　The name and its story may have come to James again through Louisa May Alcott's *Little Women*. Henry James, Sr., had been a friend of Bronson Alcott, and their two "literary" offspring had become acquainted in youth. The young James had read and reviewed Alcott's early novels—*Moods*, a novel for adult readers, and *Eight Cousins*, one of her children's books—with considerable disapproval, but several literary historians have recently pointed out how her work may have stimulated his own very productive interest in writing about girls and young women. James's review of *Moods* is reprinted in *Moods / Louisa May Alcott*, ed. Sarah Elbert (New Brunswick, N.J.: Rutgers University Press, 1991), pp. 219–24. *Little Women*, especially in its early chapters, makes frequent and significant allusions to *Pilgrim's Progress*, and Chapter 8, in which Jo March realizes for the first time the frightening depths of her capacity for violent anger, is entitled "Jo Meets Apollyon." The temptation to pride, selfishness, rage, and resentment constitute the "Apollyon" Jo must confront when she confesses that she had almost allowed her younger sister to drown out of anger with her after the little girl had destroyed the manuscript of a book Jo was writing.

19 Citations are to Roger Sharrock's edition of *The Pilgrim's Progress* (New York: Penguin, 1965), pp. 102, 105, 106.

20 Eugène Delacroix, letter to Guillemardet, 2 November 1819, quoted by Thomas Crow, *Emulation: Making Artists for Revolutionary France* (New Haven: Yale University Press, 1995), p. 292.

21 Boime, *Thomas Couture and the Eclectic Vision*, p. 158.

22 Crow, *Emulation*, pp. 291–92.

23 Walter Friedlaender, *From David to Delacroix*, trans. Robert Goldwater (New York: Schocken, 1968), p. 101.

24 There is an engraving of Cupid and Psyche by Prud'hon in the National Gallery (London).

25 There were some ways in which their stories overlapped. Gérard and Girodet had both been students of Jacques-Louis David; as aspiring artists, Gérard, Girodet, and Guérin had all competed for the prestigious Prix de Rome in the 1790s and soon thereafter produced paintings that were the sensations of the Salons of the respective years in which they were exhibited; Gérard, Girodet, and Prud'hon had all received important artistic commissions from Napoleon. Nevertheless, their styles and careers were in many ways quite divergent. Girodet had worked in intimate association with David during the Revolutionary years. Guérin was a product of the studio of Regnault, which was seen as a rival to David's. Prud'hon, a provincial and the son of a stonecutter, rose to serve as chief designer of Napoleon's coronation and of his wedding to Marie-Louise. Guérin was an important teacher of several of the leading artists of the subsequent generation, including Delacroix and Géricault.

26 Whitney Davis, "Renunciation of Reaction in Girodet," in *Visual Culture: Images and Interpretations*, ed. Norman Bryson, Michael Ann Holly, and Keith Moxey (Hanover, N.H.: Wesleyan/University Press of New England, 1994), p. 182.

27 Ibid., p. 182.

28 Ibid.

29 The Cupid in Gérard's *Cupid and Psyche* has been described by art historian Thomas Crow as clearly imitating "the *Endymion*'s sealed envelope of flesh," and Crow sees this *Cupid and Psyche* (the one that I believe James means when he speaks of "Prudhon's Cupid and Psyche") as the crucial link between Girodet's *Endymion* and the many imitations of it that followed, importantly including the two Guérin paintings just mentioned. Crow criticizes these imitations for refusing the "public meanings" in which he sees the *Endymion* fully participating. See Thomas Crow, "Revolutionary Activism and the Cult of Male Beauty in the Studio of David," in *Fictions of the French Revolution*, ed. Bernadette Fort (Evanston: Northwestern University Press, 1991), pp. 82–83. Although Crow has little to say about the various kinds of intensely homoerotic charges that impel some of the most powerful of these paintings that participate in the setting of representational terms for

the production and performance of the "public meanings" of the time, a few art historians such as Whitney Davis and Alex Potts have recently begun to insist on the necessity
of acknowledging and analyzing the effects of the articulation and representation of
homoerotic desires on the public life and public art of the period. As Crow and some of
his colleagues have recently demonstrated, many of these "public meanings" are richly
and densely intertextual, linking paintings produced either around the same time or at
quite different historical moments.

30 Davis, "Renunciation," p. 197 n. 15.

31 "But as Psyche wept in fear and trembling on that rocky eminence," Apuleius writes, "the
Zephyr's kindly breeze with its soft stirring wafted the hem of her dress this way and that,
and made its folds billow out. He gradually drew her aloft, and with tranquil breath bore
her slowly downward. She glided down over the sloping side of that high cliff, and he
laid her down in the bosom of the flower-decked turf in the valley below" (The Golden Ass,
closing passage of book 4, trans. P. G. Walsh [New York: Oxford University Press, 1995]).

32 See, for example, James's prefaces to The American, The Aspern Papers, Daisy Miller, and The
Princess Casamassima.

33 Quoted in French Painting 1774–1830: The Age of Revolution, catalog of an exhibition at the
Detroit Institute of the Arts, 1975, p. 570.

34 In speaking of "Prudhon's Cupid and Psyche" James may have also "confusedly" been
signaling toward another celebrated painting of Prud'hon's, entitled The Uplifting of Psyche (L'Enlèvement de Psyché). According to Edmond de Goncourt's catalogue raisonné of Pru-
d'hon's work, this painting was exhibited at the Salon under its full title, Psyche Uplifted by
Zephyrs, making it explicitly intertextual with Young Zephyr, which was also being exhibited
for the first time in the same Salon (1814). The "nine or ten-year-old" (Landon's esti-
mate) boy in Young Zephyr is supplemented in The Uplifting by a younger boy (a baby cupid
who peers out from beneath Psyche's knees) and two older boys, the adolescent zephyrs
who provide the main support for the body of Psyche. The nude Psyche, one hand rest-
ing on her upper chest and the other falling back over her brow, recalls in pose and
demeanor Girodet's sleeping Endymion, as the large-winged adolescent zephyr supporting her nearer side recalls the boy Eros who watches over him. The positions of sleeping
adult and hovering Eros are redistributed in a painting that Prud'hon made soon after
(ca. 1815–20) he exhibited the Young Zephyr and Psyche Uplifted by Zephyrs: This is his Venus,
Hymen and Cupid, in which a butterfly-winged baby Cupid leans over asleep on the knees
of a somewhat eery-looking Venus with Leonardesque wide-set eyes, enigmatic smile,
and shining visage who raises her left breast with her hand. With the other arm she en-
circles the waist of Hymen, another pubescent Eros who holds the hymeneal torch in one
hand and, with the other, attempts to awaken the sleeping Cupid by tickling him on the
ear. There is a strong family resemblance among the three bodies in this picture: all are
fleshy, thick, heavy-haunched. As in the case of the Young Zephyr, the conspicuous wings
of the two boys are more than countered by their no less conspicuous physical heft and
solidity; these are no airy "sprite"-bodies figuring "transcendence" of the corporeal.

35 Both of Vigée-Lebrun's portraits of herself and her daughter that hang in the Louvre are
commonly referred to as maternités. Mary D. Sheriff has recently discussed how Simone

de Beauvoir (in *The Second Sex*) dismissed this painter's work as the products of a kind of feminine false consciousness: "Madame Vigée-Lebrun never wearied of putting her smiling maternity on her canvases" (quoted by Mary D. Sheriff, *The Exceptional Woman: Elisabeth Vigée-Lebrun and the Cultural Politics of Art* [Chicago: University of Chicago Press, 1996], p. 43). In dissenting from Beauvoir's judgment, Sheriff points out how uncharacteristic these two images are in the context of Vigée-Lebrun's many other representations of herself in both painting and writing (besides numerous self-portraits, Vigée-Lebrun published an extensive memoir of her long career as a painter). Sheriff also complicates any notion of Vigée-Lebrun's two self-portraits with her daughter as simply reproducing late-eighteenth-century sentimental, Rousseauian stereotypes of "virtuous motherhood" by insisting on the way in which the artist challenges comparison with Raphael by producing a painting (the second of the two self-portraits-with-child, the *Self-Portrait à la Grecque*) modeled closely in some ways on the composition of Raphael's *Madonna della Sedia* (1514). Sheriff further repudiates the conventionalizing "good-mother" account of the painting by pointing out that in placing herself in the position of Raphael's celebrated Madonna, Vigée-Lebrun was also allowing herself to be associated with the scandalous historical figure of Raphael's fabled model, his mistress and the mother of his child, La Fornarina (see Sheriff, *The Exceptional Woman*, pp. 67–68).

36 See *Memoirs of Elisabeth Vigée-Lebrun*, trans. Sian Evans (Bloomington: Indiana University Press, 1989), p. 44.

37 Several historians have recently reminded us of the centrality of these charges in the propaganda campaign mounted against Marie Antoinette, who was formally charged at her trial with having committed incest with her son the *dauphin*. See, for example, Lynn Hunt, "The Many Bodies of Marie-Antoinette: Political Pornography and the Problem of the Feminine in the French Revolution," in *Eroticism and the Body Politic*, ed. Lynn Hunt (Baltimore: Johns Hopkins University Press, 1991), pp. 114–15.

38 See Joseph Baillio's catalog of Vigée-Lebrun's various paintings of her daughter and their probable dates in his exhibition catalog, *Elisabeth Louise Vigée-Lebrun, 1755–1842* (Fort Worth, Ind.: Kimbell Art Museum, 1982), pp. 75–76.

THREE *Flaming Closets*

1 My discussion of the Ballets Russes *Scheherazade* is indebted to Richard Buckle's account of the planning and performance of the ballet in his biography *Nijinsky* (New York: Simon and Schuster, 1971), especially pp. 137–42.

2 *Lettres à Reynaldo Hahn*, ed. Philip Kolb (Paris, 1956), p. 188; quoted in Buckle, *Nijinsky*, pp. 141–42.

3 Wollen's article has been of crucial importance to me in thinking about the kinds of continuities in gay-male performance in the twentieth century that I am considering in this project; see his "Fashion/Orientalism/The Body," *New Formations*, no. 1 (spring 1987), pp. 5–33. Dale Harris takes a more conventionally connoisseurial approach to the subject of the cultural impact of Ballets Russes orientalism in his "Diaghilev's Ballets Russes and the Vogue for Orientalism," in *The Art of Enchantment: Diaghilev's Ballets Russes, 1909–*

1929, compiled by Nancy Van Norman Baer (catalog of an exhibition held at the Fine Arts Museum of San Francisco, 1988), pp. 84–95. For accounts of the institution of the harem that tend to deconstruct Western orientalizing fantasies of it, see Malek Alloula, *The Colonial Harem*, trans. Myrna Godzich and Wlad Godzich (Minneapolis: University of Minnesota Press, 1986); and Huda Shaarawi, *Harem Years: The Memoirs of an Egyptian Feminist*, trans. and ed. Margot Badran (London, Virago Press, 1986).

4   Beaton quoted in Wollen, "Fashion/Orientalism/The Body," p. 21.

5   The 1911 avant-garde's subversion of prevailing religious and sexual certainties was registered in, among other ways, the ban that the then archbishop of Paris placed on the performance of *The Martyrdom of Saint Sebastian*. Of the many reasons he might have put forward for this ban, he announced two: (1) d'Annunzio's identification of the saint with the pagan god Adonis, and (2) the fact that a male Christian saint was to be played by a Jewish woman. Despite the official condemnation, "the show went on," to an only middling success; see Alfred Frankenstein's liner notes for Leonard Bernstein's recording of the *Martyrdom* on Columbia Masterworks discs M2L 353/M2S 753.

6   Bram Dijkstra, *Idols of Perversity: Fantasies of Feminine Evil in Fin-de-Siècle Culture* (New York: Oxford University Press, 1988), p. 53.

7   Nouvel quoted in Buckle, *Nijinsky*, p. 124.

8   Besides marking his performance in *Scheherazade*, the year 1910 also marks the beginning of Nijinsky's most productive period as a choreographer; it was then that he began to formulate the projects that would issue in 1912–13 in his three great inaugural modernist ballets, *L'après-midi d'un faune, Jeux,* and *Le sacre du printemps*. For a recent assessment of Nijinsky's achievements as a choreographer, see Lynn Garafola, "Vaslav Nijinsky," *Raritan* 8, no. 1 (summer 1988): 1–27.

9   Fokine quoted in Buckle, *Nijinsky*, p. 141.

10   Ibid.

11   Benois quoted in Buckle, *Nijinsky*, p. 141.

12   Joan Acocella writes briefly but perceptively of the way Nijinsky was cast throughout his career in roles in which he was either "something other than human: a puppet, a god, a faun, the specter of a rose," or, if human, not so in any ordinary sense, but always in either a reduced or excessive way: "a slave, an androgyne, or some other object of sexual connoisseurship." See her article "Vaslav Nijinsky," in Baer, *The Art of Enchantment*, p. 110.

13   For a history of gay and lesbian political organizing and resistance in the three decades before Stonewall, see John D'Emilio, *Sexual Politics, Sexual Communities: The Making of a Homosexual Minority in the United States, 1940–1970* (Chicago: University of Chicago Press, 1983). Eve Kosofsky Sedgwick's *Epistemology of the Closet* (Berkeley: University of California Press, 1990) provides a searching theoretical exploration of the ways in which an endemic crisis of homo/heterosexual definition has structured/fractured Western culture in the twentieth century.

14   Everyone interested in Jack Smith's work in film and performance is indebted to Stefan Brecht and J. Hoberman for their efforts in preserving at least some aspects of Smith's extremely fugitive performance art. Brecht gives a number of informative accounts of Smith's work from 1961 to 1977 in his valuable study *Queer Theatre* (Frankfurt: Suhrkamp,

1978), pp. 10–27 and 157–77. Hoberman surveys Smith's performances during the same period in his article "The Theatre of Jack Smith," *The Drama Review* 23, no. 1 (March 1979): 3–12. For further information about Smith and his performances, see Jonas Mekas's July 1970 *Village Voice* article, "Jack Smith, or the End of Civilization," reprinted in Mekas's *Movie Journal: The Rise of a New American Cinema, 1959–1971* (New York: Collier Books, 1972), pp. 388–97. Film scholar Karel Rowe, who worked briefly as Smith's assistant during the summer of 1972, provides useful information about Smith's film performances as well as a Smith filmography in his book *The Baudelairean Cinema: A Trend within the American Avant-Garde* (Ann Arbor: UMI Research Press, 1982). Joan Adler, in a piece entitled "On Location," gives an impressionistic account of the making of *Normal Love*, the unfinished film project Smith undertook after *Flaming Creatures*, in Stephen Dwoskin's *Film Is: The International Free Cinema* (Woodstock, N.Y.: Overlook Press, 1975), pp. 11–21.

15 For most of the time the film has existed, it has been even more difficult to see *Flaming Creatures* than is usual for an "underground" work. Never available for screening beyond a very small circuit of alternative venues, the film seems to have been withdrawn from circulation by Smith by the early 1970s in angry reaction to what he considered its mis-reception on the part of everyone from the New York Police Department to Susan Sontag. Smith was antagonistic to written analyses of his work; his most frequently quoted utterance has been, "Film critics are writers and they are hostile and uneasy in the presence of a visual phenomenon" (quoted, for example, in Rowe, *Baudelairean Cinema*, p. xiii). Given Smith's passionate commitment to his film's being seen rather than being made to serve as grist for the mill of what he saw as pseudo-controversy, it is more than ironic, it is deeply unfortunate that *Flaming Creatures* has, owing to its general unavailability, "lived on" to the extent that it has largely in the form of written descriptions of it. On the subject of the general suppression of many of the most radical examples of "underground" film of the 1960s, see David E. James's eloquent prefatory statement to his history of noncommercial American film of that decade, *Allegories of Cinema: American Film in the Sixties* (Princeton: Princeton University Press, 1979), p. ix. Among published descriptions of *Flaming Creatures*, the following are particularly useful: P. Adams Sitney, *Visionary Film: The American Avant-Garde 1943–1978*, 2d ed. (New York: Oxford University Press, 1979), pp. 354–57; Rowe, *Baudelairean Cinema*, pp. 49–50.

16 Rowe describes his travails in attempting to show *Flaming Creatures* in *Baudelairean Cinema*, pp. xi–xii; Hoberman discusses the prosecution of *Flaming Creatures* and other underground films of the period (chiefly Jean Genet's *Un chant d'amour* and Kenneth Anger's *Scorpio Rising*) in his and Jonathan Rosenbaum's *Midnight Movies* (New York: Harper and Row, 1983), pp. 59–61.

17 Smith made this charge against his critics in his 1973 *Village Voice* review of John Waters's *Pink Flamingos*. Brecht quotes it in *Queer Theatre*, p. 26n.

18 Sontag says *Flaming Creatures* "is about joy and innocence" in her essay "Jack Smith's *Flaming Creatures*," reprinted in *Against Interpretation* (New York: Farrar, Straus, and Giroux, 1966), p. 229. Possible political meanings and consequences get thoroughly elided from Sontag's influential account of Smith's film, which, according to her, simply eschews moralizing in order to occupy a purely aesthetic "space": "The space in which *Flaming*

Creatures moves is not the space of moral ideas, which is where American critics have traditionally located art. What I am urging is that there is not only moral space, by whose laws *Flaming Creatures* would indeed come off badly; there is also aesthetic space, the space of pleasure. Here Smith's film moves and has its being" ("Jack Smith's Flaming Creatures," p. 231). Sontag similarly writes in "Notes on 'Camp'": "Jews pinned their hopes for integrating into modern society on promoting the moral sense. Homosexuals have pinned their integration into society on promoting the aesthetic sense. Camp is a solvent of morality. It neutralizes moral indignation, sponsors playfulness" ("Notes on 'Camp'," in *Against Interpretation*, p. 290). The problem with such extreme hypostatizations is that moral and aesthetic practices cannot be rendered stable, plainly disjunct "spaces" or "senses"; categories and categorical dyads such as Jewish moral seriousness versus gay "playfulness" fall explanatorily flat, especially in view of the subsequent history of these two groups in the decades since Sontag's essay, during which time many of her New York Jewish liberal intellectual confreres of the mid- to late 1960s have turned neoconservative, and gays have been engaged in a series of political struggles that have for the most part been anything but "playful."

19 Hoberman, "The Theatre of Jack Smith," p. 4.

20 Lotringer quoted in Hoberman, "The Theatre of Jack Smith," p. 6.

21 Hoberman, "The Theatre of Jack Smith," p. 4.

22 Gerard Malanga, "Interview with Jack Smith," *Film Culture*, no. 45 (1967): 15.

23 Ibid., p. 14.

24 Ibid., p. 15.

25 *The Diary of Vaslav Nijinsky*, ed. Romola Nijinsky (Berkeley: University of California Press, 1968). See, for example, pp. 29, 51, 120, 175.

26 Norine Dresser discusses the reasons for the general appeal of the figure of the vampire to adolescents: "Teenagers find the vampire fascinating because the vampire is usually an unwilling victim of a bodily change he cannot control, a change that brings on frightening new desires and cravings, a change that sets him apart from the society he has known and makes him an outsider." See her *American Vampires: Fans, Victims and Practitioners* (New York: Norton, 1989), p. 146. "Normal" adolescent anxieties of the kind Dresser describes are of course compounded when the young person in question is gay. Surely some of the power of the vamp/vampire comedy aspect of *Flaming Creatures* derives from the intensity of these anxieties in what may seem like the archaic past in the lives of gay viewers of the film. Smith had "rehearsed" for *Flaming Creatures* by playing "The Fairy Vampire" in a brief 1961 film collaboration with Ken Jacobs called *The Death of P'town*.

27 See Chapter 3, "The Vampire," in Sumiko Higashi, *Virgins, Vamps, and Flappers: The American Silent Movie Heroine* (Montreal: Eden Press, 1978), for a compact and informative account of the cult of the film vamp ca. 1915–22.

28 Thierry de Duve, "Andy Warhol, or The Machine Perfected," *October*, no. 48 (spring 1989): 13.

29 Brecht, *Queer Theatre*, p. 177n.

30 Ibid.

31 To be fair to Brecht, one should notice that while his attempts to theorize Smith's prac-

tice can be crude (as when he collapses homosexuality into heterosexuality and consigns Smith's art simply to transvestism), his descriptions and observations of Smith's work and that of other "queer artists" are more precise than anyone else's; for example, he is the only commentator I have read who remarks that for all its apparent male-transvestite focus, the mock-rape of a female character carried out in one episode of *Flaming Creatures* culminates in a scene of lesbian affection and consolation (Brecht, *Queer Theatre*, p. 25n).

32 Maria Montez's other greatest admirer is Myra Breckinridge, who comes to inhabit Montez's body in the penultimate chapters of Gore Vidal's *Myron* (New York: Random House, 1974).

33 Quoted in Rowe's filmography of Ken Jacobs in *Baudelairean Cinema*, pp. 125–26.

34 Jack Smith, "The Perfect Filmic Appositeness of Maria Montez," Film Culture, no. 27 (winter 1962–63): 30.

35 Jack Smith and Ken Jacobs, "Soundtrack of *Blonde Cobra*," Film Culture, no. 29 (summer 1963): 2.

36 Leo Bersani, *A Future for Astyanax: Character and Desire in Literature* (Boston: Little, Brown, 1976), pp. 306–7.

37 My discussion of Smith's adaptation of *Ghosts* is indebted to Brecht's description of several quite different performances of it he saw (*Queer Theatre*, pp. 157–77), and to Hoberman's remarks on the piece ("The Theatre of Jack Smith," pp. 8–9).

38 Jack Smith, "Soundtrack of *Blonde Cobra*," in *Wait for Me at the Bottom of the Pool: The Writings of Jack Smith*, ed. J. Hoberman and Edward Leffingwell (New York: High Risk Books, 1997), p. 159.

FOUR Screen Memories

1 Andy Warhol and Pat Hackett, *POPism: The Warhol Sixties* (New York: Harcourt Brace Jovanovich, 1980), p. 116.

2 *The Complete Poems and Selected Letters and Prose of Hart Crane*, ed. Brom Weber (New York: Anchor Books, 1966), p. 21.

3 Victor Bockris, *The Life and Death of Andy Warhol* (New York: Bantam, 1989), provides numerous accounts, many of them based on the testimony of participants, of the artist's production of images of the male nude in several media throughout his career. On Warhol's sketching sessions of the fifties, see, for example, pp. 61–62; for accounts of his exhibitions of "boy drawings" of 1952, 1954, and 1956, see pp. 67–68, 78–79, and 84, respectively. For an account of some of Warhol's "Polaroid sex sessions" of the seventies, see Bob Colacello, *Holy Terror: Andy Warhol Close Up* (New York: HarperCollins, 1990), pp. 343–44. For a thoughtful analysis of some of the many ways in which Warhol's work of the fifties participated in gay male subcultural life in Manhattan and beyond, see Trevor Fairbrother, "Tomorrow's Man," in *"Success is a job in New York . . .": The Early Art and Business of Andy Warhol* (New York: Carnegie Museum of Art, 1989), pp. 55–74.

4 Warhol relates an anecdote in *POPism* that has become emblematic of his abject and anomalous relation to the New York art world at the end of the fifties; this is the often-cited tale of his asking his friend Emile de Antonio why Warhol's fellow artists and

fellow fags Robert Rauschenberg and Jasper Johns routinely snubbed him. "You're too swish, and that upsets them," de Antonio informed Warhol. Interestingly, he adds that Rauschenberg and Johns were also put off by Warhol's collecting habits (already a conspicuous aspect of his persona) and his use of his own name in his commercial work (Rauschenberg and Johns designed windows for Tiffany's under a discreet pseudonym). Conspicuous consumption of other artists' work and conspicuous success as a commercial artist both seem to be taken as intensifications of Warhol's effeminate personal mannerisms by his anxious and relatively closeted contemporaries. See Warhol and Hackett, POPism, pp. 11–13.

5   See, for example, Kenneth E. Silver, who attempts to situate what he reads as "gay identity" both in relation to Warhol's art and that of a number of his gay contemporaries and predecessors in his wide-ranging article, "Modes of Disclosure: The Construction of Gay Identity and the Rise of Pop Art," in Hand-Painted Pop: American Art in Transition, 1955–62, ed. Russell Ferguson (Los Angeles: Museum of Contemporary Art, 1992), pp. 179–203; see especially Silver's exhaustive discussion of Rauschenberg's and Johns's response to Warhol, pp. 193–97. See also Richard Meyer's analysis of Thirteen Most Wanted Men in his article "Warhol's Clones," Yale Journal of Criticism 7, no. 1 (spring 1994): 79–109.

6   Andy Warhol, The Philosophy of Andy Warhol (New York: Harcourt Brace Jovanovich, 1975), pp. 21–22.

7   For "Screen Memory" and "Primal Scene," see respective entries in Jean Laplanche and J.-B. Pontalis, The Language of Psycho-Analysis, trans. Donald Nicholson-Smith (New York: W. W. Norton, 1973). For a valuable analysis of the place of "primal-scene" theories in the writings of Henry James, Freud, and Heidegger, see Ned Lukacher, Primal Scenes: Literature, Philosophy, Psychoanalysis (Ithaca: Cornell University Press, 1986).

8   Warhol, Philosophy, p. 84.

9   See references in note 1 above to accounts of Warhol sketching male-male sex scenes in the fifties in Bockris, Life and Death of Andy Warhol, and photographing them in the seventies in Colacello, Holy Terror.

10   Ultra Violet, Famous for Fifteen Minutes: My Years with Andy Warhol (New York: Avon, 1988), pp. 154–55. Note the author's "Disclaimer," p. v: "I have relied on memory, diaries, tapes, recorded phone calls, press clippings, books, magazines, interviews, and conversations to document what I bear witness to. Some conversations are reconstructed and are not intended, nor should they be construed, as verbatim quotes."

11   Ibid., p. 155.

12   "What is Pop Art?" interviews by G. R. Swenson with Andy Warhol and other painters, Art News, November 1963, p. 60.

13   Michael Wassenaar, "Strong to the Finich: Machines, Metaphor, and Popeye the Sailor," Velvet Light Trap 24 (fall 1989): 23.

14   See Sasha Torres's essay, "The Caped Crusader of Camp: Pop, Camp, and the Batman Television Series," in Pop Out: Queer Warhol, ed. Jennifer Doyle, Jonathan Flatley, and José Esteban Muñoz (Durham: Duke University Press, 1996), pp. 238–55.

15   Fredric Wertham, Seduction of the Innocent (New York: Holt, Rinehart and Winston, 1954), and Gillian Freeman, The Undergrowth of Literature (London: Nelson, 1967).

16 Edmund Bergler, quoted by Robert Anton Wilson, "Attitudes toward Sex, Modern," in *The Encyclopedia of Sexual Behavior*, ed. Albert Ellis and Albert Abarbanel (New York: Hawthorn, 1961), p. 190.

17 Edmund Bergler, "Homosexuality and the Kinsey Report," in *The Homosexuals: As Seen by Themselves and Thirty Authorities*, ed. A. M. Krich (New York: Citadel, 1958), p. 233.

18 See, for example, Warhol's discussion of this motto in his *Philosophy*, p. 98.

19 David Bourdon, *Warhol* (New York: Harry N. Abrams, 1989), p. 82.

20 Of the terms in the first part of this sentence, "cold" is quoted in Bourdon, *Warhol*; the rest of the terms are quoted from an interview with Karp in Kim Evans's documentary on Warhol (London Weekend Television, 1987).

21 Among the key texts in the recent historiography of gay and lesbian social and political movements "before Stonewall" is *Before Stonewall*, directed by Greta Schiller and co-directed by Robert Rosenberg (1986); Allan Berube, *Coming Out under Fire: The History of Gay Men and Women in World War Two* (New York: Free Press, 1990); John D'Emilio, *Sexual Politics, Sexual Communities: The Making of a Homosexual Minority in the United States, 1940–1970* (Chicago: University of Chicago Press, 1983); Elizabeth Lapovsky Kennedy and Madeline Davis, *Boots of Leather, Slippers of Gold: The History of a Lesbian Community* (New York: Routledge, 1993); Stuart Timmons, *The Trouble with Harry Hay* (Boston: Alyson, 1990).

22 Freud, "Childhood Memories and Screen Memories," in *The Psychopathology of Everyday Life*, trans. Alan Tyson, ed. James Strachey (New York: Norton, 1960), p. 49 n. 2.

23 Warhol, quoted in Bockris, *Life and Death of Andy Warhol*, p. 154.

24 "Saturation" is Sandor Ferenczi's term for infantile sexual pleasure, in contrast with the cyclic and climactic qualities that characterize adult sexuality. See his essay "Confusion of Tongues between Adults and the Child" (1933), reprinted in Sandor Ferenczi, *Final Contributions to the Problems and Methods of Psychoanalysis*, ed. Michael Balint (New York: Brunner/Mazel, 1980), pp. 156–67.

25 Peter Brooks has written compellingly about the history and effects of "the frozen moment" of melodrama in nineteenth-century literary and theatrical culture in *The Melodramatic Imagination: Balzac, Henry James, Melodrama, and the Mode of Excess* (New Haven: Yale University Press, 1976).

FIVE Outlaw Sex and the "Search for America"

1 Although I restrict my attention in this piece to representations of male-male desire and male prostitution in novels and films of the sixties, some key texts for thinking about lesbianism and prostitution in the recent past would include Lizzie Borden's 1986 film *Working Girls* and Joan Nestle's essay, "Lesbians and Prostitutes: A Historical Sisterhood," which appears in her *A Restricted Country* (Ithaca, N.Y.: Firebrand, 1987) and has been reprinted in *Sex Work: Writings by Women in the Sex Industry*, ed. Frédérique Delacoste and Priscilla Alexander (Pittsburgh: Cleis, 1987).

2 Dyer, *Now You See It: Studies on Lesbian and Gay Film* (New York: Routledge, 1990), p. 140.

3 Ibid.

4 Lauren Berlant's illuminating analysis of the drama of desire and national identity in the

successive versions of *Imitation of Life* has informed my thinking about this relation in sixties representation; see her essay, "National Brands/National Body: *Imitation of Life*," in *Comparative American Identities: Race, Sex, and Nationality in the Modern Text*, ed. Hortense J. Spillers (New York: Routledge, 1991), pp. 110–40.

5 See Esther Newton's *Mother Camp: Female Impersonators in America* (Chicago: University of Chicago Press, 1972), and Judith Butler's rereading of Newton's work, in her *Gender Trouble: Feminism and the Subversion of Identity* (New York: Routledge, 1990), pp. 136–37. In *Now You See It*, Richard Dyer points out, as others have done, that the hustler and the drag queen are the two most heavily charged figures in sixties underground representation.

6 For a rich discussion of the sexual politics of the spectacle of bodybuilding, see Jonathan Goldberg, "Recalling Totalities: The Mirrored Stages of Arnold Schwarzenegger," *differences* 4, no. 1 (spring 1992), 172–204.

7 I am indebted in this part of my discussion to Eve Kosofsky Sedgwick, *Epistemology of the Closet* (Berkeley: University of California Press, 1990).

8 "Costume Fetishism, or, Clothes Make the Man," *Ridiculous Theatre, Scourge of Human Folly: The Essays and Opinions of Charles Ludlam*, ed. Steven Samuels (New York: Theatre Communications Group, 1992), p. 161.

9 The classic discussion of fetishism in film theory is Christian Metz's "Disavowal, Fetishism," in his *The Imaginary Signifier*, trans. Celia Britton et al. (Bloomington: University of Indiana Press, 1982), pp. 69–78.

10 John Rechy, *City of Night* (New York: Grove, 1963), p. 129.

11 "Lookin' for a good time at the movies," *Film Threat*, November 1991, p. 41.

12 Charbon was Edie Sedgwick's roommate back in Manhattan; she is said to have been cast in *My Hustler* instead of Sedgwick in order to punish Sedgwick for allegedly having made too much trouble about her status in the filmmaking operation. See Victor Bockris, *The Life and Death of Andy Warhol* (New York: Bantam, 1989), pp. 173–74.

13 Bockris, *Life and Death of Andy Warhol*, pp. 174–75.

14 See Koch's description of the "shock" of cuts and pans in the opening sequence of *My Hustler* in his *Stargazer: Andy Warhol's World and His Films* (New York: Praeger, 1973), pp. 81–82. R. Bruce Brasell's terms for the camera maneuvers in the first half of *My Hustler* are apt; as he puts it, "The gay characters in the film do not have to swish because the camera does it for them" ("My Hustler: Gay Spectatorship as Cruising," *Wide Angle* 14, no. 2 [April 1992]: 58). While I agree with Brasell that films like *My Hustler* can only be ill served by what have become "standard" theories of film spectatorship, and while I find his discussion of the second half of *My Hustler* as a prolonged cruising gesture persuasive in some ways, I am troubled by the article's apparent commitment to the binary categories that I see the film as tending to break down; see, for example, Brasell's analyses of the film in terms of public vs. private space (pp. 56–62), gazing vs. glancing (pp. 63–64), and of hustling vs. cruising (p. 62). Brasell characterizes hustling as "commodified" sex and cruising as "not an economic exchange but a bartering system," as if "barter" were not itself a kind of economic exchange and, indeed, as if it existed as a practice somewhere outside the economic realm. The implication of cruising as well as hustling in economic exchange manifests itself across the range of texts I am considering, from

Rechy to Warhol and Schlesinger. In reading these texts it seems crucial to me to resist the impulse to draw the same kinds of clear-cut distinctions between them that the dominant culture does.

15 Quoted in David E. James, *Allegories of Cinema: American Film in the Sixties* (Princeton: Princeton University Press, 1989), p. 69.

16 I do not know, but hope that Eric Emerson, exponent nonpareil of 1960s-style self-bodygrooving, is at least a collateral descendant of the R. W. Emerson who famously placed "the body" under the heading "NOT ME" in his 1836 essay "Nature," which inaugurated the Transcendentalist movement.

17 On homosexuality and "self-shattering" psychological effects see Leo Bersani, *A Future for Astyanax* (Boston: Little, Brown, 1976), pp. 306–7.

18 Warhol famously came to believe in the course of the sixties and seventies that "business" was "the best art." He also famously insisted (in his *Philosophy*) that sex was work—not "joyful," "liberated" play as many people wanted to believe, but "work" for which one should be paid, or for which one should be able to hire assistants, as one did for everything else. Sex as labor and paid labor was of course not a strange notion to Warhol, who had long cherished the fantasy (and through his films and "art-business" partially realized it) of running a male brothel in which he would be the cashier (see Bockris, *Life and Death of Andy Warhol*, p. 148). In the summer of Stonewall, Warhol experimented briefly with the business of running one of the first gay-porn-film theaters in New York, which he proudly named "Andy Warhol's Theater: Boys to Adore Galore." Some patrons came to the theater expecting to see avant-garde films and were outraged to see ten-minute gay-sex loops. According to Jim Carroll, who operated the box-office for the theater's six-week existence, male prostitution was practiced on the premises, unbeknownst to Warhol (who would probably have demanded a cut of the proceeds) (Bockris, *Life and Death of Andy Warhol*, pp. 248–49).

19 I quote Mellen's words from her book *Big Bad Wolves: Masculinity in the American Film* (New York: Pantheon, 1977), p. 289. Schlesinger's summary of his film's "message" is paraphrased by Gene Phillips in his article, "John Schlesinger: Social Realist," *Film Comment* 5, no. 4 (winter 1969).

20 Mellen discusses these negotiations in *Big Bad Wolves*, p. 287.

21 Dawson's review of *Midnight Cowboy* appeared in *Sight and Sound* 38, no. 4 (autumn 1969): 211–12.

22 Dawson, review of *Midnight Cowboy*, p. 212.

23 John Simon is to my knowledge the only commentator on the film who has previously discussed *Midnight Cowboy*'s fleeting shots of the rape of Joe Buck (his review is reprinted in his *Movies into Film: Film Criticism 1967–1970* [New York: Dial, 1971], pp. 357–60). Simon mentions how hard it is to interpret the rape shots on p. 358. Vito Russo discusses representations of male-male rape in a number of seventies buddy films, in *Celluloid Closet: Homosexuality in the Movies* (New York: Harper and Row, 1981), pp. 83–85, but he does not mention the fragmented rape scene in *Midnight Cowboy*. I have discussed in the first chapter of this book the apparent turning of a "real" scene of the rape of one man by another, in David Lynch's *Blue Velvet*, into a scene of "symbolic" rape.

24 It is important to qualify any assertion about "Middle America's" not knowing about S-M in the sixties by noting that although S-M subcultures were then hardly even at the periphery of representation, S-M desire was rampant among American boys and youths, from the bondage, beating, and torture conventions of Saturday-matinee serials and cowboys-and-Indians games to the elaborate sexual humiliation-and-pain rituals endemic to sports-club and fraternity initiations and hazing rituals.

25 John Leo Herlihy, *Midnight Cowboy* (New York: Simon and Schuster, 1965), p. 176.

26 Ibid., p. 177.

27 It is worth noting that although Buck is with a woman in the first sex scene and with a man in the second, "happy" sex does not simply get coded hetero and vanilla in the film, nor "sick" sex simply homo and S-M. When Joe finds himself impotent with his client Shirley (Brenda Vaccaro) late in the film, the "remedy" turns out to be her goading him into having rougher sex with her; the "bouncy," simple sex Joe started out having with another woman here turns into a prolonged exchange, with mounting intensity, of scratches, slaps, and bites — but it does not turn into the brutal, possibly fatal, "sex" Joe has with Towny.

28 Herlihy, *Midnight Cowboy*, p. 127.

SIX *Oralia*

1 Caws's *Joseph Cornell's Theater of the Mind* (New York: Thames & Hudson, 1993) will hereafter be cited parenthetically in the text.

2 Glueck reported her conversation with Cornell in the *New York Times* of February 11, 1972; it is quoted by Dore Ashton in *A Joseph Cornell Album* (New York: Viking, 1974), p. 35.

3 Sigmund Freud, "The Theme of the Three Caskets," in *Sigmund Freud: Character and Culture*, ed. Philip Rieff (New York: Collier, 1963), p. 69.

4 Sigmund Freud, *The Interpretation of Dreams*, trans. James Strachey (New York: Basic Books, 1955), p. 389.

5 Freud, *Interpretation of Dreams*, p. 188.

6 Although Cornell does not appear to have been a reader of Henry James's fiction, his artistic practice closely resembles James's in its seemingly inexhaustible capacity for setting up striking engagements in his work between Romantic and modernist habits of perception and composition. Cornell's contemporary R. P. Blackmur is the most inspired critic of this aspect of James's work. See his essays on James, composed between 1934 and 1964, gathered in *R. P. Blackmur: Studies in Henry James*, ed. Veronica A. Makowsky (New York: New Directions, 1983).

7 Ashton, *A Joseph Cornell Album*, p. 14; the section in *The Interpretation of Dreams* on "the work of condensation" can be found in James Strachey's translation, pp. 312–339.

8 Freud, *Interpretation of Dreams*, p. 313.

9 Dore Ashton, *A Joseph Cornell Album* (New York: Viking, 1974), p. 14.

10 Gérard de Nerval, *Aurelia/Sylvie*, trans. Kendall Lappin (Santa Monica, Calif.: Asylum Arts, 1993), p. 48.

11 Ibid., 32.

12 Ibid., p. 92; I have slightly altered the translation of the last clause here.

13 Ibid., p. 31.

14 Motherwell quoted in Caws, *Joseph Cornell's Theater of the Mind*, p. 15.

15 Cornell seems to have been fully aware of how richly his fellow New Yorker and fellow *flâneur* Whitman had prefigured his own love of the city streets, ordinary people, and the homelier versions of the urban sublime, as well as his love of music and performance. Cornell's strong identification with Emily Dickinson has been more widely remarked, but his devotion to Whitman is clear in such passages as his diary entries for August 3, 1947, where he remembers discovering Whitman and other modern American artists through Marsden Hartley's *Adventures in the Arts* (1926), or August 9 of the same year, where he remembers reading and emulating Whitman as he rode down Broadway on the old trolley-cars as a young man (145).

16 Jordan quoted in Caws, *Joseph Cornell's Theater of the Mind*, p. 281.

17 Jacques Derrida, *Dissemination*, trans. Barbara Johnson (Chicago: University of Chicago Press, 1981), p. 206.

18 Ibid., p. 206.

19 Judith Butler, "Imitation and Gender Insubordination," in *Inside/Out: Lesbian Theories, Gay Theories*, ed. Diana Fuss (New York: Routledge, 1991), p. 21; original emphasis.

20 *Stéphane Mallarmé: Selected Prose Poems, Essays, & Letters*, trans. Bradford Cook (Baltimore: Johns Hopkins University Press, 1956), p. 62. Thomas Lawson also discusses this passage at the beginning of his article on Cornell's films, "Silently, by Means of a Flashing Light," *October* 15 (1980): 49–57.

21 Butler, "Imitation and Gender Insubordination," p. 30, n. 12.

SEVEN *Tragedy and Trash*

1 Henry James, *The American Scene* (1907; reprint Bloomington: Indiana University Press, 1968), p. 139.

2 Nahma Sandrow, *Vagabond Stars: A World History of the Yiddish Theater* (New York: Harper & Row, 1977; Syracuse: Syracuse University Press, 1996), p. 135.

3 My brief account of Gordin's career depends throughout on Sandrow, "Jacob Gordin," *Vagabond Stars*, pp. 132–63.

4 The resemblance of this scene to that of Hamlet and the players suggests that this kind of conflict, between a more improvisatory actors' theater on the one hand and a more script-bound one on the other, or between a folk theater and a courtly one, has been a staple of the history of the stage in the West since the beginning of the early modern period.

5 Quoted in Sandrow, *Vagabond Stars*, p. 157.

6 Leon Edel, *Henry James: The Master, 1901–1916* (Boston: Lippincott, 1972), p. 293.

7 Henry James, *The American Scene*, p. 199.

8 Yiddish theater historian David S. Lifson also mentions the Windsor as the site of a performance of a Hurwitz play in 1917. See Lifson, *The Yiddish Theater in America* (New York: Yoseloff, 1965), p. 270.

9   Henry James, *The American Scene*, p. 194.

10 Ibid., p. 199.

11 Ibid., p. 205.

12 Leon Edel, *Henry James: The Master, 1901–1916*, pp. 293–94.

13 For a thorough account of James's relation to the Jewish question, see Eli Ben-Joseph, *Aesthetic Persuasion: Henry James, the Jews, and Race* (Lanham, Md.: University Press of America, 1996).

14 Itzkovitz reexamines the work of Willa Cather, Jean Toomer, Fannie Hurst, and other writers, as well as some extremely significant court cases (Leo Frank, Leopold and Loeb), in his forthcoming study of queerness and Jewishness in the twentieth-century United States.

15 George Chauncey, "The Bowery as Haven and Spectacle," *Gay New York: Gender, Urban Culture, and the Making of the Gay Male World 1890–1940* (New York: Basic Books, 1994), pp. 33–45. The passage cited appears on p. 33.

16 Ibid., p. 37.

17 Fred Kaplan's biography of James, *Henry James: The Imagination of Genius* (New York: William Morrow, 1992), has opened up some space for considering the role of male-homo-erotic desire earlier in the author's life by telling the story of James's infatuation with the Russian dilettante Paul Zhukovsky (or Joukowsky). Sheldon M. Novick, in his *Henry James: The Young Master* (New York: Random House, 1996), suggests James may have had an affair with Oliver Wendell Holmes, Jr., in 1865, when they were both young men. In attempting to understand the significance of queerness for James's writing, I suspect that the search for the supposedly "missing" male object of James's desires (whether William James, Zhukovsky, Holmes, or whomever) is substantially less important than acquiring an understanding of how mobile, various, and in some ways not definitively object-directed the desires of someone like James may have been. See, on this point in general, Eve Kosofsky Sedgwick's remarks in *Epistemology of the Closet* (Berkeley: University of California Press, 1990), p. 8: "It is a rather amazing fact that, of the very many dimensions along which the genital activity of one person can be differentiated from that of an other . . . precisely one, the gender of object choice, emerged from the turn of the century, and has remained, as the dimension denoted by the now ubiquitous category of 'sexual orientation.'"

18 Although there is as yet no discussion in English that I am aware of that takes up the question of the significance of any but heterosexuality in the Yiddish theater, the question has at least been raised in relation to the history of Yiddish film. Film curator and historian Eve Sicular has initiated the discussion of queer presences in the history of Yiddish film with her articles on the substantial significance of crossdressing and playing tomboys in the film career of Molly Picon, and on the sexualities of some key male figures in the Yiddish film industry. See her "Gender Rebellion in Yiddish Film," Lilith 20, no. 4 (winter 1995–96): 12–17; and also her "Outing the Archives: Adventures from the Celluloid Closet of Yiddish Film," *Davka* 1, no. 3 (winter 1997): 46–47.

19 See Richard Dyer, *Heavenly Bodies: Film Stars and Society* (New York: St. Martin's Press,

1986), ch. 2; and Miriam Hansen, *Babel and Babylon: Spectatorship in American Silent Film* (Cambridge: Harvard University Press, 1991), chs. 11 and 12.

20 Thomashefsky quoted in Sandrow, *Vagabond Stars*, p. 78.

21 Sandrow, *Vagabond Stars*, p. 96. On Thomashefsky's audience's perception of his sex appeal, see also Lifson, *The Yiddish Theatre in America*, p. 147.

22 See Adeline R. Tintner, "Photograph versus Cinematograph: Dark versus Light in 'Crapy Cornelia,'" *The Museum World of Henry James* (Ann Arbor, Mich.: UMI Research Press, 1986), p. 188.

23 Henry James, *The Scenic Art: Notes on Acting and the Drama, 1872–1901*, ed. Allan Wade (1948; New York: Hill & Wang, 1957), p. 157. Hereafter cited parenthetically in the text.

24 James's admiration for Bernhardt and his disapproval of her powers of publicity are of course related to his treatment of such matters as women's access to the public sphere and the question of whether an actress can be a genuine artist—subjects he explored in some of his fiction, especially in *The Bostonians* (1888) and *The Tragic Muse* (1890).

25 Sander L. Gilman, "Salome, Syphilis, Sarah Bernhardt, and the Modern Jewess," and Carol Ockman, "When Is a Jewish Star Just a Star? Interpreting Images of Sarah Bernhardt." Both articles appear in Linda Nochlin and Tamar Garb, eds., *The Jew in the Text: Modernity and the Construction of Identity* (New York: Thames & Hudson, 1995).

26 Arthur Gold and Robert Fizdale tell the story in *The Divine Sarah: A Life of Sarah Bernhardt* (New York: Knopf, 1991), p. 179.

27 Gertrude Stein, "Plays," *Lectures in America* (New York: Random House, 1935), pp. 115–16.

28 Quoted in Joe E. Jeffreys, "Ethyl Eichelberger: A True Story," *Dragazine*, no. 8 (1995): p. 23. Jeffreys published a fuller version of the same article in *Theatre History Studies* 14 (June 1994): 23–40. Students of Eichelberger's career, myself included, are deeply indebted to Jeffreys, whose maintenance of a full archival record of Eichelberger's performances constitutes in itself an act of queenly extravagance and devotion in the grand tradition.

29 He gives his account of his conversion experience ("I saw the Garbo film [of *Camille*] when I was in college and was destroyed by it") in "Confessions of a Farceur," *Ridiculous Theatre: Scourge of Human Folly*, ed. Steven Samuels (New York: Theatre Communications Group, 1992), p. 36. See also Gregg Bordowitz, "The AIDS Crisis Is Ridiculous," in Martha Gever, Pratibha Parmar, and John Greyson, eds., *Queer Looks: Perspectives on Lesbian and Gay Film and Video* (New York: Routledge, 1993), pp. 208–24. I wish to acknowledge the inspiration Bordowitz has given me, through both his writing and his video, *Fast Trip, Long Drop*, for thinking about queerness and Jewishness together.

30 Charles Ludlam, *The Artificial Jungle* (1988), in *The Complete Plays of Charles Ludlam* (New York: Harper & Row, 1989), p. 888.

31 Neil Bartlett, "Speaking Your Mind: Ethyl Eichelberger and Lily Savage," in Russell Ferguson et al., eds., *Discourses: Conversations in Postmodern Art and Culture* (New York: New Museum of Contemporary Art, and Boston: MIT Press, 1990), p. 267.

32 Ibid.

33 Charles Ludlam, *Ridiculous Theatre*, p. 41.

34 James remembers seeing *Uncle Tom's Cabin* in the theater in Chapter 12 of *A Small Boy and Others.*

35 Ludlam, "*Confessions of a Farceur*," p. 8.

36 Neil Bartlett, "Speaking Your Mind: Ethyl Eichelberger and Lily Savage," p. 266.

37 Marvin T. Herrick, *Tragicomedy: Its Origin and Development in Italy, France, and England* (Urbana: University of Illinois, 1955), p. 321.

38 Carl Van Vechten, "The Yiddish Theater," *In the Garret* (New York: Knopf, 1920), pp. 330–31.

39 The latter is in Sandrow, *Vagabond Stars*, p. 110.

40 Nahum Stutchkoff, *Der oytzr fun der yidisher shprakh* [*Thesaurus of the Yiddish Language*] (New York: YIVO, 1950).

41 See Leo Rosten, entry for "miesse meshina," in his *The Joys of Yiddish* (New York: McGraw-Hill, 1968), pp. 338–39 and 244, respectively.

Disorientation (continued)
    parts, fantasmatic circulation of;
    Desire: mimetic character of
Dyer, Richard (quoted), 118–19

Eakins, Thomas, 55
Eichelberger, Ethyl, 13, 167–70

Frank, Waldo (quoted), 171
Freud, Sigmund: on "box" as sexual
    symbol, 143–44; on condensation in
    dreams, 145–46; on fetishism, 122;
    on primal scene and screen mem-
    ory, 98; on sublimation, 143; on the
    uncanny, 17–18
Frigidity, 111–12

Galérie d'Apollon (in Louvre): Henry
    James's visit to, 44–48; his dream of,
    48–52
Garbo, Greta: in Camille, 167
Gaze: role of, in "cruising," 81; shat-
    tered, 123–24. See also Visual: theories
    of the
Géricault, Théodore: Raft of the Medusa,
    53–56
Girard, René, 15
Girodet, Anne-Louis: Sleep of Endymion,
    57–59
Gordin, Jacob, 156–58

Hartley, Marsden: Adventures in the Arts,
    171
Herlihy, James Leo: Midnight Cowboy,
    129–30
Hoffmann, E. T. A.: "The Sandman,"
    17–19
Houdini, Harry, 8
Hustling. See Prostitution, male

Imitation, 9; and initiation, 10–11;
    and mimicry, 151–54. See also Butler,
    Judith; Derrida, Jacques; Mallarmé,
    Stéphane
Initiation, 6–8, 15, 19–24; "into style"
    (Henry James's), 39–65. See also
    Imitation

Jacobs, Ken, 79, 86
James, Henry, 2–4, 5–8, 11–12, 15,
    23–30, 31–65, 155–66, 170; The
    American Scene, 155, 157, 163; and
    anti-Semitism, 158–59; appearance
    and manner of, 36–39; attends first
    motion picture (of prizefight), 162;
    attends performance of Uncle Tom's
    Cabin, 7–8, 170; biographers' specu-
    lations about his erotic attachments,
    190 n.17; "The Pupil," 15, 24–28;
    A Small Boy and Others, 31–65. See also
    Body, male, as spectacle; Initiation;
    Queer childhood

Lamb, Charles: "My First Play," 169–70
Ludlam, Charles, 8, 13, 167–70
Lynch, David: Blue Velvet, 15, 17–24

Mallarmé, Stéphane: "Ballets," 152–53;
    Mimique, 151–53
Masculinity: crisis of in United States
    during 1960s, 119–21
Mimesis. See Imitation
Montez, Maria, 83–86
Mourning, 3, 131–32, 172

Nancy (comic strip), 110–15
Nerval, Gérard de: Angélique, 10–11;
    Aurelia, 146–48
Nijinsky, Vaslav, 12, 68–75, 80

Orbison, Roy: "In Dreams," 17

Pasolini, Pier Paolo, 92–93
Poe, Edgar Allan, 150
Poirier, Richard: "The Performing
    Self," 4
Popeye (comic strip), 105–6
Preston, John: "The Theatre of Sexual
    Initiation," 11
Prostitution, male, 117–32
Prud'hon, Pierre-Paul: Young Zephyr,
    59–61

Queer childhood, 2–3, 155; Henry

James's, 31–33; Andy Warhol's, 97–102

Rape, male-male. *See* Scene
"Ravishment." *See* Scene
Rubinstein, Ida, 68, 71–72

Sadomasochism, male-male, 16, 21–22, 129–30; *See also* Desire: male-male
Scene: of childhood initiation, 5–9; male-male rape scene: in *Blue Velvet*, 23, in *Midnight Cowboy*, 128–29; male-male "sex scene," 11, 100; of "ravishment": in Barthes's *Lover's Discourse*, 5–6, in Couture's *Falconer*, 41–44, in Vigée-Lebrun's *Self-Portrait*, 62–64; theatrical, 5–8. *See also* Body, female, as spectacle; Body, male, as spectacle; Desire; Sadomasochism, male
Schlesinger, John: *Midnight Cowboy*, 125–32
Sexuality: climactic character of adult, 103; infantile, 103, 113–15, and "saturation," 185 n.24
Smith, Jack, 12, 76–93, 180–81 n.14; adaptation of Ibsen's *Ghosts*, 91–92; *Blonde Cobra*, 86–90; *Flaming Creatures*, 76–80; *Little Stabs at Happiness*, 86, 90
"Star": complex meaning of, for Andy Warhol, 113
Stein, Gertrude: on Sarah Bernhardt (quoted), 166
"Straightness": pretense of, between hustler and john, 121–23, 132

Subcultures, "underground": centrality of to film and fiction in 1960s United States, 117–18
Superman (comic strip), 107–10

Tomashefsky, Boris, 161–62
Tragedy and comedy, confusion of, 169–72

Uncanny, the, 5, 17–18

Vamp, figure of, 81–82
Van Vechten, Carl, quoted, 172
Velvet, 25
Vigée-Lebrun, Elisabeth: *Self-portrait à la grecque*, 62–65
Visual: fantasy of visual capture, 23–24; theories of the, 5–6, 173 n.1. *See also* Gaze

Warhol, Andy, 12, 81, 95–116, 117–25; *Chelsea Girls*, 124; *Diaries* (quoted), 175 n.7; *My Hustler*, 120–25; *Philosophy of Andy Warhol* (quoted), 97–98
Whitman, Walt: conflicts between vision and speech in "Song of Myself," 149
Winckelmann, Johann Joachim, 33–36, 58, 61
Wollen, Peter, 68–69

Yiddish theater, 13–14, 154–64, 168–69, 171–72

Michael Moon is Professor of English at Duke University. He is
the author of *Disseminating Whitman: Revision and Corporeality in
"Leaves of Grass"* and co-editor (with Cathy N. Davidson) of
*Subjects and Citizens: Nation, Race, and Gender from "Oroonoko"
to Anita Hill* (Duke, 1995).

Library of Congress Cataloging-in-Publication Data
Moon, Michael.
A small boy and others : imitation and initiation in American
culture from Henry James to Andy Warhol / Michael Moon.
p.   cm. — (Series Q)
Includes index.
ISBN 0-8223-2161-0 (cloth : alk. paper).
— ISBN 0-8223-2173-4 (paper : alk. paper)
1. Gays in popular culture.   2. Gay men in literature.
3. Homosexuality in motion pictures.   I. Title.   II. Series.
HQ76.25.M66   1998   306.76'6'0973—dc21   97-37858 CIP